iOS
Animations
by Tutorials

Third Edition

By Marin Todorov

iOS Animations by Tutorials Third Edition

Marin Todorov

Copyright ©2016 Razeware LLC.

Notice of Rights

Notice of Liability

Trademarks

ISBN: 978-1-942878-30-8

Dedications

"To my father."

— *Marin Todorov*

About the team

Marin Todorov is the author of this book. Marin is one of the founding members of the raywenderlich.com tutorial team. He is an independent iOS consultant and publisher, and also has a background in web and desktop development. Besides crafting code, Marin also enjoys blogging, writing books and speaking at conferences. He happily open sources code.

Erik Kerber is the tech editor of this book. Erik is a software developer in Minneapolis, MN, and the lead iOS developer for the Target app. He does his best to balance a life behind the keyboard with cycling, hiking, scuba diving, and traveling.

Rich Turton is an iOS developer for MartianCraft, prolific Stack Overflow participant and author of a development blog, Command Shift. When he's not in front of a computer he is usually building Lego horse powered spaceships (don't ask!) with his daughter.

Chris Belanger is the editor of this book. Chris is the Book Team Lead and Lead Editor for raywenderlich.com. If there are words to wrangle or a paragraph to ponder, he's on the case. When he kicks back, you can usually find Chris with guitar in hand, looking for the nearest beach, or exploring the lakes and rivers in his part of the world in a canoe.

Vicki Wenderlich created many of the illustrations in this book. Vicki discovered a love of digital art many years ago, and has been making app art and digital illustrations ever since. She is passionate about helping people pursue their dreams, and makes app art for developers on her website http://www.gameartguppy.com.

Table of Contents:

Introduction

There's no denying it: creating animations is one of the most enjoyable parts of iOS development!

Animations are fun to create, they breathe life into your user interface, and most importantly, they make your interface a delight to use. Who doesn't love an app that gives you a little visual thrill when you open a menu or swipe right?

You've probably seen impressive animations in many third-party apps, as well as in Apple's own built-in apps such as Passbook:

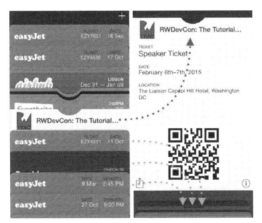

When used properly, animations can convey information to your users and draw their attention to important parts of the interface.

To create responsive and attractive user interfaces, you'll need to use all kinds of animations, from very subtle effects, to extremely expressive ones that leap off the screen.

In this book, you'll learn about various iOS animation techniques, from simple view animations, to vivid 3D animations, to view controller animations that make the navigation in your app look and feel great.

By the end of this book, you'll have worked through the chapter content and you'll have hands-on experience solving the challenges at the end of the chapters — and you'll be well on your way to coming up with stunning animations for your ownapps!

What you need

To follow along with the tutorials in this book, you'll need the following:

- **A Mac running the latest point release of OS X El Capitan or later**: You'll need this to be able to install the latest version of Xcode.

- **Xcode 8 or later**: Xcode is the main development tool for iOS. You can download the latest version of Xcode for free on the Mac app store here: https://itunes.apple.com/app/xcode/id497799835?mt=12

- Basic knowledge of Swift and iOS development. This book is about animations specifically; to understand the animation code and how the accompanying demo projects work you will need at least a basic understanding of Swift and Cocoa Touch.

If you want to try things out on a physical iOS device, you'll need a developer account with Apple, which you can obtain for free. However, all the sample projects in this book will work just fine in the iOS Simulator bundled with Xcode, so the paid developer account is completely optional.

Who this book is for

This book is for iOS developers who already know the basics of iOS and Swift, and want to dive deep into animations.

If you're a complete beginner to iOS, we suggest you first read through the latest edition of The iOS Apprentice. That will give you a solid foundation of building iOS apps with Swift from the ground up.

If you know the basics of iOS development but are new to Swift, we suggest you read through Swift Apprentice first, which goes through the features of Swift using playgrounds to teach the language. You can find both of these books at our online store:

http://www.raywenderlich.com/store

How to use this book

Each chapter in this book includes a starter project and covers a small number of animation techniques in detail; this lets you work through the chapters in the book in any order.

However, for beginners, we do suggest that you work through the chapters in order, since the concepts build upon each other. Also, remember you'll get the most out of the book if you follow along with the tutorials and perform the hands-onchallenges.

For advanced developers, there's still value in the early chapters since that cover the basics, since you might not yet be familiar with the Swift syntax for these familiar animation APIs. However if you're comfortable with that, feel free to jump ahead to the topics that interest you the most.

What's in store

This book is divided into six sections. You can find more details on each section in its introduction, which also includes a short description of its chapters. Here's a brief overview.

Section I: View Animations

The first section of the book covers view animations in UIKit. View animations are the simplest type of animations in iOS, but still very powerful; you can easily animate almost any view element and change things such as its size, position and color.

Section II: Auto Layout

Auto Layout is becoming more common in apps, and there are some special techniques to animate views that are sized and positioned with auto layout constraints. This section provides a crash course in Auto Layout and then covers theanimation techniques that play nicely with Auto Layout.

Section III: Layer Animations

Views on iOS are backed by layers, which offer a lower-level interface to the visual content of your apps. When you need more flexibility or performance, you can use layer animations rather than view animations. In this section, you'll learn about layers and the Core Animation API.

Section IV: View Controller Transitions

Animating views and layers is impressive, but you can dial it up to 11 and animate entire view controllers! In this section, you'll learn the techniques for transitioning between view controllers, as well as transitioning between changes in device orientations, all in the same view controller.

Section V: Animations with UIViewPropertyAnimator

UIViewPropertyAnimator, introduced in iOS10, and helps developers create interactive, interruptible view animations. Since all APIs in UIKit just wrap that lower level functionality, there won't be many surprises for you when looking at UIViewPropertyAnimator. This class does make certain types of view animations a little easier to create, so it is definitely worth looking into.

Section VI: 3D Animations

In this section, you'll move beyond two dimensions and learn about 3D animations and effects with CATransform3D. Although Core Animation isn't a true 3D framework, it lets you position things in 3D-space and set perspective – which leads to some very slick and impressive effects!

Section VII: Further types of animations

There are two more animation techniques that are part of Core Animation and UIKit, but don't really fit into sections I and III. In this section, you'll get an impressive snowy effect working with particle emitters, and then learn about flipbook-style frame animation with UIImageView.

Book source code and forums

You can get the source code for the book here:

www.raywenderlich.com/store/ios-animations-by-tutorials/source-code

You'll find all the code from the chapters, as well as solutions to the challenges for your reference.

We've also set up an official forum for the book at www.raywenderlich.com/forums. This is a great place to ask any questions you have about the book, or to submit any errors you might find.

PDF Version

We also have a PDF version of this book available, which can be handy if you want a soft copy to take with you, or you want to quickly search for a specific term within the book.

Buying the PDF version of the book also has a few extra benefits: free PDF updates each time we update the book, access to older PDF versions of the book, and you can download the PDF from anywhere, at anytime.

Visit the book store page here: raywenderlich.com/store/ios-animations-by-tutorials.

License

By purchasing iOS Animations by Tutorials, you have the following license:

- You are allowed to use and/or modify the source code in iOS Animations byTutorials in as many apps as you want, with no attribution required.

- You are allowed to use and/or modify all art, images and designs that are included in iOS Animations by Tutorials in as many apps as you want, but must includethis attribution line somewhere inside your app: "Artwork/images/designs: fromiOS Animations by Tutorials book, available at http://www.raywenderlich.com."

- The source code included in iOS Animations by Tutorials is for your personal use only. You are NOT allowed to distribute or sell the source code in iOS Animations by Tutorials without prior authorization.

- This book is for your personal use only. You are NOT allowed to sell this book without prior authorization, or distribute it to friends, co-workers or students; they would need to purchase their own copy.

All materials provided with this book are provided on an "as is" basis, without warranty of any kind, express or implied, including but not limited to the warranties of merchantability, fitness for a particular purpose and non-infringement. In no event shall the authors or copyright holders be liable for any claim, damages or other liability, whether in an action of contract, tort or otherwise, arising from, out of or in connection with the software or the use or other dealings in the software.

All trademarks and registered trademarks appearing in this book are the property of their respective owners.

About the cover

The American lobster is a fascinating creature; it can live up to 70 years, doesn't slow down with age and grows throughout its life.

Lobsters escape threats by swimming backwards at speeds up to 10 mph, and can resort to cannibalism to survive by eating other, younger lobsters. They are found in all...oh, admit it, you and I both know that the BEST thing about lobsters is that they are tasty as heck!

Lobster bisque à la Marin

- 4 tbsp. butter
- 1/4 c. mushroom, diced
- 1/2 c. onion, diced
- 1/4 c. celery, diced
- 1/4 c. carrot, diced
- 16 oz. chicken stock
- pinch salt
- pinch cayenne pepper
- 3/4 c. milk
- 1 c. heavy cream
- 1/2 c. dry white wine
- 2 c. lobster meat, shredded

Sauté the mushroom, onion, celery and carrot in the butter. Add the chicken stock, salt, and cayenne pepper. Bring to a boil, then reduce heat to minimum and simmer for 15 minutes.

Add lobster meat and purée the bisque with an immersion blender until creamy. Stir in the milk, cream and white wine. Cook over low heat for about half an hour, stirring often, until thickened.

Section I: View Animations

The five chapters will introduce you to the animation API of UIKit. This API is specifically designed to help you animate your views with ease while avoiding the complexity of Core Animation, which runs the animations under the hood.

Though simple to use, the UIKit animation API provides you with lots of flexibility and power to handle most, if not all, of your animation requirements.

Animations are visible, onscreen effects that apply to all of the views, or visible objects, in your user interface:

You can animate *any* object on screen that ultimately inherits from UIView; this includes UILabel, UIImageView, UIButton, and any custom classes you might have created yourself.

In the five chapters of this section on view animations, you'll learn how to use animation to improve a fictional airline app, **Bahama Air**, by adding various animations to its UI elements.

First, you'll add animations to the login screen:

You'll work on this screen in the following chapters:

- **Chapter 1, Getting Started**: You'll learn how to move, scale and fade views. You'll create a number of different animations to get comfortable with Swift and the basic UIKit APIs.

- **Chapter 2, Springs**: You'll build on the concepts of linear animation and create more eye-catching effects using spring-driven animations. Boiiing! :]

- **Chapter 3, Transitions**: You'll learn about several class methods in UIKit that help you animate views in or out of the screen. These one-line API calls make transition effects easy to achieve.

Once you've completed your work on the login screen, you'll move on to the **Bahama Air** flight status screen. You'll work with the existing screen and make it more exciting by adding animations that follow on from the theme of the login screen.

You'll start with a visually static version of the screen and add a number of compelling, advanced animations to improve the user experience:

- **Chapter 4, View Animations in Practice**: You've learned most of what you need to know about animations in UIKit. This chapter teaches you how to combine techniques you're familiar with in creative ways to build up even cooler animations.

- **Chapter 5, Keyframe Animations**: You'll use keyframe animations to unlock the ultimate achievement of impressive UI: creating elaborate animation sequences built from a number of distinct stages.

Once you've worked through all chapters in this section you'll have some in-depth experience on animation that you can carry forward to the rest of this book.

This section shows you how easy it is to add animations to your views – read on to Chapter 1 to get started!

Chapter 1: Getting Started with View Animations

In this chapter you'll dip your toes into the bottomless sea of view animations. Don't be misled by the chapter's title, however — getting started with such a powerful and rich API means there's a lot of interesting material to cover!

In this chapter and accompanying project, you'll learn how to do the following:

- Set the stage for a cool animation.

- Create move and fade animations.

- Adjust the animation easing.

- Reverse and repeat animations.

There's a fair bit of material to get through, but I promise it will be a lot of fun. Are you up for the challenge?

All right! Time to get started.

Your first animation

Open the starter project located in the Resources folder for this chapter. Build and run your project in Xcode; you'll see the login screen of a fictional airline app like so:

The app doesn't do much right now; it just shows a login form with a title, two text fields, and a big friendly button at the bottom.

There's also a nice background picture and four clouds. The clouds are already connected to outlet variables in the code named `cloud1` through `cloud4`.

Open **ViewController.swift** and have a look inside. At the top of the file you'll see all the connected outlets and class variables. Further down, there's a bit of code in `viewDidLoad()` which initializes some of the UI. The project is ready for you to jump in and shake things up a bit!

Enough with the introductions — you're undoubtedly ready to try out some code!

Your first task is to animate the form elements onto the screen when the user opens the application. Since the form is now visible when the app starts, you'll have to move it off of the screen just before your view controller makes an appearance.

Add the following code to `viewWillAppear()`:

```
heading.center.x  -= view.bounds.width
username.center.x -= view.bounds.width
password.center.x -= view.bounds.width
```

This places each of the form elements outside the visible bounds of the screen, like so:

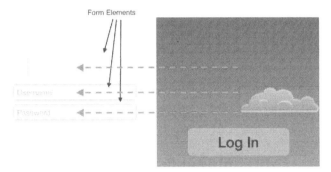

Since the code above executes before the view controller appears, it will look like those text fields were never there in the first place.

Build and run your project to make sure your fields truly appear offscreen just as you had planned:

Perfect — now you can animate those form elements back to their original locations via a delightful animation.

Add the following code to the end of `viewDidAppear()`:

```
UIView.animate(withDuration: 0.5) {
    self.heading.center.x += self.view.bounds.width
}
```

To animate the title into view you call the **UIView** class method `animate(withDuration:animations:)`. The animation starts immediately and animates over half a second; you set the duration via the first method parameter in the code.

It's as easy as that; all the changes you make to the view in the animations closure will be animated by UIKit.

Build and run your project; you should see the title slide neatly into place like so:

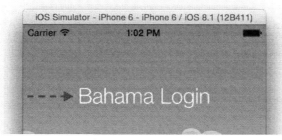

That sets the stage for you to animate in the rest of the form elements.

Since `animate(withDuration:animations:)` is a class method, you aren't limited to animating just one specific view; in fact you can animate as many views as you want in your animations closure.

Add the following line to the animations closure:

```
self.username.center.x += self.view.bounds.width
```

Build and run your project again; watch as the username field slides into place:

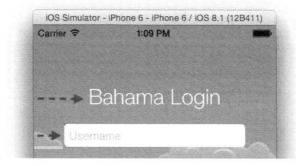

Seeing both views animate together is quite cool, but you probably noticed that animating the two views over the same distance and with the same duration looks a bit stiff. Only kill-bots move with such absolute synchronization! :]

Wouldn't it be cool if each of the elements moved independently of the others, possibly with a little bit of delay in between the animations?

First **remove** the line you just added that animates `username`:

```
self.username.center.x += self.view.bounds.width
```

Then add the following code to the bottom of `viewDidAppear()`:

```
UIView.animate(withDuration: 0.5, delay: 0.3, options: [],
    animations: {
        self.username.center.x += self.view.bounds.width
    },
    completion: nil
)
```

The class method you use this time looks familiar, but it has a few more parameters to let you customize your animation:

- `withDuration`: The duration of the animation.

- `delay`: The amount of seconds UIKit will wait before it starts the animation.

- `options`: Lets you customize a number of aspects about your animation. You'll learn more about this parameter later on, but for now you can pass an empty array [] to mean "no special options".

- `animations`: The closure expression to provide your animations.

- `completion`: A code closure to execute when the animation completes. This parameter often comes in handy when you want to perform some final cleanup tasks or chain animations one after the other.

In the code you added above you set `delay` to 0.3 to make the animation start just a hair later than the title animation.

Build and run your project; how does the combined animation look now?

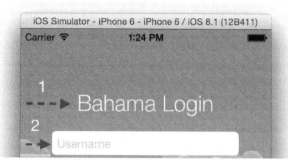

Ah — that looks much better. Now all you need to do is animate in the password field.

Add the following code to the bottom of `viewDidAppear()`:

```
UIView.animate(withDuration: 0.5, delay: 0.4, options: [],
    animations: {
        self.password.center.x += self.view.bounds.width
    },
    completion: nil
)
```

Here you've mostly mimicked the animation of the username field, just with a slightly longer delay.

Build and run your project again to see the complete animation sequence:

That's all you need to do to animate views across the screen with a UIKit animation!

That's just the start of it — you'll be learning a few more awesome animation techniques in the remainder of this chapter!

Animatable properties

Now that you've seen how easy animations can be, you're probably keen to learn how else you can animate your views.

This section will give you an overview of the animatable properties of a `UIView`, and then guide you through exploring these animations in your project.

Not all view properties can be animated, but all view animations, from the simplest to the most complex, can be built by animating the subset of properties on a view that *do* lend themselves to animation, as outlined in the section below.

Position and size

You can animate a view's position and frame in order to make it grow, shrink, or move around as you did in the previous section. Here are the properties you can use to modify a view's position and size:

- **bounds**: Animate this property to reposition the view's content within the view's frame.

- **frame**: Animate this property to move and/or scale the view.

- **center**: Animate this property when you want to move the view to a new location on screen.

Don't forget that in Swift, several **UIKit** properties such as `size` and `center` are mutable . This means you can move a view vertically by changing `center.y` or you can shrink a view by decreasing `frame.size.width`.

Appearance

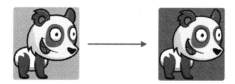

You can change the appearance of the view's content by either tinting its background or making the view fully or semi-transparent.

- **backgroundColor**: Change this property of a view to have UIKit gradually change the background color over time.

- **alpha**: Change this property to create fade-in and fade-out effects.

Transformation

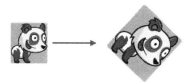

Transforms modify views in much the same way as above, since you can also adjust size and position.

- **transform**: Modify this property within an animation block to animate the rotation, scale, and/or position of a view.

These are affine transformations under the hood, which are much more powerful and allow you to describe the scale factor or rotation angle rather than needing to provide a specific bounds or center point.

These look like pretty basic building blocks, but you'll be surprised at the complex animation effects you're about to encounter!

Animation options

Looking back to your animation code, you were always passing [] in to the options parameter. options lets you customize how UIKit creates your animation. You've only adjusted the duration and delay of your animations, but you can have a lot more control over your animation parameters than just that.

Below is a list of options declared in the `UIViewAnimationOptions` set type that you can combine in different ways for use in your animations.

Repeating

You'll first take a look at the following two animation options:

- `.repeat`: Include this option to makes your animation loop forever.

- `.autoreverse`: Include this option only in conjunction with `.repeat`; this option repeatedly plays your animation forward, then in reverse.

Modify the code that animates the password field `viewDidAppear()` to use the `.repeat` option as follows:

```
UIView.animate(withDuration: 0.5, delay: 0.4,
   options: .repeat,
   animations: {
      self.password.center.x += self.view.bounds.width
   },
   completion: nil
)
```

Build and run your project to see the effect of your change:

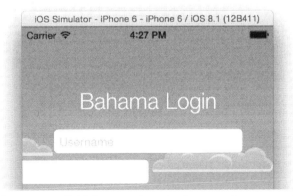

The form title and username field fly in and settle down in the center of the screen, but the password field keeps animating forever from its position offscreen.

Modify the same code you changed above to use both `.repeat` and `.autoreverse` in the `options` parameter as follows:

```
UIView.animate(withDuration: 0.5, delay: 0.4,
   options: [.repeat, .autoreverse],
   animations: {
      self.password.center.x += self.view.bounds.width
```

```
    },
    completion: nil
  )
```

Note how if you want to enable more than one option you need to use the set syntax and list all options separated with a comma and enclose the list in square brackets.

> **Note:** If you only need a single option, Swift allows you to omit the square brackets as a convenience. However, you can still include them in case you add more options in the future. That means [] for no options, [.repeat] for a single option, and [.repeat, .autorepeat] for multiple options.

Build and run your project again; this time the password field just can't make up its mind about staying on the screen!

Animation easing

In real life things don't just suddenly start or stop moving. Physical objects like cars or trains slowly accelerate until they reach their target speed, and unless they hit a brick wall, they gradually slow down until they come to a complete stop at their final destination.

The image below illustrates this concept in detail:

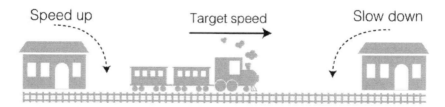

To make your animations look more realistic, you can apply the same effect of building momentum at the beginning and slowing down before the end, known in general terms as **ease-in** and **ease-out**.

You can choose from four different easing options:

- .curveLinear: This option applies no acceleration or deceleration to the animation. The only time in this book you'll use this option is in the final challenge of Chapter 3: "Transitions".

- .curveEaseIn: This option applies acceleration to the start of your animation.

- .curveEaseOut: This option applies deceleration to the end of your animation.

- .curveEaseInOut: This option applies acceleration to the start of your animation *and* applies deceleration to the end of your animation.

To better understand how these options add visual impact to your animation, you'll try a few of the options in your project.

Modify the animation code for your password field once again with a new option as follows:

```
UIView.animate(withDuration: 0.5, delay: 0.4,
  options: [.repeat, .autoreverse, .curveEaseOut],
  animations: {
    self.password.center.x += self.view.bounds.width
  },
  completion: nil
)
```

Build and run your project; notice how smoothly the field decelerates until it reaches its rightmost position, before returning to the left side of the screen:

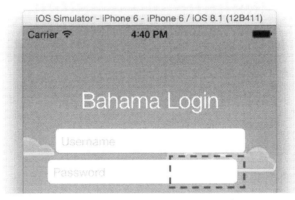

This looks much more natural since that's how you expect things to move in the real world.

Now try the opposite. Ease-in the animation when the field is still outside of the screen by modifying the same code as above to change the .curveEaseOut option to .curveEaseIn as follows:

```
UIView.animate(withDuration: 0.5, delay: 0.4,
  options: [.repeat, .autoreverse, .curveEaseIn],
  animations: {
    self.password.center.x += self.view.bounds.width
  },
  completion: nil
)
```

Build and run your project; observe how the field jumps back from its rightmost position with robotic vigor. This looks unnatural and isn't as visually pleasing as the previous animation.

Finally give .curveEaseInOut a try. It combines the two options you already know into one very natural looking easing. .curveEaseInOut is also the default easing function UIKit applies to your animations.

You've seen how the various animation options affect your project and how to make movements look smooth and natural.

Before you move on, change the options on the piece of code you've been playing with back to []:

```
UIView.animate(withDuration: 0.5, delay: 0.4, options: [],
  animations: {
    self.password.center.x += self.view.bounds.width
  },
  completion: nil
)
```

Now that you know how basic animations work, you're ready to tackle some more dazzling animation techniques.

Animating views from point A to point B? Pshaw — that's so easy! :]

In the next chapter, you'll explore how to drive your animations using springs. *Boing...boing...boing...boing...!*

Challenges

If this chapter is the first time you've animated a view in iOS, your head might be spinning a little. Don't worry, though, because no matter your initial skillset, you'll be well on your way to animation mastery in just a few chapters.

For now though, there's one very simple challenge waiting for you where you'll create an animation of your very own.

Challenge 1: Fade in the clouds

In **ViewController** you have four outlets: cloud1, cloud2, cloud3, and cloud4. Your task is to fade those in when the application starts.

You can pretty much decide on the exact form your solution will take, but here's a list of the basic steps you'll need to follow:

1. Set the `alpha` property to `0.0` for all four cloud views in `viewWillAppear()`.

2. In `viewDidAppear()`, make four separate calls to `animate(withDuration:delay:options:animations:completion:)`. You'll get a nice-looking effect if you use a duration of `0.5` for all four animations and delays of `0.5`, `0.7`, `0.9`, and `1.1` respectively.

3. In each `animations` closure change the `alpha` of the respective cloud view to `1.0`. This will fade the cloud in.

When you run the project you should see a nice transition effect that animates the clouds, one after another:

All views on the screen should animate nicely. Well almost...the Log In button isn't animating!

Don't worry — you'll fix that in the next chapter. :]

Chapter 2: Springs

In the previous chapter, you learned how to create basic animations with UIKit. By providing start and end values along with a durations, delays, and other options, **UIKit** automatically creates animations for you.

So far, your animations have been fluid movements in a single direction. When you animated a view's position, it was a straightforward movement from point A to point B, like so:

In this chapter you'll learn how to create more complex animations, which move views as if they were attached to a spring, as demonstrated below:

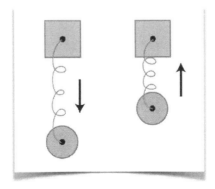

If you took the basic animation from point A to point B and added a bit of springiness to it, the motion of the animation would follow a path indicated by the red arrows below:

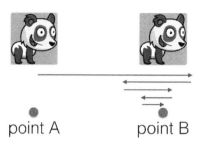

The view heads from point A to point B, but overshoots point B by a small amount. The view then heads back to point B and overshoots by a little less this time. This back-and-forth oscillation repeats until the view has come to rest at point B.

It's a nice effect; it adds a snappy, real-world feel to your animations. This chapter will show you how to use this effect to add a little bit of playfulness to your UI.

Spring animations

You'll continue on with the project from the previous chapter; if you didn't complete the exercises in Chapter 1 (including the challenge at the end of the chapter), then grab the starter project from the Resources folder for Chapter 2 and start from there.

Build and run your project; you should see the views on screen (except the Log In button) animate as soon as the app opens like so:

Your job is to take care of the last non-animated element on this screen: the Log In button.

Open **ViewController.swift** and add the following code to the bottom of `viewWillAppear()`:

```
loginButton.center.y += 30.0
loginButton.alpha = 0.0
```

Just as you did in the previous chapter, you set the start position of the button a bit lower on the y-axis and set its alpha value to zero so that it will start out as invisible.

Now move to `viewDidAppear()` and add the following code:

```
UIView.animate(withDuration: 0.5, delay: 0.5,
  usingSpringWithDamping: 0.5, initialSpringVelocity: 0.0,
  options: [], animations: {
    self.loginButton.center.y -= 30.0
    self.loginButton.alpha = 1.0
}, completion: nil)
```

There are two key points in this piece of code.

First, you've animated two different properties at the same time! That was easier than you thought, right?

Second, you used a new animation method for the first time: `animate(withDuration:delay:usingSpringWithDamping:initialSpringVelocity:options:animations:completion:)`. Saying that method name too quickly just might injure your tongue! :]

The above method looks much like the ones you used in the previous chapter of the book, but it sports a couple of new parameters:

- `usingSpringWithDamping`: This controls the amount of damping, or reduction, applied to the animation as it approaches its final state. This parameter accepts values between `0.0` and `1.0`. Values closer to `0.0` create a bouncier animation, while values closer to `1.0` create a stiff-looking effect. You can think of this value as the "stiffness" of the spring.

- `initialSpringVelocity`: This controls the initial velocity of the animation. A value of `1.0` sets the velocity of the animation to cover the total distance of the animation in the span of one second. Bigger and smaller values will cause the animation to have more or less velocity.

Build and run your project; check out how the button moves now:

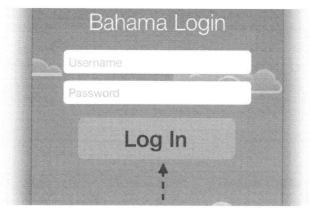

Since your animation has an initial velocity of `0.0` and a neutral damping of `0.5`, the animation doesn't look very eye-catching.

You should be able to dress up this animation a little by trying some different values for the velocity and damping.

Change the duration to `3.0` and the damping to `0.1`. This is just to let you observe the effect of your changes in slow motion instead of at normal speed.

Build and run your project again; note how the opacity of the button changes as it moves up. This is because the spring behavior affects **all** properties you animate; in your case, this affects *both* the vertical position of the button *and* its alpha value.

Now set `initialSpringVelocity` to `1.0` and build and run your project again:

You'll notice that the button bounces a bit more when it animates and moves beyond the password field; this is because it has more momentum at the beginning of its movement and takes longer to settle down into its final position.

Play around with some different values for damping and velocity until you understand how changes in these parameters affect the look and feel of your animation.

When you're done, set the values for the velocity and damping back to their original values, like so:

```
UIView.animate(withDuration: 0.5, delay: 0.5,
  usingSpringWithDamping: 0.5, initialSpringVelocity: 0.0,
  options: [], animations: {
    self.loginButton.center.y -= 30.0
    self.loginButton.alpha = 1.0
}, completion: nil)
```

Animating user interactions

You don't have to limit your spring animations to the initial placement of your views. In fact, animating views in response to user input can really make your interface come alive. In this section you'll animate the Log In button in response to a tap.

Add the following code to `login()`:

```
UIView.animate(withDuration: 1.5, delay: 0.0,
  usingSpringWithDamping: 0.2, initialSpringVelocity: 0.0,
  options: [], animations: {
    self.loginButton.bounds.size.width += 80.0
}, completion: nil)
```

The above animation increases the button's width by 80 points over a duration of a second and a half. The button will bounce around a fair bit as well since the damping is set to just `0.2`. Increasing the bounds grows the frame on its left and right sides.

Build and run your project; tap the button to see your animation in action:

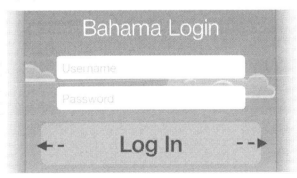

The button grows and bounces in a blobby fashion when you tap it; it's a neat way to provide tap feedback to the user.

Next you'll combine this animation with a few more spring movements to really bring the button to life.

Add the following code to the end of `login()`:

```
UIView.animate(withDuration: 0.33, delay: 0.0,
  usingSpringWithDamping: 0.7, initialSpringVelocity: 0.0,
  options: [], animations: {
    self.loginButton.center.y += 60.0
}, completion: nil)
```

The above animation moves the button 60 points down when tapped. Notice that the duration for this animation is much shorter than the one that animates the button width.

This is intentional, since the desired effect is to make the button jump away from the tap and bounce a bit once it's settled into its new vertical position.

Build and run your project; tap the button and see how it moves in response to your touch this time:

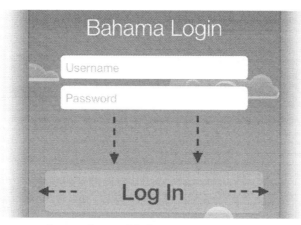

That looks really nice — but you're quickly becoming an animation master and you *know* that you can do even better!

Another great way of providing user feedback is through color change. You'll tint the button as it moves by animating the `backgroundColor` property of the button.

Add the following code to the last animation you added, inside the `animations` closure expression:

```
self.loginButton.backgroundColor =
UIColor(red: 0.85, green: 0.83, blue: 0.45, alpha: 1.0)
```

Build and run your project again; you'll see the button move, change shape *and* change color, all at the same time:

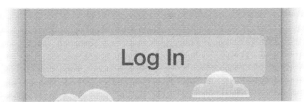

There's one last bit of feedback to add here: an activity indicator. The Log In button is supposed to start a user authentication activity over the network, so it would be nice to show an activity indicator to the user to let them know that there's an action in progress.

Scroll up and have a look at viewDidLoad() and find the existing code for the progress indicator. spinner contains an instance of UIActivityIndicatorView that's all ready for your use. You haven't seen it on the screen yet because its alpha is set to 0.0.

Head back to login() and add the following code to the last animations closure expression:

```
self.spinner.center = CGPoint(
    x: 40.0,
    y: self.loginButton.frame.size.height/2
)
self.spinner.alpha = 1.0
```

This animation moves the spinner slightly to the left and fades it in. This should be enough to attract the user's attention and let them know their request is being processed.

Build and run your project; check out the final version of your spiffy new animation:

Take a moment to reflect on what you've accomplished here. You've added three simultaneous animations to the button view to make it grow in width, move down the screen, and change color.

You've also animated and faded in an activity spinner, which is itself a subview of the button view.

All animations are combined automatically by UIKit and run flawlessly to create one fluid visual effect.

There's no need for you to worry about the implementation details of your animations; you can instead focus on designing great animations and wowing your users thanks to UIKit!

Keep it up UIKit,
You rock my world!

Challenges

Challenge 1: Convert text field animations to spring-animations

The spring animation APIs in UIKit are quite similar in usage to their standard animation counterparts. Thus it shouldn't be much of a problem for you to convert the animations you have running on the `username` and `password` fields to spring animations.

To complete this challenge you will need to do the following:

1. Add the `usingSpringWithDamping` and `initialSpringVelocity` parameters to the animation for the username field. Use `0.0` for the spring initial velocity. Try out `0.2`, `0.6` and `0.9` for the spring damping and choose the value that looks most like a pleasant and subtle spring effect to you.

2. Repeat the same for the `password` field animation using the damping and velocity of your choice.

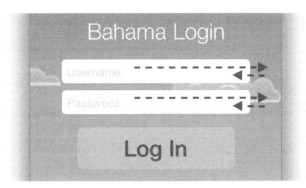

By this point in the book you've gained a solid foundation of spring animation. The more you play with this type of animation, and the more you experiment with different combinations of damping and velocity, the more comfortable you'll be designing the perfect spring animation for the views in your own apps.

Are you ready to *spring* into the next chapter? :] In Chapter 3, you'll learn about the next type of animation in UIKit: **transitions**.

Chapter 3: Transitions

In the previous two chapters, you learned how to create animations based on the animatable properties of views such as `position` and `alpha`. But how would you handle the case where you want to animate the addition or removal of a view?

You *could* use the methods from the previous chapters and animate views in and out of your interface. However, this chapter will show you how to use transitions to animate *any* set of changes to your view.

Transitions are predefined animations you can apply to views. These predefined animations don't attempt to interpolate between the start and end states of your view. Instead, you'll design the animations so that the various changes in state appear natural.

Example transitions

To better understand when you'd use transitions, this section walks you through the various animation scenarios where you could make use of transition animations.

Adding a new view

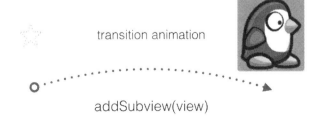

transition animation

addSubview(view)

To animate the addition of a new view on the screen, you call a method similar to the ones you used in the previous chapters. The difference this time is that you'll choose one of the predefined transition effects and animate what's known as an **animation container view**.

The transition animates the container view, and any new views you add to it as subviews appear while the animation runs.

To better explain how you'd animate container views and when you'd execute the transition between subviews, consider the following code snippet:

```
var animationContainerView: UIView!

override func viewDidLoad() {
  //set up the animation container
  animationContainerView = UIView(frame: view.bounds)
  animationContainerView.frame = view.bounds
  view.addSubview(animationContainerView!)
}

override func viewDidAppear(_ animated: Bool) {
  super.viewDidAppear(animated)

  //create new view
  let newView = UIImageView(image: UIImage(named: "banner")!)
  newView.center = animationContainerView.center

  //add the new view via transition
  UIView.transition(with: animationContainerView,
    duration: 0.33,
    options: [.curveEaseOut, .transitionFlipFromBottom],
    animations: {
      self.animationContainerView.addSubview(newView)
    },
    completion: nil
  )
}
```

In this hypothetical situation, you create a new view named `animationContainerView` in `viewDidLoad()` of your view controller. You then position and add this container to the view.

Later, when you want to create an animated transition, you create a new view to animate; here it's named `newView`.

To create the transition, you call `transition(with:duration: options:animations:completion:)`. This is almost identical to the standard **UIView** animation method, but in this case you supply an extra parameter `view`, which serves as the container view for the transition animation.

There's a new animation option here, `.transitionFlipFromBottom`, which you haven't seen yet. This is one of the predefined transitions discussed in the introduction of this chapter. `.transitionFlipFromBottom` flips the view over with the bottom edge of the view serving as the "hinge" around which the view flips.

Finally, you add a subview to your animation container within your animations block, which causes the subview to appear during the transition.

The full list of predefined transition animation options are as follows:

```
.transitionFlipFromLeft
.transitionFlipFromRight
.transitionCurlUp
.transitionCurlDown
.transitionCrossDissolve
.transitionFlipFromTop
.transitionFlipFromBottom
```

Removing a view

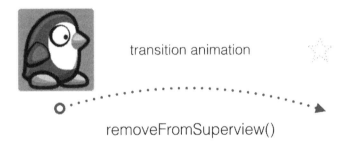

transition animation

removeFromSuperview()

Removing a subview from the screen with a transition animation works much like adding a subview. To do this with a transition animation, you simply call `removeFromSuperview()` inside the animation closure expression like so:

```
//remove the view via transition

UIView.transition(with: animationContainerView, duration: 0.33,
  options: [.curveEaseOut, .transitionFlipFromBottom],
  animations: {
    self.newView.removeFromSuperview()
  },
  completion: nil
)
```

As in the previous example, the wrapper transition will perform the flip animation and the newView will disappear at the end of it all.

Hiding/showing a view

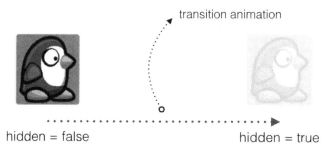

transition animation

hidden = false   hidden = true

So far in this chapter, you've learned only about transitions that alter the view hierarchy. That's why you needed a container view for the transitions — this puts the hierarchy change in context.

In contrast, you don't need to worry about setting up a container view to hide and show views. In this case, the transition uses the view *itself* as the animation container.

Consider the following code to hide a subview using a transition:

```
//hide the view via transition

UIView.transition(with: self.newView, duration: 0.33,
  options: [.curveEaseOut, .transitionFlipFromBottom],
  animations: {
    self.newView.isHidden = true
  },
  completion: nil
)
```

Here you pass in the view you intend to show or hide as the first argument to `transition(with:duration:options:animations:completion:)`. All you do after that is set the `isHidden` property of your view in the animations block and *voilà*, the transition animation kicks off.

Replacing a view with another view

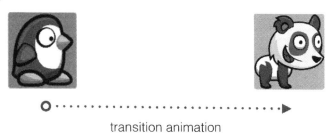

transition animation

Replacing one view with another view is also an easy process. You simply pass in the existing view as the first argument and set the `toView:` parameter as the view you wish to replace it with as shown below:

```
//replace via transition
UIView.transition(from: oldView, to: newView, duration: 0.33,
    options: .transitionFlipFromTop, completion: nil)
```

It's becoming quite apparent how much of the heavy lifting UIKit does for you! :]

In the remainder of this chapter, you'll work on showing and hiding UI elements via transitions and learn some new animation skills you can bring into your own projects!

Mixing in transitions

You'll continue to work on the Bahama Air login screen project in this chapter; you've already created a number of compelling animations to the views on this screen to add a bit of pizzazz to the login form and to make the button react to being tapped.

Next, you're going to simulate a bit of user authentication and animate several different progress messages. Once the user taps the Log In button, you'll show them messages including "Connecting…", "Authorizing…" and "Failed".

If you haven't worked through the previous chapters, you can begin with the starter project in the Resources folder for this chapter. If you've followed the examples in the last few chapters in your own project, great job! :] You can simply continue working with your existing project.

Open **ViewController.swift** and look at `viewDidLoad()`. Part of this method adds a hidden image view stored in the class variable status. The code then creates a text label and adds it as a sub-view to `status`.

You'll use status to show the progress messages to the user. The messages are sourced from the messages array, which is another class variable included in the starter project.

Add the following method to ViewController:

```
func showMessage(index: Int) {
  label.text = messages[index]

  UIView.transition(with: status, duration: 0.33,
    options: [.curveEaseOut, .transitionCurlDown],
    animations: {
      self.status.isHidden = false
    },
    completion: {_ in
      //transition completion
    }
  )
}
```

This method takes one parameter called index, which you use to set the value of label to the contents of messages based on index.

Next you call transition(with:duration:options:animations: completion:) to animate the view. To show the banner as it transitions you set isHidden to false within the animations block.

There's another new animation option above: .transitionCurlDown. This transition animates the view like a sheet of paper being flipped down on a legal pad and looks like the following:

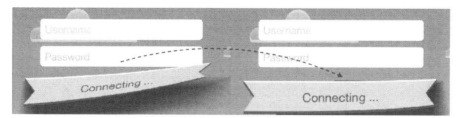

It's time to exercise your new showMessage(index:) method. Find the following block of code in login():

```
animations: {
  self.loginButton.bounds.size.width += 80.0
}, completion: nil)
```

This is your existing animations block that makes the login button bounce when the user taps it. You'll add something new — a completion closure — to this animation that calls showMessage(index:).

Replace the completion's `nil` argument value with the following closure expression:

```
completion: {_ in
  self.showMessage(index: 0)
}
```

The closure takes one Boolean parameter, which tells you whether the animation finished successfully or was cancelled before it ran to completion.

> **Note:** The completion closure above has a single parameter for `completed`. Because you don't care whether it finished or not, Swift allows you to skip binding the parameter by putting "_" in its place.

Inside the closure you simply call `showMessage` with index `0` to show the very first message from the messages array.

Build and run your project; tap the Log In button and you'll see the status banner appear with your first progress message:

Did you see how the banner curled down like a sheet of paper? That's a really nice way to bring attention to messages that are usually just shown as a static text label.

> **Note:** Some of your animations seem to run really quickly, don't they? Sometimes it's tricky to ensure the animation happens at just the right location, and in the correct sequence. Or maybe you just want things to happen slower so you can appreciate the effect!
>
> To slow down all animations in your app without changing your code, select **Debug/Toggle Slow Animations** in **Frontmost App** from the iPhone Simulator menu. Now tap the Login button in your app and enjoy the animations and transitions in vivid slow motion!

For the next animation, you'll first need to save the banner's initial position so you can place the next banner in just the right spot.

Add the following code to the end of `viewDidLoad()` to save the banner's initial position to the property called `statusPosition`:

```
statusPosition = status.center
```

Now you can begin to devise a mixture of view animations and transitions.

Add the following method to remove the status message from the screen via a standard animation:

```
func removeMessage(index: Int) {
  UIView.animate(withDuration: 0.33, delay: 0.0, options: [],
    animations: {
      self.status.center.x += self.view.frame.size.width
    },
    completion: {_ in
      self.status.isHidden = true
      self.status.center = self.statusPosition

      self.showMessage(index: index+1)
    }
  )
}
```

In the code above you use your old friend `animate(withDuration:delay:options:animations:completion:)` to move `status` just outside of the visible area of the screen.

When the animation completes in the `completion` closure, you move status back to its original position and hide it. Finally you call `showMessage` again, but this time you pass the index of the next message to show.

Combining standard animations with transitions is quite easy: you simply call the appropriate API and UIKit calls the corresponding Core Animation bits in the background.

Now you need to complete the chain of calls between `showMessage` and `removeMessage` to mimic a real authentication process.

Find `showMessage(index:)` and replace the comment `//transition completion` with the following code:

```
delay(seconds: 2.0) {
  if index < self.messages.count-1 {
    self.removeMessage(index: index)
  } else {
    //reset form
  }
}
```

Once the transition completes, you wait for 2.0 seconds and check if there are any remaining messages. If so, remove the current message via removeMessage(index:). You then call showMessage(index:) in the completion block of removeMessage(index:) to display the next message in sequence.

> **Note:** delay(seconds:completion:) is a convenience function that runs a block of code after an elapsed delay; it's defined at the top of **ViewController.swift**. Here you're using it to simulate the usual network access delay.

Build and run your project once more; enjoy the resulting animation sequence, which updates the authentication progress messages like so:

Transitions are a small but important subset of animation knowledge to keep in your figurative toolbox, since they're the only way to create 3D-styled animations in UIKit.

If you're looking forward to learning more elaborate 3D effects, you'll have the opportunity to do that in Section VI, "3D Animations", which discusses Core Animation and 3D layer transformations in detail.

Before you move on to the next section, give the challenges in this chapter a try. Since you've learned so much about animation in the last three chapters, one challenge isn't enough — I've given you three!

These challenges give you the chance to wrap up development on your Bahama Air login screen — and also to take on your first über haxx0r challenge. Woot! :]

Challenges

Challenge 1: Pick your favorite transition

So far you've seen only one of the built-in transition animations. Aren't you curious to see what the others look like?

In this challenge you can try out all the other available transition animations and use your favorite to animate the progress message banner.

Open `ViewController` and find the line in `showMessage(index:)` where you specify the transition animation `.transitionCurlDown`:

```
UIView.transitionWithView(status, duration: 0.33, options:
  [.curveEaseOut, .transitionCurlDown], animations: …
```

Replace `.transitionCurlDown` with any of the other transition animations available, then build and run your project to see how they look. Here's the list of available transitions:

```
.transitionFlipFromLeft
.transitionFlipFromRight
.transitionCurlUp
.transitionCurlDown
.transitionCrossDissolve
.transitionFlipFromTop
.transitionFlipFromBottom
```

Which one do you think works best with the other animations on this screen?

In case you don't have a favorite, try my favorite transition: `.transitionFlipFromBottom`. I think it fits really well with the banner graphic:

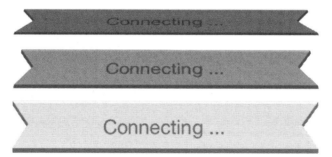

Challenge 2: Reset the form to its initial state

For this challenge, you'll reset the form to its initial state by undoing all the animations that run once you tap the Log In button. That way, if the login fails, the user would see all of the animations happen again when they tap the Log In button a second time.

Here's a list of the general steps you'll need to complete this challenge:

1. Create a new empty method `resetForm()` and call it from your code where the placeholder comment `//reset form` lives.

2. In `resetForm()` use `transition(with:duration:options:
   animations:completion:)` to set the visibility of status to hidden and center to
   `self.statusPosition`. This should reset the banner to its initial state. Use a `0.2`
   seconds duration for that transition.

3. It would be nice if the transition that hides your banner uses the exact opposite
   animation of the one that shows the banner. For example, if you show the banner via
   `.transitionCurlDown`, then use `.transitionCurlUp` to hide it. The reverse
   of `.transitionFlipFromBottom` would be `.transitionFlipFromTop` …and so
   forth.

4. Next, add a call to `animate(withDuration:delay:options:
   animations:completion:)` in `resetForm()`. Make the following adjustments
   inside the animations closure block:

- Move `self.spinner` — the activity indicator inside the Log In button — to its
  original position of (`-20.0, 16.0`).

- Set the alpha property of `self.spinner` to `0.0` to hide it.

- Tint the background color of the Log In button back to its original value:
  `UIColor(red: 0.63, green: 0.84, blue: 0.35, alpha: 1.0)`.

- Continue to reset all changes you made to the Log In button and decrease the
  `bounds.size.width` property by `80.0` points.

- Finally, move the button back up to its original spot under the password field and
  decrease `center.y` by `60.0` points.

If you precisely reversed all of the animations in the authentication process, the screen
should animate as below once all authentication messages have displayed:

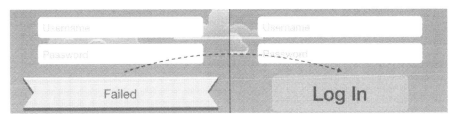

Well done! And now for this chapter's über challenge…

Über haxx0r challenge: animate the clouds in the background

Wouldn't it be cool if those clouds in the background moved slowly across the screen and reappeared from the opposite side?

Yeah, it would totally be cool — and that's your challenge!

The four cloud image views are already wired to four outlets in `ViewController` so you're good to go. You can try to make the clouds move on your own, using your newfound knowledge of transition animations, or you can follow the recipe below:

1. Create a new method with signature `animateCloud(cloud: UIImageView)` and add your code inside that.

2. First, calculate the average cloud speed. Assume the cloud should cross the entire length of the screen in about `60.0` seconds. Call that constant `cloudSpeed` and set it to `60.0 / view.frame.size.width`.

3. Next, calculate the duration for the animation to move the cloud to the right side of the screen. Remember, the clouds don't start from the left edge of the screen, but from random spots instead. You can calculate the correct duration by taking the length of the path the cloud needs to follow and multiplying the result by the average speed: `(view.frame.size.width - cloud.frame.origin.x) * cloudSpeed`.

4. Then call `animate(withDuration:delay:options:animation:completion:)` with the duration you just calculated above. You'll need to create an instance of `TimeInterval` from it as the compiler won't have decided the correct type for you: `TimeInterval(duration)`. For the options parameter use `.curveLinear`; this is one of the very few times you'll use an animation with no easing. Clouds are naturally quite far in the background, so their movement should look absolutely even-keeled.

5. Inside the animations closure expression set the `frame.origin.x` property of the cloud to `self.view.frame.size.width`. This moves the cloud to just outside the screen area.

6. Inside the completion closure block move the cloud to just outside the opposite edge of the screen from its current position. Don't forget to skip the closure parameter by using "_" as you did earlier in this chapter. To position the cloud properly set its `frame.origin.x` to `-cloud.frame.size.width`.

7. Still working in the completion closure, add a call to `animateCloud()` so that the cloud re-animates across the screen.

8. Finally, add the following code to the end of `viewDidAppear()` to start the animations for all four clouds:

```
animateCloud(cloud1)
animateCloud(cloud2)
animateCloud(cloud3)
animateCloud(cloud4)
```

This should make all four clouds traverse the screen slowly to create a nice, unobtrusive effect.

If you completed the challenges for this chapter, congratulations! They were tough! :]

There past few chapters had a lot of information to digest, but you took a stiff, static login form and turned it into an eye-catching and fun experience for the user:

It's time to take a short break from new material and put all your view animation knowledge to the test! In the next chapter, you'll use a wide assortment of the practical things you've learned to add some serious polish to the Bahama Air app.

Chapter 4: View Animations in Practice

You'll take a short breather in this chapter to learn a few techniques that combine the skills you've already gained to produce some new and impressive effects.

Having said that, please note that this chapter is *optional*. If you would like to keep on learning about new APIs, feel free to skip to the next chapter — no hard feelings! :]

However, if you want to flex your animation muscles and learn a few new tips and tricks, then you'll most definitely enjoy working on the project in this chapter, which takes the app for your made-up airline Bahama Air to a new level.

In this chapter you are going to add some cool animations to dress up a flight summary screen, like the one shown below:

There are a few new effects to be found in this chapter that build on the animation foundations you learned in the previous chapters:

1. **Crossfade animation:** An animation that blends one image into another.

2. **Cube transition animation:** A transition animation that creates a faux 3D transition effect.

3. **Fade and bounce transition:** A slightly different take on the combination of simple animations, auxiliary views and everything else you learned up to this point.

This chapter is juicy with code, so head on in to the next section to get started right away!

Crossfading animations

Open the starter project from the **Resources** folder for this chapter. Build and run your project to get acquainted with what you have to work with. The app currently shows the flight summary for a trip from London to Rome with a layover in Paris.

The flight summary screen alternates between the two connecting flights and shows items such as the destination, flight number and gate number:

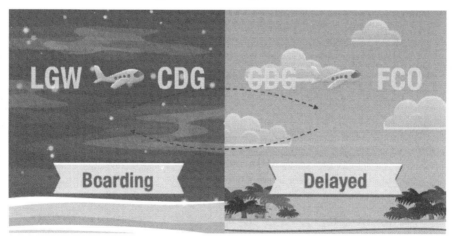

Your first task is to smoothly transition, or **blend**, between the two background images.

Your first instinct might be to simply fade out the present image and then fade in the new one. But this approach would show the content behind the image as the alpha approached zero; you want the content behind this screen to remain hidden during the entire animation.

Fading the images out, then fading them in again would result in an odd-looking transition like the following:

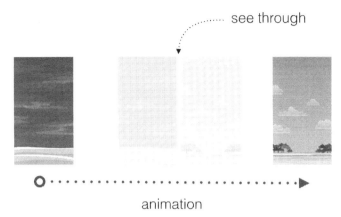

Obviously, you'll need a different approach to solve this problem.

Open **ViewController.swift** and add the following new method to handle your new crossfade effect:

```swift
func fade(imageView: UIImageView, toImage: UIImage, showEffects:
Bool) {
  UIView.transition(with: imageView, duration: 1.0,
    options: .transitionCrossDissolve,
    animations: {
      imageView.image = toImage
    },
    completion: nil
  )

  UIView.animate(withDuration: 1.0, delay: 0.0,
    options: .curveEaseOut,
    animations: {
      self.snowView.alpha = showEffects ? 1.0 : 0.0
    },
    completion: nil
  )
}
```

The method takes the following three parameters:

1. `imageView`: This is the image view you are going to fade out.

2. `toImage`: This is the new image you want visible at the end of the animation.

3. `showEffects`: This is a boolean flag indicating whether the scene should show or hide the snowfall effect. The snowfall animation should only run on the first connecting flight's screen, where presumably the airport is experiencing bad weather.

The transition animation you use this time is of type `.transitionCrossDissolve` — this allows you to simply change the image view's image to the one supplied as a parameter and UIKit automatically creates a cross-fade transition.

Additionally, you fade `snowView` in or out in parallel with the rest of the animation depending on the value of `showEffects`.

> **Note:** That snowfall effect looks pretty cool, right? You'll learn how to make a similar effect in Chapter 22, "Particle Emitters".

So where do you trigger `fade(imageView:,toImage:,showEffects:)` from? Currently `changeFlight(to:)` switches all the data about the two connecting flights.

Since you are going to eventually animate all of the UI elements on this screen, update the signature of that method as follows:

```
func changeFlight(to data: FlightData, animated: Bool = false) {
```

Above, you supply a default value of false for the new animated parameter so that existing calls to this method work as they did before, with no animation.

Next, find the code inside `changeFlight(to:,animated:)` that updates both the image view and the snow view:

```
bgImageView.image = UIImage(named: data.weatherImageName)
snowView.isHidden = !data.showWeatherEffects
```

Wrap it in an `if` statement that optionally animates the transition as shown below:

```
if animated {
  fade(imageView: bgImageView,
    toImage: UIImage(named: data.weatherImageName)!,
    showEffects: data.showWeatherEffects)
} else {
  bgImageView.image = UIImage(named: data.weatherImageName)
  snowView.isHidden = !data.showWeatherEffects
}
```

This method calls `fade(imageView:, toImage:, showEffects:)` when `animated` is true and passes in the proper parameters from `data`.

If you want to see what's inside of data, have a look inside **FlightData.swift**. The FlightData structure is the model that represents a single flight; there's two of those flights already pre-defined in **FlightData.swift**: `londonToParis` and `parisToRome`.

Back in **ViewController.swift** you still need to make one more change before you can see the crossfade effect on screen You need to add the animated parameter to the line where you call changeFlight(to:, animated:).

In changeFlight(to:animated:) change the call to self.changeFlight near the end of the method inside the delay call as follows:

```
self.changeFlight(to: data.isTakingOff ?
  parisToRome : londonToParis, animated: true)
```

Build and run your app; you should now see the image views transition smoothly:

The images blend beautifully into each other, and since you fade the snow effect at the same time, the animation looks seamless. You can even see it snow in Rome for a split second! :]

You've learned an important technique here: transitions can be used to animate changes to non-animatable properties of your views.

> **Note:** If you want to have some fun, you can try also some of the transition effects from the previous chapter. Keep in mind that transitions like .transitionFlipFromLeft are simply too distracting for the current project. .transitionCrossDissolve is a subtle "background" effect which only enhances the animations, which will happen in the foreground.

That takes care of the image view, but the text labels for the flight number and gate number look like they could use some creative animation:

You'll take care of those next with a faux-3D transition.

Cube transitions

The effect you are going to build in this section makes it look like the flight and gate information is on adjacent sides of a cube that rotates around its center to reveal the next value. When complete, your animation will work as illustrated below:

This is not a real 3D effect, but it looks pretty close and it's a great opportunity for you to try animations featuring auxiliary views.

Your approach will be to add a temporary label, animate the heights of the two labels simultaneously, remove the temporary label and, in the end, clean up after yourself.

This will be also the first animation you create that has a **direction**, since you'll play it both forwards and backwards. The direction will determine whether the temporary label appears from the top or bottom.

Start by adding the following enumeration inside the `ViewController` class:

```
enum AnimationDirection: Int {
  case positive = 1
  case negative = -1
}
```

Your animation method will take a parameter that sets the animation direction.

Next, add the initial version of that method as shown below:

```
func cubeTransition(label: UILabel, text: String, direction:
AnimationDirection) {

  let auxLabel = UILabel(frame: label.frame)
  auxLabel.text = text
  auxLabel.font = label.font
  auxLabel.textAlignment = label.textAlignment
  auxLabel.textColor = label.textColor
  auxLabel.backgroundColor = label.backgroundColor
}
```

The method takes three parameters:

1. `label`: The label that you want to animate.

2. `text`: The new text to display on the label.

3. `direction`: The location from where you animate the new text label; this is either the top or the bottom of the view.

To start, you'll create a new label `auxLabel` and copy all key properties of the existing label to it, including `frame`, `font`, and `alignment`.

The single difference between the two labels is the text they each contain: the auxiliary label will contain the new text.

Having the two labels appear at the same position is not what you want. Instead, you need to move the auxiliary label away from the existing view and make it really tiny.

Keep going with the transition! Add the following code to end of `cubeTransition`:

```
let auxLabelOffset = CGFloat(direction.rawValue) *
  label.frame.size.height/2.0

auxLabel.transform = CGAffineTransform(scaleX: 1.0, y: 0.1)
  .concatenating(
    CGAffineTransform(translationX: 0.0, y: auxLabelOffset)
)

label.superview?.addSubview(auxLabel)
```

In the code above, you first calculate the vertical offset for the auxiliary label. The raw value of `direction` is either 1 or −1, which gives you the proper vertical offset to position the temporary label.

Next, you adjust the transform of the auxiliary label to create a faux-perspective effect. When you scale the text on its Y-axis alone, it'll look squashed like you're viewing the plane of the text on edge:

LGW ········▶ LGW

scale(1.0, 1.0)   scale(1.0, 0.1)

Finally, you add the newly created label at the same level in the hierarchy as the existing label.

Next add the following animation code to the end of `cubeTransition`:

```
UIView.animate(withDuration: 0.5, delay: 0.0,
  options: .curveEaseOut,
```

```
    animations: {
      auxLabel.transform = .identity
      label.transform =
        CGAffineTransform(scaleX: 1.0, y: 0.1).concat(
        CGAffineTransform(translationX: 0.0, y: -auxLabelOffset)
      )
    },
    completion: {_ in
      label.text = auxLabel.text
      label.transform = .identity

      auxLabel.removeFromSuperview()
    }
  )
```

In the `animations` block you reset the `transform` of `auxLabel`; this makes the new text grow in height and positions it exactly on top of the old one.

Speaking of the old text, you also apply a transform to label that scales it down and moves it in the direction opposite to where the new text appears.

Insert the following code in `changeFlight(to:animated:)` inside the `if` statement, just below where you call `fadeImageView`:

```
let direction: AnimationDirection = data.isTakingOff ?
  .positive : .negative

cubeTransition(label: flightNr, text: data.flightNr, direction:
direction)
cubeTransition(label: gateNr, text: data.gateNr, direction:
direction)
```

In the same method, **move the existing code** that sets the `flightStatus`, `flightNr`, `gateNr`, `departingFrom`, `arrivingTo` text **inside** the `else` statement, otherwise those statements will change the label's text immediately and spoil your animation.

The completed `else` block should look now like this:

```
} else {
  bgImageView.image = UIImage(named: data.weatherImageName)
  snowView.isHidden = !data.showWeatherEffects

  flightNr.text = data.flightNr
  gateNr.text = data.gateNr

  departingFrom.text = data.departingFrom
  arrivingTo.text = data.arrivingTo

  flightStatus.text = data.flightStatus
}
```

Build and run your project; enjoy the results of your labor as you watch the gate number and flight number animate via your fancy faux-3D transition:

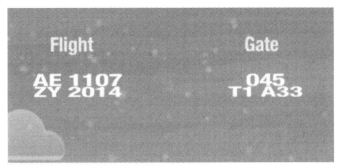

Notice how running the animation both forwards and backwards gives a real impression that you're switching between two alternate states. This screen is becoming more and more alive, thanks to you!

You're not quite done yet; you'll finish off this chapter by adding a composite animation to the three-letter airport codes on the screen to make the screen transitions feel organic and snappy!

Fade and bounce transitions

The final animation in this chapter makes use of labels, auxiliary views, and everything else you've learned up to this point. Consider it a chapter review, if you will! :]

Start by adding the following new method for the new transition animation:

```
func moveLabel(label: UILabel, text: String, offset: CGPoint) {
    let auxLabel = UILabel(frame: label.frame)
    auxLabel.text = text
    auxLabel.font = label.font
    auxLabel.textAlignment = label.textAlignment
    auxLabel.textColor = label.textColor
    auxLabel.backgroundColor = UIColor.clear()

    auxLabel.transform = CGAffineTransform(translationX: offset.x,
y: offset.y)
    auxLabel.alpha = 0
    view.addSubview(auxLabel)
}
```

The new method takes three parameters:

1. `label`: The label you want to animate.

2. `text`: The new text you want to display.

3. `offset`: The arbitrary offset you'll use to animate the auxiliary label.

The code above is pretty simple: just as you did in the previous section, you create an auxiliary label and copy all properties to it from the existing one. To create the label transform, you simply use the `offset` parameter.

Finally, just before you add the new label to the view controller's view, you hide it by setting its `alpha` property to `0.0`.

That sets the stage for your animations. Next you're going to exchange the places of the original and auxiliary labels. This time, instead of using the same animation for both labels, you'll create separate animations for each and move them independent of each other. This will result in an interesting and organic visual effect.

First add the following code to the end of `moveLabel`:

```
UIView.animate(withDuration: 0.5, delay: 0.0,
  options: .curveEaseIn,
  animations: {
     label.transform = CGAffineTransform(translationX: offset.x,
y: offset.y)
     label.alpha = 0.0
  },
  completion: nil
)
```

This animation moves the label away from its original position and fades it out.

Next, add the following code to animate the auxiliary label:

```
UIView.animate(withDuration: 0.25, delay: 0.1,
  options: .curveEaseIn,
    animations: {
      auxLabel.transform = .identity
      auxLabel.alpha = 1.0
    },
    completion: { _ in
      //clean up
    }
  )
```

You reset the auxiliary label's transform above, effectively moving it to its original location. You also fade the text in by animating its alpha value.

Note that this animation kicks off after a 0.1 second delay and it lasts only 0.25 seconds. This means that the two labels will overlap while exchanging places, creating a subtle yet pleasing "ghost" effect:

Before you can test your new animation, you need to add the code to remove the auxiliary label when the animation is complete.

Find the comment //clean up in the completion block of the code you just added and replace it with the following code:

```
auxLabel.removeFromSuperview()
label.text = text
label.alpha = 1.0
label.transform = .identity
```

This wraps up the transition nicely, returns the label to its initial state and sets the new text of the label.

Now find changeFlight(to:,animated:) and add the following code to the bottom of your if animated { statement:

```
let offsetDeparting = CGPoint(
  x: CGFloat(direction.rawValue * 80),
  y: 0.0)

moveLabel(label: departingFrom, text: data.departingFrom,
  offset: offsetDeparting)

let offsetArriving = CGPoint(
  x: 0.0,
  y: CGFloat(direction.rawValue * 50))

moveLabel(label: arrivingTo, text: data.arrivingTo,
  offset: offsetArriving)
```

This new method takes an arbitrary offset as a parameter. This lets you create two different animations for the departure and arrival airports.

For the departure label, you create a horizontal movement; for the arrival airport, you create a vertical movement instead.

That's all the code you need! Build and run your app to see all labels animate via your snappy new transition effect:

Take a moment to appreciate that even in this impressive-looking animation, you've *still* only animated a few properties on any given view. You've worked with bounds, frame, center, transform, `backgroundColor` and alpha — but you've managed to create some very impressive animations with those properties alone!

Animating each property on its own might not always result in mind-blowing effects, but using a combination of a number of simple animations and using subtle yet powerful techniques such as adding auxiliary views and transitions can produce impressive visual effects.

Let your imagination... take flight! :]

Challenges

Challenge 1: Animate the flight status banner

So far there's still one UI element that doesn't animate when the screen switches between the two connecting flights — the flight status:

The piece of text on the banner saying "Boarding" is a `UILabel`; as such, you can use either of the two label animations you created in this chapter to show the alternate flight statuses.

I believe you can figure out how to animate the banner on your own; use the `flightStatus` outlet to access the label and `data.flightStatus` to get the new text to animate to.

Feel free to experiment and play around further. The more experience you gain, the better understanding you will have of animations in UIKit!

Now that you're a pro at animations and transitions, it's time for the final topic on view animations — combining multiple animation steps together with **keyframes**.

Chapter 5: Keyframe animations

Much of the time, you'll find that you need to support multiple, sequential animations for your views. Up until this point you've used the completion closure to **chain** multiple animations to each other.

This approach works in a pinch for chaining two simple animations, but it can lead to some incredibly messy and complicated code when you want to group three, four or more animations together.

Let's see how it would look like if you wanted to chain multiple animations together and move a view in a rectangular pattern:

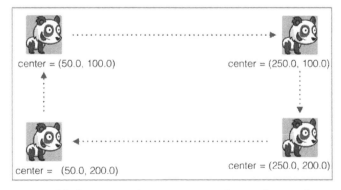

To achieve this you could chain several animations and completion closures together like so:

```
UIView.animate(withDuration: 0.5,
  animations: {
    view.center.x += 200.0
  },
  completion: { _ in
```

```
UIView.animate(withDuration: 0.5,
  animations: {
    view.center.y += 100.0
  },
  completion: { _ in
    UIView.animate(withDuration: 0.5,
      animations: {
        view.center.x -= 200.0
      },
      completion: { _ in
        UIView.animate(withDuration: 0.5,
          animations: {
            view.center.y -= 100.0
          }
        )
      }
    )
  }
)
```

Look at all that nesting! And that's for a simple rectangle-shaped path; can you imagine what that would look like for a more complicated movement?

Instead, you can split the total animation into four distinct stages, or **keyframes**, and then combine the individual keyframes into a **keyframe animation**.

Keyframe animations

Consider another animation that depicts the take-off sequence of a plane. The distinct stages of this animation would look like the following:

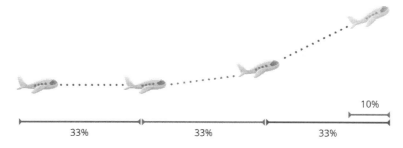

The first stage of the animation sequence accelerates the plane on the runway. The second stage gives the plane a little altitude and tilts it upward. The third stage continues to tilt the plane and boosts the plane skyward at a much faster rate.

There's a fourth and final stage in the final 10% of the animation that fades the plane out of view, as if it were moving behind some low-hanging clouds.

The complete animation could be overwhelming to create, but breaking down the animation into the various stages makes it a lot more manageable. Once you've defined the keyframes for each stage, you've got the problem mostly solved.

You'll learn about keyframes and how to assemble them into a keyframe animation by creating an airplane animation similar to the above — but it will be far more complex. Don't worry, you're more than capable of handling this! :]

Setting up your keyframe animation

If you worked through the project in the last chapter, you can use that as your starting point; if you didn't do that, or if you want to start fresh, you can use the starter project for this chapter.

Build and run your project; you should see the two alternating connecting flights:

You'll make the airplane take off from its starting position, circle around, then land and taxi back to the starting point. This animation will run each time the screen switches between connecting flights.

The complete animation will look something like this:

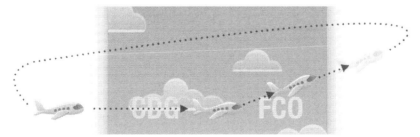

Open **ViewController.swift**; all the code for this animation will live in a new class method named `planeDepart()`.

Find `changeFlight(to:,animated:)` and you'll see an `if animated` statement near the top containing all of the animated changes. Add the following line at the top of the `if` block (be careful to place it *inside* the block):

```
planeDepart()
```

Now add the following initial version of your new animation method `planeDepart()` as shown below:

```
func planeDepart() {
  let originalCenter = planeImage.center

  UIView.animateKeyframes(withDuration: 1.5, delay: 0.0,
    animations: {
      //add keyframes
    },
    completion: nil
  )
}
```

You store the original position of the airplane in `originalCenter` so you'll know where your animation should finish.

You also use `animateKeyframes(withDuration:delay:options:animations:completion:)` to create your first keyframe animation. The parameter list is identical to the ones you've used all along in this book to create your view animations. You set the duration to 1.5 seconds, add no other options and add an empty `animations` closure.

The options for keyframes are different; they come from the `UIViewKeyFrameAnimationOptions` enumeration instead of `UIViewAnimationOptions`. You'll learn about the fine details of keyframe options a little later in this chapter.

Adding keyframes

It's time to add your first keyframe. Replace the `//add keyframes` comment with the following code:

```
UIView.addKeyframe(withRelativeStartTime: 0.0, relativeDuration:
0.25,
  animations: {
    self.planeImage.center.x += 80.0
    self.planeImage.center.y -= 10.0
  }
)
```

This is the first of several calls to `addKeyframe(withRelativeStartTime: relativeDuration:animations:)` you'll be adding.

The animation keyframe above is little different than the animation methods you've used so far.

`addKeyframe(withRelativeStartTime:relativeDuration:animations:)` is the first time you've used relative durations in the animations in this book. The start time of the keyframe, as well as its duration, are expressed as percentages relative to the entire duration of the animation. For example, `0.1` would be 10%, `0.25` would be 25%, and `1.0` would be 100% of the total duration.

Working with relative values lets you specify that a keyframe should last for a fraction of the total time; UIKit takes the relative durations of each keyframe and automagically figures out the exact durations for each keyframe, saving you a ton of work.

In the final bit of code above you set the start time to `0.0` — meaning "immediately" — and the duration to `0.25`, representing 25% of the total animation time:

Since you set the duration of the complete animation to `1.5` seconds, the first keyframe will last for approximately `0.375` seconds. Later on, if you decide to modify the total duration of the animation to a different value, the individual keyframe animations will recalculate their duration times accordingly.

Build and run your project and check out the first frame of your animation:

Running the first keyframe sets in motion the code in the animations closure: the airplane moves `80` points to the right and `10` points up.

This is, of course, only the first step in creating the complete animation sequence. To create the second keyframe, add the following code to the keyframe block, underneath the previous addKeyframe call:

```
UIView.addKeyframe(withRelativeStartTime: 0.1, relativeDuration:
0.4) {
    self.planeImage.transform = CGAffineTransform(rotationAngle:
-.pi / 8)
}
```

The second keyframe starts 10% of the way into the animation and lasts for 40% of the total duration. This keyframe rotates the airplane as it moves off the runway:

Build and run your project now and see how the two keyframes look when they run together:

Keep building your sequence by adding the third keyframe as follows:

```
UIView.addKeyframe(withRelativeStartTime: 0.25,
relativeDuration: 0.25) {
    self.planeImage.center.x += 100.0
    self.planeImage.center.y -= 50.0
    self.planeImage.alpha = 0.0
}
```

In this stage of the animation, you keep the airplane moving along but start to fade it out.

Build and run your project and see how the three keyframes in your animation look:

The plane flies out of sight and disappears. Now you'll need to bring it back and land it safely on the next connecting flight screen.

Before you show the airplane on the screen, you'll have to reset the orientation of the plane — that is, undo the rotation you've applied — and move it to the left of the visible area.

Since the airplane is invisible with its alpha set to 0 for the moment, you can move it around without the user seeing anything. Add the following keyframe to your animation:

```
UIView.addKeyframe(withRelativeStartTime: 0.51,
  relativeDuration: 0.01) {
    self.planeImage.transform = .identity
    self.planeImage.center = CGPoint(x: 0.0, y: originalCenter.y)
}
```

This keyframe runs after all three previous frames have completed and lasts just a small fraction of a second; it resets the plane transform and moves it to the left edge of the screen.

Now you can add the final keyframe and taxi the airplane frame and taxi back to the original location:

```
UIView.addKeyframe(withRelativeStartTime: 0.55,
  relativeDuration: 0.45) {
    self.planeImage.alpha = 1.0
    self.planeImage.center = originalCenter
}
```

This keyframe fades the airplane back in while moving it to the original starting point of the animation.

Build and run your project to see the completed animation sequence as shown below:

Take a minute to review the code you wrote. It's easy to follow and decode; you can modify, rearrange or alter the timing of any of the sections above without too much work on your part.

It's a short step to imagine your animation as a series of separate animations with delays in between, or even as a set of animations triggered from completion closures. Keyframes are an incredibly useful and flexible way to design and control your animations.

Calculation modes in keyframe animations

Keyframe animations don't support the built-in easing curves that are available in standard view animations. This is by design; keyframes are supposed to start and end at specific times and flow into each other.

If each stage of your animation above had an easing curve, the plane would jerk around instead of moving smoothly from one animation into the next. If you *could* apply easing to the entire animation, that would result in your animation durations being ignored — and that's not what you want.

Instead, you have several **calculation modes** to choose from; each mode offers a different method to calculate intermediate frames of the animation as well as different optimizers for smooth movement and even pacing. Check out the documentation by searching for `UIViewKeyframeAnimationOptions` for more details.

Now that you know how to group together any number of simple animations using keyframe animations, you can build just about any sequence that comes to mind. If you want to test your knowledge of keyframes and keyframe animations, give the challenge below a try before moving on to the next section.

Challenges

Challenge: Animate the flight departure times

There's still one UI element on screen that isn't animated: the black flight summary status bar at the top of the screen that shows the flight departure times.

Your challenge is to add a keyframe animation to move the summary offscreen each time the connecting flight data changes. Then you'll change the text to reflect the departure time of the next flight animate it back on screen like so:

The departure summary label is already connected to an outlet called `summary`.

If you need a general structure for your solution, here's a basic recipe you can follow:

• Create a new method `summarySwitch(to: String)` to animate the summary label.

• Inside the method, define a keyframe animation with two keyframes — one to animate the text out of the screen and another to animate it back in.

• Finally, make a call to `delay(seconds:completion:)` outside of the keyframe animation and change the text of the summary label in the closure parameter. You need to time the text change to happen exactly when the label is offscreen.

• Call `summarySwitch(to)` from within the "animated" part of `changeFlight(to:,animated:)`

Don't forget to move the existing non-animated call inside the `else` statement.

How did you do? If you succeeded, congratulations! You've managed to animate every single UI element in the project.

The next section of this book delves into the seemingly complex world of Auto Layout and animations; you'll learn that Auto Layout isn't nearly as mystifying as you might have thought, and you'll learn to animate constraints just as easily as you animate views!

Section II: Auto Layout

Auto Layout has been around for a while now – it was first introduced in iOS 6 and has gone through a series of successful iterations with each release of iOS and Xcode.

The core idea behind Auto Layout is incredibly simple: it lets you define the layout of the UI elements of your app based on relationships you create between each of the elements in the layout.

Although you may have used Auto Layout for static layouts, you'll go beyond that in this section and work with constraints in code to animate them!

You'll need a slightly better understanding of the Auto Layout paradigm than the average iOS developer in order to make your animations play nicely with Auto Layout.

Fortunately, you'll find working with Auto Layout constraints in code isn't as hard as it sounds at first, and it's a fairly straightforward process once you work through a few examples.

In this section of the book you are going to work on a little project named **Packing List**.

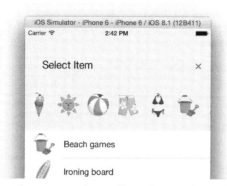

There are two chapters in this section that will guide you through creating animations that co-exist with Auto Layout:

- **Chapter 6, Introduction to Auto Layout** – This will be your crash course on Auto Layout; the great part is that you can carry these concepts on to other areas besides animation.

- **Chapter 7, Animating Constraints** – Once you've worked through the project in Chapter 6, you'll add a number of animations to it and put your newfound knowledge to good use.

By the end of this section, you'll have tamed Auto Layout and will know how to bend it to your will to create some really amazing animations.

Chapter 6: Introduction to Auto Layout

This chapter is for the readers that need an *iOS Animations by Tutorials* crash course on Auto Layout. You will need to have the skills taught in this chapter in order to proceed to the next one, where you'll learn about animations in Auto Layout.

If you are already well-versed in building Auto Layout interfaces, you can skip ahead to Chapter 7, "Animating Constraints".

For those of you out there still reading and eager to dive into using Auto Layout, imagine first, if you will, a world *without* Auto Layout...

You're in charge of creating a new app for your company. Your design, built with Interface Builder, would look like something like the following:

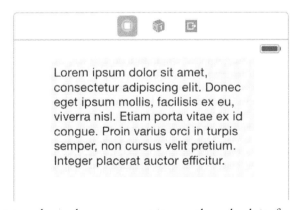

With the view positioned exactly as you want it, you then check its frame in the Size Inspector.

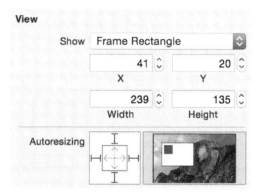

The position and size of your view are expressed in absolute values of points. That *looks* okay, so you launch the iPhone 6 Simulator to see your beautiful app in action:

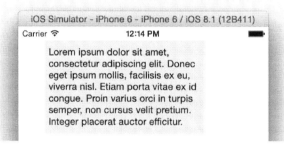

What happened? You view is no longer centered. The problem is that the view's position is expressed in points; you had designed your app in Interface Builder with the iPhone 5s in mind, but since the iPhone 6 has a different screen resolution, your view appears off-center.

When you press Cmd + Right arrow to rotate the Simulator, the situation gets even worse:

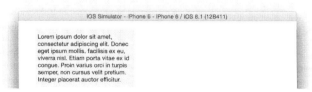

The auto-resizing and re-positioning system in Interface Builder provides a partial solution to these kinds of problems. However, if you're serious about creating dynamic and beautiful user interfaces that work with multiple device sizes and orientations, then you'll need to start using Auto Layout.

Auto Layout to the rescue

Since you're no longer living in the Twilight Zone and Auto Layout is a reality, consider the same project from before, but this time using Auto Layout:

With Auto Layout it's easy to indicate that the `center.y` property of the text view should equal the `center.y` value of its superview. This means the text view will *always* be centered within its superview – independent of the screen on which the app runs.

You could also choose to set the width of the text view to 90% of the width of its superview; this leaves a nice 5% margin of white space around the text.

With this simple set of rules in hand, Auto Layout happily rearranges the elements in your UI to look good on any device, in any orientation:

"So what's the catch?" you might be thinking. Well, there isn't a catch *per se*, it's just that you need to *think differently*.

Once you place your app in the hands of Auto Layout, you no longer set the bounds, frame or center properties of a view. If you were to try, UIKit will force a layout pass on your UI using Auto Layout, which will set everything back to the positions and sizes determined by your constraints.

Not being able to change these properties means that you can't *animate* those properties either! Therefore to move your views around or change their shape, you'll instead alter the Auto Layout rules — or *constraints* — that define where a view appears as well as its size.

But before you can animate constraints, you first need to learn how to create constraints, and more importantly, how they work.

Auto Layout Constraints

Open the starter project for this chapter in Xcode, then build and run your project to see what it looks like:

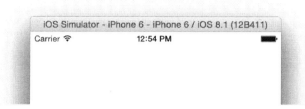

That's right — the project has no UI at all. Your job in this chapter is to build a simple interface with Auto Layout and learn how constraints work.

The project *does*, however, include some starter code:

- **ViewController.swift**: This class contains a few outlets to be connected to the views you'll create in Interface Builder. Further, it contains table view delegate and data source methods, which you will use once you add a table view to the user interface.

- **HorizontalItemList.swift**: This is a scroll view subclass, which shows a scrollable list of images. You'll use this class in the next chapter.

Your goal is to build a very simple dynamic UI, which will have the following appearance on different devices and orientations:

Adding the top menu

First you're going to add the top menu to the interface file. Visually, the menu will resemble a navigation bar.

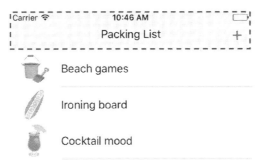

In the next chapter, you're going to make it expand and contract, and offer the user much more than a plain old navigation bar.

Open **Main.storyboard** and drag a custom view onto the existing view controller:

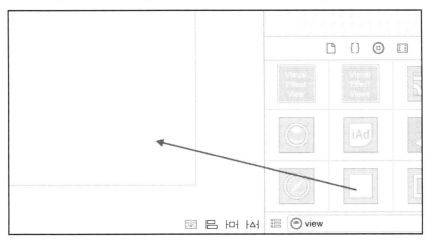

Use the Attributes Inspector to change the background color of the view to **Group Table View Background Color**:

Resize the new view to more or less resemble a navigation bar in size; you don't need to worry about the exact dimensions right now. Make sure to snap the view to the top, left and right edges.

Now that you can actually see the view, you can constrain it to stay always in that top area where you mocked it up in Interface Builder.

Creating your first constraint

Select the view, and then click on the **Pin** button — the second button from the left — in the toolbar in the bottom right corner of Interface Builder (a.k.a. the square TIE fighter button):

In the resulting popup menu, uncheck **Constrain to margins** and click the **left**, **top**, and **right** indicators to create three constraints as shown below:

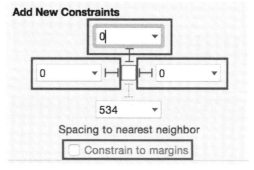

Click the **Create 3 Constraints** button to add them to your view and close the popup.

Each constraint is a relationship expressed as an equation; the top constraint you just created would be represented like so:

```
View.Top = 1 * Superview.Top + 0
```

The top position of your new view will always be 0 pt, because the top of the superview is also 0 pt.

Constraining the menu height

Select your view again and click again on the **Pin** button to get the constraints popup.

This time you want to create a constraint to fix the **Height** of the menu view to a constant value. In the popup, you will see the height of the view you set while positioning the view. Check the checkbox next to **Height** and then click **Add 1 Constraint** at the bottom:

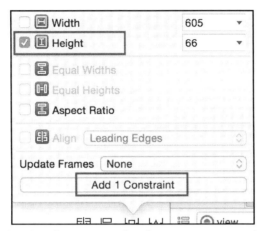

Now you've fixed the height of your menu bar forever. However, what if you wanted the height to be precisely `60pt`? Let's look into how to edit the already created Height constraint.

Deselect the current UI element and select your view once more then switch to the Size Inspector, the second tab from the right in the assistant editor:

Here you'll see all the constraints for the selected view:

You probably don't have the Height fixed to **60pt** so let's fix that. Click the **Edit** button on the offending constraint and set it to **60pt**, like so:

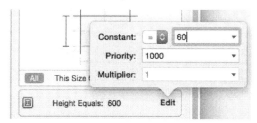

As soon as you do that you'll see the menu resize accordingly:

Build and run your project in any of the iPhone Simulators to see that the layout is preserved across different screen sizes:

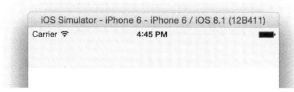

It works! The menu view is always pinned to the top and sides and has a height of **60pt**. And even better — you *understand* how it works. :] Now you can start to populate that menu.

Adding the menu title

Drag a label onto the menu view, set its Text to **Packing List**, the Alignment to **Center**, and the Font size to **21.0** points. Your label should look as follows:

Now you need to center the label in its parent view. Select the label, and while holding the Ctrl key, drag with the mouse (in a diagonal direction) to the menu bar like so:

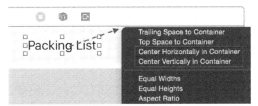

Click **Center Horizontally in Container** to center the label horizontally within the menu. Then, while holding the Ctrl key, drag again and click **Center Vertically in Container** to align the label vertically within the menu.

This creates constraints that fix the label's center coordinate to the center coordinate of the menu:

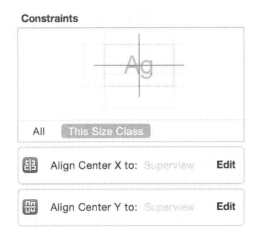

Things don't look quite right in Interface Builder; unless you placed the label precisely in the center of the menu view you'll probably see something like the following:

Resolving Auto Layout issues

While designing in Interface Builder it's possible that dragging views around can result in a difference between where views are placed in Interface Builder, and where your constraints would place them at runtime (i.e. the view is positioned manually on a spot that doesn't reflect the applied constraints).

In the image above, the label just happens to be placed precisely in the vertical center of the menu, so Interface Builder notes this with a **blue guide** indicating the vertical constraint has been satisfied.

The **orange guide**, however, indicates that the horizontal alignment constraint is "broken". Interface Builder shows you the current frame of your view in solid orange along with the frame that the constraint expects in a dashed orange line.

To fix this, ensure the label is selected, then click the **Resolve Auto Layout Issues** button in the bottom right corner of Interface Builder as shown below:

The menu popup presents you with lots of options, but all you want to do here is move the label to the position required by your constraint. Click **Update Frames** and your label will automatically jump to the correct position:

The two new constraints on your label translate to the following equations:

$$Superview.CenterX = 1.0 * UILabel.CenterX + 0.0$$

$$Superview.CenterY = 1.0 * UILabel.CenterY + 0.0$$

There's just a bit more tweaking required; you'll need to move the label down just a touch to leave a bit more headroom at the top.

Positioning elements with Auto Layout

You now need to position the label vertically in the menu. If you're new to Auto Layout, it may be tempting to just drag the label to the position you want. It is important, however, that you **don't**! :] Doing so will break the constraints you've already created, so you'll have to work with the Auto Layout constraints to make it happen.

Select the label, switch to the Size Inspector in the assistant editor, and then double click the constraint called **Align Center Y.** You should see the constraint displayed in a form like below:

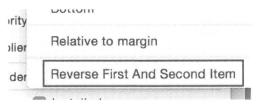

What's this First Item/Second Item business?

A relationship in Auto Layout, like any relationship in the world, has two sides to it. Constraint rules indicate the relationship between your two UI elements. For example, a rule could be: set the view's height (the first item) to half that of its superview (the second item).

Take a look at the constraint relationship above; the first item in the constraint is the Superview. That's not right — you want the constraint to be based from the point of view of your Label instead.

When creating a constraint, Xcode isn't always consistent with the order of the first and second item.

If you have the Packing List label as the first item, great! If not, that's a relatively easy thing to fix. Click on the dropdown menu under **First Item** and select **Reverse First And Second Item:**

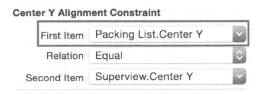

This switches the position of the first and second items. Now you can edit the equation from the point of the view of the label and move the label down a little.

Before moving on, double check that the label is your first item:

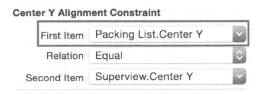

Set **Constant** to 5 as shown below:

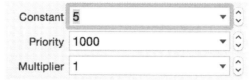

From now on the label will always be 5 points off the vertical center of its parent view.

Next, you'll add the + button on the right hand side of the screen.

Adding a menu button

Drag a button onto the menu view. Set its Title to **+**, Font Size to **27.0**, and align it as shown below:

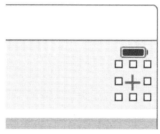

Click the Pin button and check the **Trailing Space** constraint. Click **Create 1 Constraint** to pin the button to the right edge of the view controller.

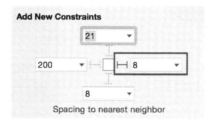

So far you've created only constraints between a view and its superview. But you don't have to *constrain* yourself in this way anymore — pardon the pun ! :] You can create relationships between views on the same level of the view hierarchy as well.

For example, it would be a good idea to vertically align the + button to the title label. This way if you change your mind about the 5 pt offset you added to the label and make it 10 pt instead, the button will automatically follow and stay aligned with the title.

Aligning views with Auto Layout

Select the button and hold Ctrl on your keyboard as you drag with the mouse from the button to the label. Release the mouse button when the label activates and you will see a popup menu like so:

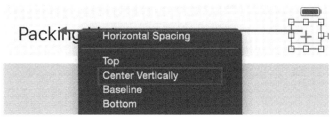

Click on **Center Vertically** to align the button vertically to the label.

Make sure the constant is **0** (zero) and the **First Item** of the new constraint is the + button, as shown in the image below:

This is important because you want to attach the button the title, instead of vice versa. If you see **Packing List.Center Y** as the first item, click on the drop down next to it and then click **Reverse First and Second Item** to switch the two items.

Now select the button again and click on the **Resolve Auto Layout Issues** button, then from the popup menu select **Update Frames**:

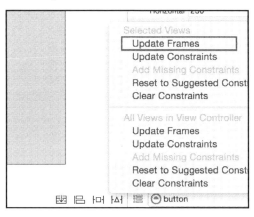

This ought to remove any warnings in Interface Builder. You are almost done with creating the user interface; the only missing element is the table view.

Adding and constraining a table view

Drag a table view and drop it in the empty view controller space:

Since you're getting quite skilled at using Auto Layout in Interface Builder, you'll likely breeze through the steps to set up your table view.

Click the **Pin** button and uncheck **Constrain to Margins**, enable the **top**, **left**, **bottom**, and **right** constraints and set them all to **0**; just be careful *not* to press Enter prematurely before entering all values:

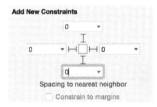

Click **Create 4 Constraints** to add the constraints to your view and close the popup:

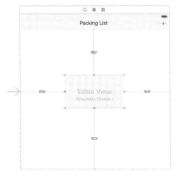

Note that the constraints you create via the **Pin** button popup relate to the table's nearest neighbor, not necessarily its parent view. In the case of the left, right, and bottom constraints above this is the superview — the view controller's view.

In the case of the top constraint above, there's a neighboring view closer to the table's top – the menu. So Interface Builder automatically picks up that view for the top constraint.

There's one final step. Select the table view again, open the **Resolve Auto Layout Issues** popup and click **Update Frames**.

You should see the table align properly within the view controller's view like so:

You're done setting up the basic constraints for your app! You now have a good understanding of how Auto Layout works and how to setup constraints and relationships between views in Interface Builder. Thanks to these new skills of yours, you'll get to create some cool new animations for your Packing List project in the next chapter.

Finalizing the UI

There's just one more thing to take care of before you move on: you need to connect the existing outlets to their corresponding UI elements.

Ctrl-drag with the mouse from the view controller object to the table view, then select **tableView** from the popup menu:

Then **Ctrl-drag** from the view controller to the title and select **titleLabel**:

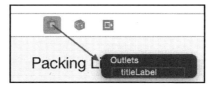

Do the same for the + button and select **buttonMenu**:

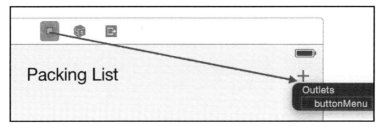

Now **Ctrl-drag** from the button back to the view controller and select **actionToggleMenu** :

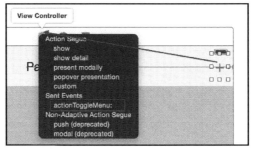

Next, drag from the table view to the view controller and select **dataSource**:

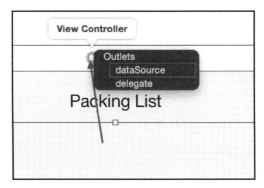

Once again, **Ctrl-drag** from the table view to the view controller but this time select **delegate**:

All that's left is to give your table a prototype cell. Drag a **table view cell** object onto the table view, like so:

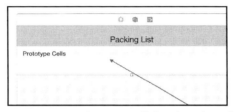

Then open the Attributes Inspector and enter **Cell** for the **Identifier**:

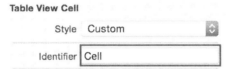

At long last, build and run your project; the existing table view code in **ViewController.swift** will pick up the newly connected outlets and populate the table with data:

The app not only *looks* good, but it has a rock-solid layout thanks to Auto Layout. Give the app a whirl in different Simulators — both iPhone and iPad — and change the orientation to check it out for yourself!

Challenges

Your challenge this time is simple: simply head on in to the next chapter! By now you understand Auto Layout in some detail, which is an important prerequisite for the work you're about to do in the next chapter, which deals with animations and Auto Layout.

See you in the next chapter! :]

Chapter 7: Animating Constraints

In the previous chapter, you learned how to use Auto Layout to create a responsive user interface for your Packing List project. You'll take it up a notch in this chapter and add a number of bouncy animations to your app.

You've learned that in order for Auto Layout to work properly, you can't fiddle directly with the view's frame or center properties; instead, you have to work with the layout constraints to create your desired animations.

So far you've seen how to animate view properties: you can animate numeric properties, such as `alpha`, from one float value to another. Instances of `CGPoint`, like in the case of the center property, can be modified progressively until the center value reaches the target position.

Naturally, your next question would be "That's great — but how do I animate a *constraint*?"

Animating constraints is no more difficult than animating properties; it's just a little different. Usually you simply replace an existing constraint with a new one and let Auto Layout animate the UI between the two states.

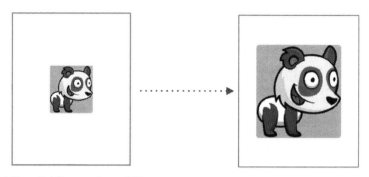

width = 0.4 *superview.width   width = 0.8 *superview.width

The sole exception is when you **only** need to change a single property of the constraint, such as constant, in the constraint's equation. In that case, you simply modify the constraint directly in code and animate the change.

In this chapter, you'll add an animation to expand the Packing List menu bar and reveal a list of items; the user can then tap an item to add it to their packing list as shown below:

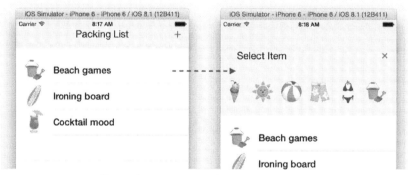

This interaction — as well as a few more visual treats — will be driven by fluid and eye-catching animations.

What are you waiting for? Time to get packing! :]

Animating Interface Builder constraints

If you completed the project from the previous chapter, you can carry on where you left off; otherwise, you can use the starter project from this chapter. Before you start, make sure the menu in your app looks like the images below across different iPhone simulators:

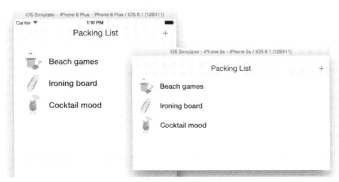

Your first task is to expand the menu when the user taps the + button. In order to do that, you'll need to change the height of the menu bar by animating its height constraint.

Making the menu expand

Open **ViewController.swift** and scroll to the top of the class. Under the rest of the outlets add the following line of code:

```
@IBOutlet weak var menuHeightConstraint: NSLayoutConstraint!
```

NSLayoutConstraint is the class that represents the constraints you create in Interface Builder. Just like any other button, image view, or label, you can also create an outlet to a constraint.

Open **Main.storyboard** and select the menu view:

Open the Size Inspector tab and double click on the Constraint that says **Height Equals: 60**. This will open the familiar view of the constraint's equation:

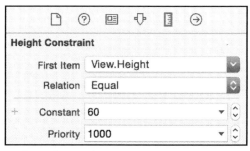

Switch to the last tab on the right — the **Connections Inspector**:

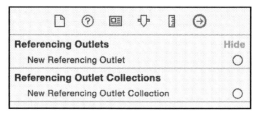

From here you can connect the constraint to its outlet in ViewController.

Drag from the small circle next to **New Referencing Outlet** to the view controller object:

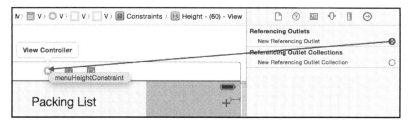

From the popup menu, select the only available option: **menuHeightConstraint**. You've now created your outlet, as shown in the image below:

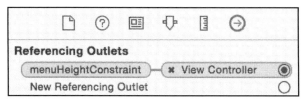

Open **ViewController.swift** and add the following three lines to `actionToggleMenu()`:

```
isMenuOpen = !isMenuOpen
menuHeightConstraint.constant = isMenuOpen ? 200.0 : 60.0
titleLabel.text = isMenuOpen ? "Select Item" : "Packing List"
```

In the code above, you first toggle the Boolean variable isMenuOpen, which tracks whether the menu is currently expanded or collapsed.

Next, you modify the constraint's `constant` property to either 200.0 pt or 60.0 pt, depending on the state of `isMenuOpen`, to make the menu expand or collapse as required.

In the final line of code you toggle the menu title between **Packing List** and **Select Item** as appropriate.

Build and run your project; tap the + button a few times and the menu should expand and contract as you had planned:

To animate the layout changes, you'll need your old friend `animate(withDuration:animations:)` or any of the similar APIs.

Animating layout changes

Add the following code to the bottom of `actionToggleMenu`:

```
UIView.animate(withDuration: 1.0, delay: 0.0,
  usingSpringWithDamping: 0.4, initialSpringVelocity: 10.0,
  options: .curveEaseIn,
  animations: {
    self.view.layoutIfNeeded()
  },
  completion: nil
)
```

In the code above, you create a spring animation (just as you learned about in Chapter 2, "Springs") and force an update of the layout from within the animations closure. This is all it takes to animate your constraint modifications.

Still a little fuzzy on what's happening above? Here's a bit more background on how the animation works.

When you modify pertinent view properties inside an animation closure, they'll be animated as you would expect, and Auto Layout will still set the bounds and center of your views once it finishes its calculations.

In this case, you've already updated the constraint value, but iOS hasn't had a chance to update the layout yet. By calling layoutIfNeeded() from within the animation closure, you set the center and bounds of *every* view involved in the layout. That's it — there's no magic happening in the background! :]

If you *hadn't* called layoutIfNeeded(), UIKit would have performed a layout anyway since you changed a constraint, which marked the layout as **dirty**.

Build and run your project again; tap the + button and you'll see the menu expand and contract with a bouncy animation.

You can even see that the menu title temporarily overlays the system menu on its way back up:

Of course, once the animation settles down it all looks good again.

Did you notice that the table view *also* shrank and grew along with the menu? Instead of covering up the table, the menu actually *pushed* the table view away as it expanded.

This is because of the existing constraint you added in the previous chapter that attaches the top of the table to the bottom of the menu. When the menu grows, the table shrinks to satisfy the constraint.

Two animations for the price of one! :]

To spice things up a bit, you'll now mix constraint animations with some non-constraint animations to see what new effects you can create.

Your next task is to rotate the + button by 45 degrees when the menu expands so it resembles an **x** — i.e. a close button.

Rotating view animations

Since you already know how to rotate views by adjusting their transform, add the following code to the final `animations` closure:

```
let angle: CGFloat = self.isMenuOpen ? .pi / 4 : 0.0
self.buttonMenu.transform = CGAffineTransform(rotationAngle:
angle)
```

When the menu expands, you set the angle of the rotation to 45 degrees (or π/4 radians); when it contracts, you simply set the rotation back to 0. Then you update the transform on the button to set the view in motion.

Build and run your project; tap the + button to see how the rotation animation looks alongside the call to `layoutIfNeeded()`:

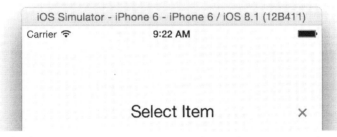

The animation looks gorgeous; you can temporarily set the animation duration to 5–6 seconds to see exactly how the + sign rotates to become an **x**. You can also see the button bounce around its center thanks to the spring animation that drives both the constraint and rotation animations.

Inspecting and animating constraints

Working with outlets in a visual fashion is a relatively easy way to connect up your outlets, but sometimes you can't use Interface Builder to connect all the bits of your UI to your outlets. You might add constraints from code, or maybe you just don't want to Control-drag and create a massive number of outlets!

In these cases, you need to inspect the existing constraints at runtime and modify in code the ones you want to animate.

Luckily, the `UIView` class has a property named `constraints`, which gives you a list of all constraints that affect the given view. How convenient is that? :]

Add the following code to the top of `actionToggleMenu()`:

```
titleLabel.superview?.constraints.forEach { constraint in
  print(" -> \(constraint.description)\n")
}
```

This one-liner loops over all constraints affecting the menu bar view and prints them one by one to Xcode's output console.

Build and run your project; tap the + button to see all constraints neatly listed like so:

```
▽  ▶  ▐▐  △  ⊥  ⊥  ◫  ◁  ▦ PackingList
-> <NSLayoutConstraint:0x7fa10a424f20 V:[UIView:0x7fa10a421490(200)]>

-> <NSLayoutConstraint:0x7fa10a42afb0 UILabel:0x7fa10a4154b0'Select Item'.centerX == UIView:
0x7fa10a421490.centerX>

-> <NSLayoutConstraint:0x7fa10a42b090 UILabel:0x7fa10a4154b0'Select Item'.centerY == UIView:
0x7fa10a421490.centerY + 5>

-> <NSLayoutConstraint:0x7fa10a42b1f0 UIButton:0x7fa10a516c40'+'.centerY == UILabel:
0x7fa10a4154b0'Select Item'.centerY>

-> <NSLayoutConstraint:0x7fa10a42b240 H:[UIButton:0x7fa10a516c40'+']-(8)-|   (Names: '|':UIView:
0x7fa10a421490 )>
```

It looks a bit messy, but read through the output carefully and you'll be able to figure out what each constraint does. Take the following constraint as an example:

```
UIView:...centerX == UILabel:...'Select Item'.centerX
```

It's clear that this is a constraint between a `UIView` and a `UILabel`; the description also includes the current text of the label. `centerX` is also mentioned a few times...aha! This must be the constraint that horizontally centers the title within the menu bar. It's time to animate this bad boy.

Animating UILabel constraints

Find the following line near the top of `actionToggleMenu(_:)`:

```
isMenuOpen = !isMenuOpen
```

Then add the following code *below* that line:

```
titleLabel.superview?.constraints.forEach { constraint in
  if constraint.firstItem === titleLabel &&
    constraint.firstAttribute == .centerX {
    constraint.constant = isMenuOpen ? -100.0 : 0.0
    return
  }
}
```

Here you loop over the list of constraints affecting the menu bar view, but this time you are looking for a certain constraint to adjust.

Do you recall the equation for the horizontal center constraint? It looked something like the following:

Superview.CenterX = 1.0 * UILabel.CenterX + 0.0

The `NSLayoutConstraint` properties map to the above equation in a very straightforward manner:

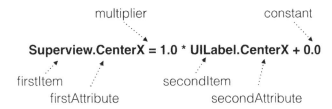

The `if` condition makes more sense now when you look back at the last piece of code you added: for each constraint, you check if the `secondItem` is the title label and if the constraint aligns with the title's `CenterX`.

When you find the correct constraint, you adjust `constant` to 100 pt to push the title to the left when the menu opens.

> **Note:** There's slightly easier way to dynamically find an existing constraint and work with it; you'll look into that next.

Build and run your project; tap the + button to see how your new constraint logic works:

Remember you're calling `layoutIfNeeded()` from within a spring animation API, so the title animation bounces a bit.

> **Note:** If by any chance your animation doesn't kick in, check out the Center Horizontally in Superview constraint on the label; make sure the label is the first item and the menu bar view is the second.

Your UI is starting to look really cool, but you know you can take this even further. The next section shows you how to *replace* constraints to create some neat animations.

Animating by replacing constraints

At this point in the chapter, you've only modified the `constant` property of your constraints. Ironically, the `constant` property is a *mutable* property in the `NSLayoutConstraint` class!

If you want to modify the multiplier, or change a constraint in any other way, you'll need to remove the constraint then add a new one in its place.

To learn how to do that, you'll animate the vertical alignment of the menu title to move it up a bit as the menu opens. This should leave enough empty space at the bottom of the menu to show some more content, which you'll add later in this chapter.

This time around, you'll use a different technique to make sure you've got the correct constraint.

In Interface Builder you can assign an identifier to each constraint, which can help you easily get hold of it at run time.

Open **Main.storyboard** and find the **Align Center Y** constraint of the title label:

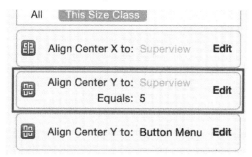

Double click the constraint and in the **Identifier** text box enter **TitleCenterY**:

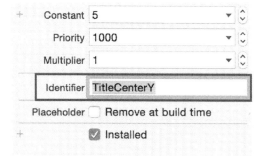

Back in **ViewController.swift** find the following spot in the code within `actionToggleMenu`, at the end of the `for` loop:

```
titleLabel.superview?.constraints.forEach { constraint in
  if constraint.firstItem === titleLabel && constraint.firstAttribute == .centerX {
    constraint.constant = isMenuOpen ? -100.0 : 0.0
    return
  }                  ←——————————————————    add code here
}
```

Insert the following code at the point indicated above:

```
if constraint.identifier == "TitleCenterY" {
  constraint.isActive = false
  //add new constraint
  continue
}
```

You check if the identifier of the constraint is the same as the one you want to replace and if so, you remove the constraint. You do that by setting `isActive` to `false`; this causes the view hierarchy to remove the constraint. If you don't also have a reference to it, the constraint object will be deleted from memory.

Build and run your project; tap + and observe what happens:

Since there's no longer a constraint to keep the view aligned, the title simply bounces to the top of its superview. The + button obediently tags along because its own `CenterY` is attached to the title's `CenterY`.

Amusing as the effect is, you'll need to add a new constraint and fix the layout.

Adding constraints programmatically

When the menu is retracted you want the title vertically centered within the menu view like so:

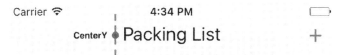

Or, to express the constraint via its equation:

```
Title.CenterY = Menu.CenterY * 1.0 + 0.0
```

But when the menu expands, you'd like to move the title a bit upwards to make space for the list of packing items later on:

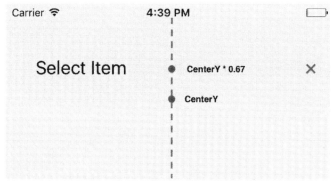

Here's the constraint's equation spelled out in detail:

```
Title.CenterY = Menu.CenterY * 0.67 + 0.0
```

Find the placeholder comment //add new constraint in the code you just added, and replace it with the following:

```
let newConstraint = NSLayoutConstraint(
    item: titleLabel,
    attribute: .centerY,
    relatedBy: .equal,
    toItem: titleLabel.superview!,
    attribute: .centerY,
    multiplier: isMenuOpen ? 0.67 : 1.0,
    constant: 5.0)
newConstraint.identifier = "TitleCenterY"
newConstraint.isActive = true
```

NSLayoutConstraint's initializer takes a cartload of parameters, but happily they map exactly to all parts of the constraint's equation. The parameters are as follows:

- item: The first item in the equation; in this case, the title label.

- attribute: The attribute of the first item of the new constraint.

- relatedBy: A constraint can represent either a mathematical equality or an inequality.

In this book, you'll only use equality expressions, so here you use `.equal` to represent this relationship.

- `toItem`: The second item in the constraint equation; in this case, it's your title's superview.

- `attribute`: The attribute of the second item of the new constraint.

- `multiplier`: The equation multiplier as discussed earlier.

- `constant`: The equation constant.

As an additional step you give the constraint the identifier **TitleCenterY**. You will use that identifier the next time the user toggles the menu to find and replace the constraint you just created.

Finally you need to set the active property on the constraint to true and that tells Auto Layout to apply it to the current layout.

> **Note:** If you've used Auto Layout from code before you might be accustomed to a method called addConstraint on UIView to add your constraints.
>
> The preferred approach is to add constraints by setting their active property or calling `NSLayoutConstraint.activate(_:)` with an array to activate many constraints at once.

Build and run your project; open the menu and the title should move up to a spot just above the vertical center of the menu bar as shown below:

Adding menu content

Your next job is to show a list of items in the menu; these are all possible items you can add to your packing list. The `HorizontalItemList` class that came with your starter project will assist you in displaying that list of items.

> **Note**: This chapter won't cover `HorizontalItemList` in detail; its implementation isn't relevant to creating animations. However, you're still welcome to peek into **HorizontalItemList.swift** if you want to see how it works!

Still in **ViewController.swift**, scroll to the bottom of `actionToggleMenu` and add the following code:

```
if isMenuOpen {
  slider = HorizontalItemList(inView: view)
  slider.didSelectItem = {index in
    print("add \(index)")
    self.items.append(index)
    self.tableView.reloadData()
    self.actionToggleMenu(self)
  }
  self.titleLabel.superview!.addSubview(slider)
} else {
  slider.removeFromSuperview()
}
```

If the menu is about to open, you create a new instance of `HorizontalItemList` in `slider` to hold your new items, assign a closure expression to `didSelectItem` and then finally add slider to the menu bar.

`didSelectItem` runs when the user taps an image in the list; in this event, you add the image index to the list of selected items and reload the table view. In the else branch, when the menu is about to close, you simply remove the image list from its parent view.

Build and run your project; add a few items to see what the list of images looks like:

You're nearly done; the final section of this chapter will walk you through dynamically creating and animating views in code.

Animating dynamically created views

Your ultimate task, which will use everything you've learned up to this point and close out the chapter nicely, will be to create a new view, add some constraints to the view and animate it on the screen.

`showItem(_:)` in `ViewController` is called when you tap a table row. Your task is to create an image view with the tapped image index and display it at the bottom of the screen as shown below:

Add the following code to `showItem(_:)` to create an image view out of the selected image:

```
let imageView = UIImageView(image: UIImage(named:
"summericons_100px_0\(index).png"))
imageView.backgroundColor = UIColor(red: 0.0, green: 0.0, blue:
0.0, alpha: 0.5)
imageView.layer.cornerRadius = 5.0
imageView.layer.masksToBounds = true
imageView.translatesAutoresizingMaskIntoConstraints = false
view.addSubview(imageView)
```

In the code above, you load the selected image and create an image view from it. You give it a semi-transparent black background and round the corners slightly. Notice that you *don't* set the position of the image view in its parent view.

Next you'll create the constraints for the image view, one by one. Add the following code directly below the code you just added:

```
let conX = imageView.centerXAnchor.constraint(equalTo:
view.centerXAnchor)
```

This method uses the new NSLayoutAnchor class, which makes creating common constraints really easy. Here, you're creating a constraint between the center x anchor of the image view and the view controller's view.

Next, add the code below to give the image view a bottom constraint:

```
let conBottom = imageView.bottomAnchor.constraint(equalTo:
  view.bottomAnchor, constant: imageView.frame.height)
```

This constraint sets the bottom of the image view to match the bottom of the view controller's view, plus the image height; this positions the image just off the bottom edge of the screen, which will serve as the starting point of the animation.

Next you are going to fix up the image width. Add the following code:

```
let conWidth = imageView.widthAnchor.constraint(equalTo:
  view.widthAnchor, multiplier: 0.33, constant: -50.0)
```

This sets the image width to 1/3 of the screen width less 50 pt. The target size is 1/3 of the screen; you'll animate away the 50 pt difference to make the image "grow" into place later.

Finally, you just need to set the height of the image. Since the images are square you can just set the height as equal to the image width.

Add one final bit of code for the last constraint, then activate them all in a group:

```
let conHeight = imageView.heightAnchor.constraint(equalTo:
imageView.widthAnchor)

NSLayoutConstraint.activate([conX, conBottom, conWidth,
conHeight])
```

This last constraint is a little different from the rest, as it's the first time you've created a relationship between two properties of the same view. Don't worry — this will still work out just fine. :]

Build and run your project; tap a table row and you'll see your new image view appear like so:

This is, of course, just the starting position of your animation. Your job now is to make the image pop up from the bottom.

Adding additional dynamic animations

Add the following code to showItem(_:):

```
UIView.animate(withDuration: 0.8, delay: 0.0,
   usingSpringWithDamping:  0.4, initialSpringVelocity: 0.0,
   animations: {
     conBottom.constant = -imageView.frame.size.height/2
     conWidth.constant = 0.0
     self.view.layoutIfNeeded()
   },
   completion: nil
)
```

Changing constant on conY moves the image up, and the adjustment to conWidth grows the image width by 50 pt to make the image return to its original size. You don't need to set the height as it's automatically constrained to the image width.

Finally you call layoutIfNeeded(), which kicks off the animations. Build and run your project; tap a few table rows to see your image animate:

Hang on! The image view starts from the top left of the screen then flies into the middle! What happened?

Think about it for a moment: you added a view, set some constraints, then altered those constraints and animated a layout change. However, the view never got the chance to perform its initial layout, so your image started from its default position at (0, 0) in the top left. Ah — that's why it's flying in like that.

To fix this, you need to make sure your initial layout happens before the animation starts. Add the following code *before* the animation call:

```
view.layoutIfNeeded()
```

This will immediately set your initial layout before anything else happens. All constraint changes you make between the call to `layoutIfNeeded()` and the next one will be part of your animation.

Build and run your project now and the animations should work as intended.

It's a little annoying that the images keep piling up on top of each other; you'll fix this in the challenge at the end of this chapter.

Don't forget to try the project in different simulators and orientations; your constraint animations should look good in all of them:

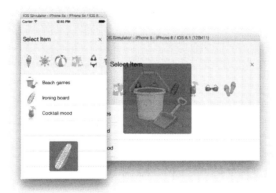

Challenges

Challenge 1: Animate the image out of the screen

OK — now you get to fix those pesky image views that stay stuck on the screen.

In `showItem(_:)`, keep the image visible for 1 second and then animate it back out of the screen.

Use the animation method that lets you set a delay for the animation, animate the image back out of the screen, and finally remove the image view from the view hierarchy in the animation completion closure.

That's all you need to know to complete the challenge. Good luck!

You now have a good understanding of how to create view animations in Auto Layout projects. Although not all projects in this book make use of Auto Layout, try to use it when you can to keep your skillset fresh!

Section III: Layer Animations

Now that you are proficient in creating view animations, it's time to dig a bit more deeply and look into the Core Animation APIs on a lower, more powerful level.

In this section of the book, you'll learn about animating layers instead of views and how to make use of special layers.

Views vs. layers

A layer is a simple model class that exposes a number of properties to represents some image-based content. Every UIView is backed by a layer, so you can think of layers as the lower-level behind the scenes class behind your content.

- A layer is different from a view (with respect to animations) for the following reasons:

- A layer is a model object – it exposes data properties and implements no logic. It has no complex Auto Layout dependencies nor does it handle user interactions.

- It has pre-defined visible traits – these traits are a number of data properties that affect how the contents is rendered on screen, such as border line, border color, position and shadow.

- Finally, Core Animation optimizes the caching of layer contents and fast drawing directly on the GPU.

To compare views and layers side by side:

Views

- Complex view hierarchy layouts, Auto Layout, etc.

- User interactions.

- Often have custom logic or custom drawing code that executes on the main thread on the CPU.

- Very flexible, powerful, lots of classes to subclass.

Layers

- Simpler hierarchy, faster to resolve layout, faster to draw.

- No responder chain overhead.

- No custom logic by default. and drawn directly on the GPU.

- Not as flexible, fewer classes to subclass.

If you need to choose between views and layers here is my tip: *choose view animations any time you can to do the job*; you will know when you need more performance or flexibility and have to switch to layer animations instead.

Don't stress yourself about it though, because you can mix and match view and layer animations freely.

By the end of this section, you will know how – and when! – to animate your views, and when it's appropriate to use layers.

Section overview

In the first four chapters, you'll re-create and improve upon some of the view animations you played with earlier in this book in your Bahama Air projects:

- **Chapter 8, Getting Started with Layer Animations** You'll start with the simplest layer animations, but also learn about debugging animations gone wrong.

- **Chapter 9, Animation keys and delegates** Here you gain more control over the currently running animations and use delegate methods to react to animation events.

- **Chapter 10, Groups and advanced timing** In this chapter you combine a number of simple animations and run them together as a group.

- **Chapter 11, Layer Springs** – In this chapter you learn how to use `CASpringAnimation` to create powerful and flexible spring layer animations.

- **Chapter 12, Keyframe animations and struct properties** - Here you'll learn about layer keyframe animations, which are powerful and slightly different than view keyframe animations. There's some special handling around animating struct properties, which you'll also learn about.

Next, you'll move on to playing with specialized layers:

- **Chapter 13, Shapes and masks** – Draw shapes on the screen via CAShapeLayer and animate its special path property.

- **Chapter 14, Gradient animations** – Learn how to use `CAGradientLayer` to help you draw and animate gradients.

- **Chapter 15, Stroke and path animations** – Here you will draw shapes interactively and work with some powerful features of keyframe animations.

- **Chapter 16, Replicating animations** – you'll learn how to create multiple copies of your layer content and then animate them in sync.

You're in for an amazing ride – *buckle up*! :]

Chapter 8: Getting Started with Layer Animations

Layer animations work much like view animations; you simply animate a property between a start and an end value over a defined period of time and let Core Animation take care of the rendering in between.

However, layers have a bigger number of animatable properties than views; this gives you a lot of choice and flexibility when it comes to designing your effects; many specialized CALayer subclasses add other properties that you can use in your animations.

This chapter will introduce you to the basics of CALayer and Core Animation. You'll get a feel for working with animations in layers; you'll learn how to move layers around, fade them in and out and create animations comparable to the ones you created using UIKit.

Animatable properties

Some of the animatable properties in CALayer correspond directly to the view properties you worked with in previous chapters, such as frame, position and opacity. You'll see both the familiar and the new animatable properties used in layer animation in this chapter.

You'll re-create some of the earlier view animations but with layers, so you can draw the parallels and see for yourself where the similarities end — and where the new possibilities begin.

Position and size

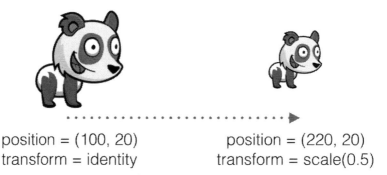

position = (100, 20)   position = (220, 20)
transform = identity   transform = scale(0.5)

Animating the position, size, or transform of a layer equally affects any view contained within that layer, just as if you had directly animated the view itself.

- `bounds`: modify this to animate the bounding frame of the layer.

- `position`: modify this to animate the position of the layer within its parent layer. You can animate `position.x` or `position.y` separately if you want to control movement on only one axis.

- `transform`: modify this to move, scale, and rotate the layer. You can even animate layers in 3D space, which you can't do with views alone. You'll learn about 3D layer transforms in Section IV, "3D Animations".

Border

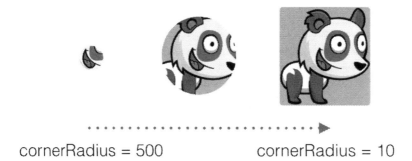

cornerRadius = 500   cornerRadius = 10

You can easily animate a layer's border to change its color, width and corner radius:

- `borderColor`: modify this to change the border tint.

- `borderWidth`: modify this to grow or shrink the width of the border.

- `cornerRadius`: modify this to change the radius of the layer's rounded corners.

Shadow

shadowOffset = (0, 0)   shadowOffset = (20, 20)

You can animate all aspects of the layer's shadow:

- **shadowOffset**: Modify this to make the shadow appear closer to or further away from the layer.

- **shadowOpacity**: Modify this to make the shadow fade in or out.

- **shadowPath**: Modify this to change the shape of the layer's shadow. You can create different 3D effects to make your layer look like it's floating with different shadow shapes and positions.

- **shadowRadius**: Modify this to control the blur of the shadow; this is especially useful when simulating movement of the view towards or away from the surface where the shadow is cast.

Contents

opacity = 1.0   opacity = 0.25

Finally, there are a few properties that control how the layer's contents are rendered:

- **contents**: Modify this to assign raw TIFF or PNG data as the layer contents.

- **mask**: Modify this to establish the shape or image you'll use to mask the visible contents of the layer; you'll use this property to create some very cool effects in Chapter 13, "Shapes and Masks".

- `opacity`: Modify this to animate the transparency of the layer contents.

Keep in mind that this is only a *partial* list of properties you can animate; subclasses of `CALayer` usually have other properties that you can animate as well.

The properties listed above are enough to get you started; it's time to get to work on your first animation with layer properties.

Your first layer animation

You'll begin with the completed Bahama Air login screen project from the end of Chapter 3, "Transitions". As always, you can build on your previous work or open the starter project included with this chapter.

Build and run your project to see the familiar sight of the Bahama Air login screen:

Your job is to remove the existing view animations and replace them one-by-one with layer-based animations.

Open **ViewController.swift** and find `viewWillAppear()`.

Remove the line below that moves the heading out of the screen bounds:

```
heading.center.x -= view.bounds.width
```

There's no need to perform this action anymore since you can specify *both* the start and end values in your layer animation.

Next, scroll down to `viewDidAppear()` and remove the animation call that moves `heading` as shown below:

```
UIView.animate(withDuration: 0.5) {
    self.heading.center.x += self.view.bounds.width
}
```

Build and run your project; watch the animation screen and check that the form title is no longer animated:

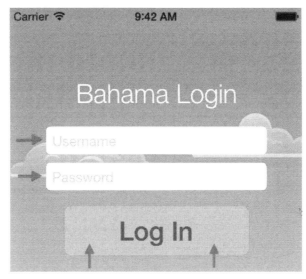

Now that you've stripped out the old view animation code, it's time to add some layer animations! Find `viewWillAppear()` and add the following code at the top of the method, underneath the call to `super`:

```
let flyRight = CABasicAnimation(keyPath: "position.x")
flyRight.fromValue = -view.bounds.size.width/2
flyRight.toValue = view.bounds.size.width/2
flyRight.duration = 0.5
```

Animation objects in Core Animation are simply data models; you create an instance of the model and set its data properties accordingly.

An instance of `CABasicAnimation` describes a *potential* layer animation: one that you might choose to run now, at a later time, or not at all.

Since the animation isn't bound to a specific layer, you can re-use the animation on other layers and each layer will run a copy of the animation independently.

In an animation model you can specify the property to animate as the `keypath` argument; that's convenient, as you'll always be animating *something* in the layer.

Here, you're animating only the x component of the position. Core Animation conveniently exposes the individual members of position, bounds, and transform so you can animate them each separately.

Next, you set the `fromValue` and `toValue` for the property you've specified on `keypath`. In this case, you want it to start offscreen to the left and end up in the center of the screen.

Finally, the concept of the animation duration hasn't changed; here you set the duration to 0.5 seconds.

Now that your animation is all set up, you can add it to a layer in your app and see how it looks. Add the following line below the code you just added to add your animation to your title layer:

```
heading.layer.add(flyRight, forKey: nil)
```

`add(_:forKey:)` makes a copy of the animation object and tells Core Animation to run it on the layer. The key argument is for your use only; it lets you identify the animation later on if you need to change or stop the animation.

Build and run your project; you'll see the form title move to the center of the screen as shown below:

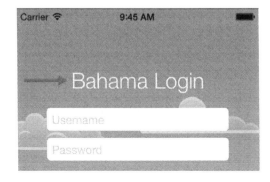

As expected, the layer — and its contained view — animate smoothly into position. This shows you how closely a view and its backing layer are bound.

> **Note:** Animating structs such as `CGRect` or `CATransform3D` isn't as straightforward as it is with object values, like you did above. You'll see how to animate structs in Chapter 12, "Keyframe Animations and Struct Properties".

Now that you have the basics nailed down, things are only going to get more interesting! :]

More elaborate layer animations

You've handled the title layer on your login screen; your next task is to take care of the username field.

Scroll to `viewWillAppear()` and **remove** the following line:

```
username.center.x -= view.bounds.width
```

Then **remove** the following view animation from the `username` field in `viewDidAppear()`:

```
UIView.animateWithDuration(0.5, delay: 0.3,
  usingSpringWithDamping: 0.6, initialSpringVelocity: 0,
  options: .CurveEaseOut,
  animations: {
    self.username.center.x += self.view.bounds.width
  },
  completion: nil
)
```

Before you rush through and blindly copy and paste the code to create a `CABasicAnimation` for the username field, consider the following two facts:

• A `CABasicAnimation` object is just a data model, which is *not* bound to any particular layer.

• `add(_:forKey:)` makes a *copy* of the animation object.

It turns out that you can simply take the animation from your heading layer, adjust the animation a bit if needed and reuse it to animate your username field onto the screen.

Add the following code in the same spot where you deleted the code above in `viewWillAppear()`:

```
username.layer.add(flyRight, forKey: nil)
```

Build and run your project to see the resulting effect of re-using your layer animation:

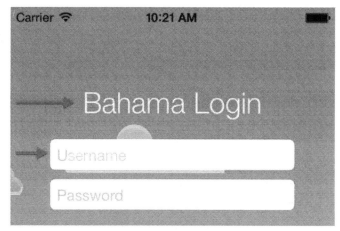

Well, the animation runs, but the title and username field slide onto the screen like those oh-so-unpopular synchronized kill-bots. You'll need to recreate the timing offset you had in the original animation.

Add the following line just **before** the line where you add the `flyRight` animation to your `username` layer:

```
flyRight.beginTime = CACurrentMediaTime() + 0.3
```

The `beginTime` property of your animation sets the absolute time the animation should start; in this case you get the current time with `CACurrentMediaTime()` and add to it the desired delay in seconds.

Build and run your app again to see how things look; it appears in the center of the screen, as it was designed in Interface Builder, and starts animating 0.3 seconds later. What gives?

It's time to learn about another layer animation property called `fillMode`; below are a few examples of how this property works.

Using fillMode

The `fillMode` property lets you control the behavior of your animation at the beginning and end of its sequence.

The constant `kCAFillModeRemoved` is the default value of `fillMode`. This starts the animation at the defined `beginTime` — or instantly, if you haven't set `beginTime` — and removes the changes made during the animation when the animation completes:

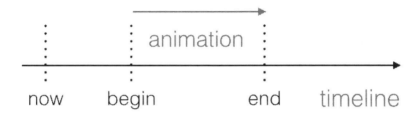

This is the approach you've used so far in this chapter. There are three other options in addition to `kCAFillModeRemoved` that you can use in your animations:

kCAFillModeBackwards

`kCAFillModeBackwards` displays the first frame of your animation instantly on the screen, regardless of the actual start time of the animation, and starts the animation at a later time:

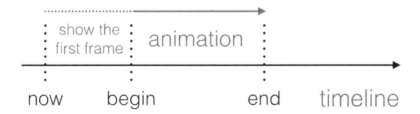

kCAFillModeForwards

`kCAFillModeForwards` plays the animation as usual, but retains the final frame of the animation on the screen until you remove the animation:

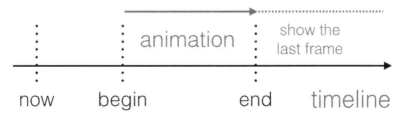

In addition to setting `kCAFillModeForwards`, you'll need to make some other changes to the layer to get the last frame to "stick". You'll learn about this a little later in the chapter.

kCAFillModeBoth

`kCAFillModeBoth` is a combination of `kCAFillModeForwards` and `kCAFillModeBackwards`; as you'd expect, this makes the first frame of the animation appear on the screen immediately and retains the final frame on the screen when the animation is finished:

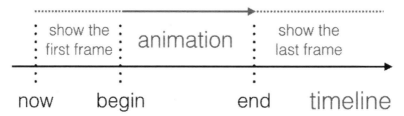

To fix the issue you discovered earlier, you'll use `kCAFillModeBoth`.

Add the following line of code to where you set up `flyRight` (`fromValue`, `toValue`, `duration`, etc.) and before you add it to a layer:

```
flyRight.fillMode = kCAFillModeBoth
```

Build and run your project; you'll see that the `username` field doesn't appear at first and the animation only starts after a 0.3-second delay. Also, the fields remain in position when the animation completes.

You can now animate your password field in a similar fashion. **Remove** the following line from `viewWillAppear()`:

```
password.center.x -= view.bounds.width
```

Then find and **remove** the following code in `viewDidAppear()`:

```
UIView.animate(withDuration: 0.5, delay: 0.4,
  options: .curveEaseOut, animations: {
    self.password.center.x += self.view.bounds.width
}, completion: nil)
```

...and replace it with the following code in `viewWillAppear()`:

```
flyRight.beginTime = CACurrentMediaTime() + 0.4
password.layer.add(flyRight, forKey: nil)
```

Build and run your project; you'll see all three layers flying in, with the password field arriving just a tenth of a second behind the username field:

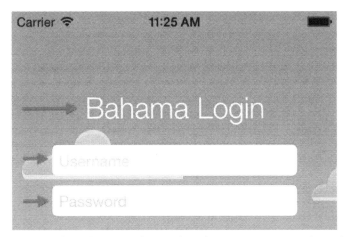

So far, your animations have happened to end at the exact position where the form elements were originally positioned in Interface Builder. However, many times this won't be the case. In the next section of this chapter, you'll discover how to handle the situation where layers end at a different position — and you'll learn how to debug your animations along the way!

Debugging basic animations

Head into `viewWillAppear()` and add the following code to the end of the method (just for testing purposes):

```
username.layer.position.x -= view.bounds.width
password.layer.position.x -= view.bounds.width
```

Now the username and password layers are initially located outside the screen bounds. That means you can **remove** the following line from `viewDidAppear()` that sets `fromValue`:

```
flyRight.fromValue = -view.bounds.size.width/2
```

You might think that this new code wouldn't affect anything, but build and run your project to see what happens.

Hey — what's going on? All the form elements animate as they did before, but the username and password fields disappear at the end of the animation without a trace!

You'll need to debug the app in order to find out what's happening with your UI.

Add the following code to the end of `viewWillAppear()`:

```
delay(seconds: 5.0)
  print("where are the fields?")
}
```

`delay(seconds:completion:)` is a little function included in the starter project; it simply executes the closure expression after a given delay.

Next, add a breakpoint to that `print` statement so that you'll be dropped into the debugger 5 seconds after the view appears.

To add a breakpoint to your code, just click on the gutter of your editing pane and a blue indicator will show up on that line to represent your breakpoint:

```
112
113        delay(5.0) {
114            print("where are the fields?")
115        }  ← click the gutter here
116
```

The line numbers you see in your project might differ from the ones in the screenshot above. Just be sure to set the breakpoint on the line that prints the message.

Now run the project and wait. When execution reaches the line with the breakpoint, the Xcode window will jump in front of the iPhone Simulator and show you the position where you set the breakpoint:

```
112
113        delay(5.0) {
114            print("where are the fields?")    Thread 1: breakpoint 1.1
115        }
116
```

You are not interested in the code *per se*; instead, you need to debug the UI of your application and find out what happened to the missing text fields.

Find the Debug Navigator on the left hand side of the Xcode window; it will show you the current app memory footprint and CPU usage. If you don't see the Debug Navigator, ensure the sixth tab on the right is selected as shown below:

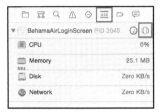

Next, click the second button to the right as indicated above; the button icon might differ for you, but it will still appear in the same position. You'll see a list of debugging modes available to you:

Click **View UI Hierarchy** to open the UI debugger:

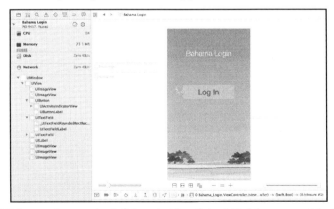

You'll see the UI hierarchy on the left hand side of the UI debugger, with the current runtime layout displayed in the center of the screen, including any hidden or transparent views as well as views outside the screen bounds.

For example, you can see the spinner view inside the Log In button, which is hidden at the time the breakpoint fired, but you can still see it in the debug view.

Let's look for the text fields now.

Aha — there are those pesky fields; they're outside the visible screen area. Select a field to inspect its live properties in the Object Inspector and other field properties in the Size Inspector in the next tab:

Your code change caused the fields to jump back to their initial position once the animation completed. But — why?

The answer to that lies in the next section, where you'll learn about the difference between your real UI elements and the animations on screen. Click on the blue breakpoint to disable it so you can keep on running the project without breaks.

Animations vs. real content

When you animate a text field, you're not actually seeing the field itself animated; instead, you're seeing a cached version of it known as the **presentation layer**. The presentation layer is removed from the screen once the animation completes and the original layer shows itself again.

To start, remember you're setting the text field to be positioned offscreen in `viewWillAppear(_:)`:

When the animation starts, a pre-rendered animation object replaces the field and the original text field is temporarily hidden:

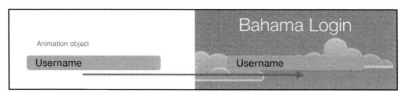

You can't tap the animated field, enter any text or engage any other specific text field functionality, because it's *not* the real text field, just a "phantom" visible representation.

As soon as the animation completes, it disappears from the screen and the original text field is un-hidden. The text field is right where you left it: offscreen to the left!

To solve this conundrum, you'll need to use another `CABasicAnimation` property: `isRemovedOnCompletion`.

Setting `fillMode` to `kCAFillModeBoth` instructs your animation to remain on screen after it completes and also show the animation's first frame before its start. To complete the effect, you'll need to set `removedOnCompletion` accordingly; the combination of the two will leave the animation visible on the screen.

Add the following line to `viewDidAppear()`, just after you set the `fillMode`:

```
flyRight.isRemovedOnCompletion = false
```

`isRemovedOnCompletion` is true by default, so the animation disappears as soon as it completes. Setting it to false and combining it with the proper `fillMode` keeps the animation on the screen — and visible as well.

Build and run your project now; you should see that all elements remain on the screen as expected once the animation completes:

Success! Now tap on the username field to enter your username — oh, wait. Remember the earlier note about the difference between the actual text field and the presentation layer? You can't do anything with this pre-rendered image of a text field.

To complete the desired effect, you'll need to remove the animation and show the real text field in its place.

Updating the layer model

Once you remove a layer animation from the screen, the layer falls back to its current values for position and other properties. This means that you'll usually need to update the properties of your layer to reflect the final values of your animation.

Remove the line below from your project:

```
flyRight.isRemovedOnCompletion = false
```

Although you know how `isRemovedOnCompletion` works when set to `false`, try to avoid it whenever possible. Leaving animations on the screen affects performance, so you'll let them be removed automatically and update the original layer's position instead.

Next, find the line of code that adds the animation to `username` in `viewDidAppear()` and add the following line after it:

```
username.layer.position.x = view.bounds.size.width/2
```

Next, add the code for the password field. Find the line that adds the animation to password and add the following line after it:

```
password.layer.position.x = view.bounds.size.width/2
```

This will set the actual layers to be positioned in the middle of the screen where they belong.

Build and run your project; Uh oh. The fields have stopped animating altogether! What's going on?

You removed the line that sets `fromValue` some time ago, but the code above updates the main layer's position; this causes the animation to start from the center of the screen. To fix this, add the following line just after you initialize `flyRight` and set its `toValue`:

```
flyRight.fromValue = -view.bounds.size.width/2
```

Build and run your project again, and this time you'll see the fields animate as expected.

> **Note:** If the keyboard doesn't appear when you tap on a text field in the Simulator, you can activate it manually by navigating the menu to Hardware\Keyboard\Toggle Software Keyboard.

When possible, design your layers in Interface Builder with their final values, and use fromValue for the starting and in-between values. This reduces the complexity of keeping your model and presentation layers in sync.

Best practices

Whoa — this was a long chapter! You tried out a ton of different layer animation techniques, and that's just the start!

At this point you might be feeling a bit overwhelmed and asking yourself "Should I use fillMode? Should I be removing my animations? And how do I update my layer to have smooth animation completion?"

As a rule of thumb: remove your animations and consider never using fillMode, except if the effect you want to achieve is not possible otherwise. fillMode makes your UI elements lose their interactivity and also makes the screen not reflect the actual values in your layer object.

In some rare cases when you animate non-interactive visual elements fillMode will save your bacon; you'll read more about this in Chapter 16, "Replicating animations."

As for updating your layer properties: consider always doing that immediately after you add the animation to your layer. Sometimes you might get the odd flash between the initial and final animation values.

In this case, try updating your layer property to the final animation value even before adding the animation.

Challenges

You covered a lot of ground in this chapter; if you want to really test that you've retained all of the concepts covered in each section, feel free to take on the challenges below.

Refer back to the various sections if you need some assistance, but if you've followed along with the exercises in this chapter, you're more than capable of working through each of the three challenges in this chapter! :]

Challenge 1: Fade in the clouds with layer animations

In this challenge, you'll replace the UIKit cloud animations from Chapter 1, "Getting Started with View Animations" with layer animations instead.

If you need a recipe to follow, the steps below should give you a good starting point:

1. Remove the four UIKit animations that fade in `cloud1`, `cloud2`, `cloud3`, and `cloud4` from `viewDidAppear()`.

2. Remove the four lines from `viewWillAppear()` that set the clouds' `alpha` property to `0.0`.

3. At the bottom of `viewWillAppear()`, create a `CABasicAnimation` with `opacity` as the `keypath`.

4. Set `fromValue` to `0.0`, `toValue` to `1.0`, and `duration` to `0.5`. You'll need to set `fillMode` to `kCAFillModeBackwards` to hide the clouds when the app starts.

5. Set the animation's `beginTime` to `CACurrentMediaTime() + 0.5` and add the animation to `cloud1`.

6. Set the animation's `beginTime` to `CACurrentMediaTime() + 0.7` and add the animation to `cloud2`.

7. Set the animation's `beginTime` to `CACurrentMediaTime() + 0.9` and add the animation to `cloud3`.

8. Set the animation's `beginTime` to `CACurrentMediaTime() + 1.1` and add the animation to `cloud4`.

The end result should recreate the initial cloud transition with layer animations as shown below:

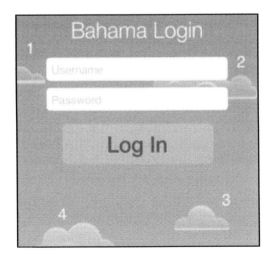

Challenge 2: Animating colors

In this challenge you'll re-create the Log In button tint animation.

First, **remove** your old UIKit code as shown below:

```
self.loginButton.backgroundColor = UIColor(red: 0.85, green:
0.83, blue: 0.45, alpha: 1.0)
```

Then scroll down to `resetForm()` and **remove** the following line:

```
self.loginButton.backgroundColor = UIColor(red: 0.63, green:
0.84, blue: 0.35, alpha: 1.0)
```

Create a new top-level function in **ViewController.swift** (e.g. a top-level function will be located outside the class body; add it below the delay function):

```
func tintBackgroundColor(layer: CALayer, toColor: UIColor)
```

In this new method, create a basic animation and run it on the layer parameter, keeping in mind these key requirements:

- Animate the `backgroundColor` property.

- Set `fromValue` to the current background color: `layer.backgroundColor`.

- Set `toValue` to `toColor.CGColor`; Core Animation uses `CGColor` values for colors.

- Set the animation `duration` for `1.0` second.

- Add the animation to `layer`.

- Don't forget to set the `backgroundColor` property on the layer itself so it retains the final animation color.

Now that `tintBackgroundColor` is complete, you can use it on your Log In button. To do that add, the following code to the very bottom of `login()`:

```
let tintColor = UIColor(red: 0.85, green: 0.83, blue: 0.45,
alpha: 1.0)

tintBackgroundColor(layer: loginButton.layer, toColor:
tintColor)
```

Build and run your project; you'll see the button change its tint as soon as you tap it:

Now find the call to `animate(...)` within `resetForm()` and replace `completion: nil` with the following code:

```
completion: {_ in
    let tintColor = UIColor(red: 0.63, green: 0.84, blue: 0.35,
alpha: 1.0)
    tintBackgroundColor(layer: self.loginButton.layer, toColor:
tintColor)
}
```

This will tint the button back to green when the animation is complete. As an added bonus, since your new function `tintBackgroundColor` is a top-level function, you can re-use it anywhere you like in your project!

Challenge 3: Animating corner radius

In this challenge you won't recreate one of your existing view animations; instead, you'll animate the layer specific property `cornerRadius`. Just like you did in Challenge 2 above, create the following new top-level function in **ViewController.swift**:

```
func roundCorners(layer: CALayer, toRadius: CGFloat)
```

This method will take a layer parameter and run a basic animation on it that animates the corner radius from its current value to the supplied `toRadius`.

Simply repeat the routine from Challenge 2, but follow these requirements instead:

• Animate the `cornerRadius` property.

• Set `toValue` to `toRadius`.

• Set the animation `duration` to `0.33` seconds.

• Add the animation to `layer`.

• Don't forget to set the `cornerRadius` on the layer.

Once you've completed `roundCorners()`, add the following line to the bottom of `login()`:

```
roundCorners(layer: loginButton.layer, toRadius: 25.0)
```

This should round the button when you tap it. To reverse the effect when the authentication process is done, add the following code to `resetForm()` after the call to `tintBackgroundColor`:

```
roundCorners(layer: self.loginButton.layer, toRadius: 10.0)
```

Build and run your project; you'll see the button appear with its initial color and corner radius:

Now tap the button to see it change in shape and color:

Once all animations complete, the button will return to its initial color and corner radius.

That's it for this chapter; by now you have a solid understanding of how to create basic layer animations, which is the perfect starting point to tackle the animation keys and delegate methods in the next chapter!

Chapter 9: Animation Keys and Delegates

One of the tricky parts about UIKit animations and the corresponding closure syntax is that once you create and run a view animation you can't pause it, stop it or access it in any way.

With Core Animation, however, you can easily inspect animations that are running on a layer and stop them if you need to. Furthermore, you can even set a delegate object on your animations and react to animation events. In contrast to the completion block you've seen in view animations, you can receive delegate callbacks for when an animation begins and ends (or is interrupted).

In this chapter you'll continue to work with the Bahama Air login project and use animation delegates to make your animations more interactive.

Introducing animation delegates

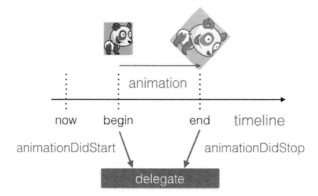

`CAAnimation` and its subclass `CABasicAnimation` implement the delegate pattern and let you respond to animation events.

`CAAnimationDelegate` features two methods that you can implement if you need either or both of them:

```
func animationDidStart(_ anim: CAAnimation)
func animationDidStop(_ anim: CAAnimation, finished flag: Bool)
```

You can either open the starter project for this chapter, or carry on with your own project if you've completed the previous chapter and its challenges.

Your first task is to make each form element pulse once when it reaches its final position on the screen using `animationDidStop()`.

Open **ViewController.swift** and add the following code to `viewWillAppear()`, just before the line where you add the animation to your `heading` layer:

```
flyRight.delegate = self
```

Then add the delegate method to the class in an extension to your view controller:

```
extension ViewController: CAAnimationDelegate {
  func animationDidStop(_ anim: CAAnimation,
    finished flag: Bool) {
    print("animation did finish")
  }
}
```

This simply prints out a line to the console to show that you are, in fact, calling your delegate method.

Build and run your project; you should see the following output in the Xcode console:

Okay, so your delegates are being called — but how do you discern *which* animation stopped in the code above? Remember, you added the same animation to three different layers! The following section shows you how to manage this with key-value pairs.

Key-value coding compliance

The `CAAnimation` class and its subclasses are written in Objective-C and are key-value coding compliant, which means you can treat them like dictionaries and add new properties to them at run time.

You'll use this mechanism to assign a name to the `flyRight` animation so that you can identify it out of the pack of other active animations.

Scroll back to `viewWillAppear()` and add the following code just after the line where you set `flyright`'s delegate:

```
flyRight.setValue("form", forKey: "name")
flyRight.setValue(heading.layer, forKey: "layer")
```

In the code above, you create the key name on the `flyRight` animation and set it to `form`. Now you can check for this name key from your delegate callbacks to identify the animation as belonging to one of your form controls.

You also assign `heading.layer` to the layer key so you have a reference back to the layer the animation belongs to.

You can leave the name unchanged, but you should update the layer key each time you add the animation to a layer.

Find the line where you add the animation to the `username` layer, and add the following just before it:

```
flyRight.setValue(username.layer, forKey: "layer")
```

Similarly, find the line where you add the animation to the `password` layer, and add the following just before it:

```
flyRight.setValue(password.layer, forKey: "layer")
```

Now each copy of `flyRight` carries a reference to the layer on which it runs.

Switching on key values

Now that you have the keys set on your animation, you can check for them in the animation delegate methods.

Add the following code to the bottom of `animationDidStop`:

```
guard let name = anim.value(forKey: "name") as? String else {
    return
}

if name == "form" {
    //form field found
}
```

In the code above you use `value(forKey:)` to get the value of name from the animation and attempt to cast the value to String. The `guard` is used simply because `value(forKey:)` returns an optional in the case there is no value assigned for the provided key, or if the downcast fails.

The optional binding statement takes care of these checks for you. If you can unwrap the value, then you have a value you can test for. If not, then your code carries on.

Now you have a spot to run some code when the form animation completes. Replace the comments `//form field found` with the following:

```
let layer = anim.value(forKey: "layer") as? CALayer
anim.setValue(nil, forKey: "layer")

let pulse = CABasicAnimation(keyPath: "transform.scale")
pulse.fromValue = 1.25
pulse.toValue = 1.0
pulse.duration = 0.25
layer?.add(pulse, forKey: nil)
```

Once that's done, you set the value of `layer` to `nil` to remove the reference to the original layer.

> **Note:** Remember that `value(forKey:)` always returns an `AnyObject?`; therefore you must cast the result to your desired type. Don't forget that the cast operation can fail, so you must use optionals in the example above to handle error conditions, such as when the name key exists but the layer key does not.

Finally, you create an animation that bumps the scale of the layer by a tiny bit (a factor of `1.25`), then animates the layer back to its original size (a factor of `1.0`).

Note that you're using optional chaining here with `layer?` — that means the `add(_:forKey:)` call will be skipped if there isn't a layer stored in the animation. And since you set the layer to `nil` earlier, this pulse animation will only happen the first time the form field flies in from the right.

Build and run your project; you should see that any time a `flyRight` animation completes, the element will pulse once before it comes to rest:

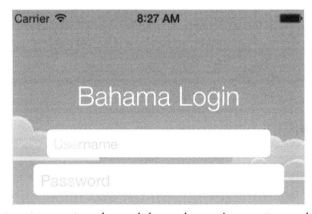

This gives the animations a nice edge and draws the user's attention to these controls.

That takes care of animations that have already stopped; but how can you work with animations that are *still running*? That's where **animation keys** come in.

Animation Keys

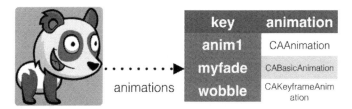

key	animation
anim1	CAAnimation
myfade	CABasicAnimation
wobble	CAKeyframeAnimation

You've probably noticed that add(_:key:) has two parameters; so far, you've only been using the first to pass in the animation object itself.

The key parameter is a string identifier that lets you access and control the animation after it's been started.

In this part you'll create another layer animation, learn how to run more than one animation at a time, and discover how to use animation keys to control running animations.

You're going to add a new animated label to your form that gives some basic instructions to the user, as shown below:

Your new label will animate slowly from right to left. As soon as the user starts to enter their username or password, this label will stop moving and jump directly to its final position. There's no need to continue the animation once the user knows what to do.

NO INSTRUCTIONS NECESSARY...

I GOT THIS

First you'll need to add some code that sets up the label to animate. Add the following property to the end of the property declarations at the top of `ViewController`:

```
let info = UILabel()
```

This is the label that will be used to display instructions to the user.

Next, add the following code to the bottom of `viewDidLoad` to set up the various properties of your label:

```
info.frame = CGRect(x: 0.0, y: loginButton.center.y + 60.0,
width: view.frame.size.width, height: 30)
info.backgroundColor = UIColor.clear
info.font = UIFont(name: "HelveticaNeue", size: 12.0)
info.textAlignment = .center
info.textColor = UIColor.white
info.text = "Tap on a field and enter username and password"
view.insertSubview(info, belowSubview: loginButton)
```

This adds the label just underneath the login button. When the user taps the login button, it will move down and cover the instructions, since the user won't need them anymore.

Now you need to slide the instructions in from the right when the app first opens. Find `viewDidAppear()` and add the following code to the end of that method:

```
let flyLeft = CABasicAnimation(keyPath: "position.x")
flyLeft.fromValue = info.layer.position.x +
view.frame.size.width
flyLeft.toValue = info.layer.position.x
flyLeft.duration = 5.0
info.layer.addAnimation(flyLeft, forKey: "infoappear")
```

This animates your label much like your form fields, only your label will slide in from the right side of the screen and fly to the left. Note that you set the animation's key to `infoappear`; you'll use this value to find and then stop the animation when the user starts to enter text in either the username or password field.

Adding a second layer animation

You'll now add a second animation to the label that will fade in the instructions while the label slides in. Add the following code to the end of `viewDidAppear`:

```
let fadeLabelIn = CABasicAnimation(keyPath: "opacity")
fadeLabelIn.fromValue = 0.2
fadeLabelIn.toValue = 1.0
fadeLabelIn.duration = 4.5
info.layer.add(fadeLabelIn, forKey: "fadein")
```

The code above fades in the label from a barely visible opacity of `0.2` to a fully visible opacity of `1.0`. The above animation runs on a different property — `opacity` — than in the previous animation — `position` — and has an entirely different duration. This shows you it's possible to run multiple animations independently of each other on the same layer.

> **Note:** If you need to synchronize animations on a layer, then you'll need to use **animation groups** to achieve this. This technique is covered in the next chapter.

Run the project to see the combined animations in action:

So far, so good. Now comes the tricky part: Cancelling the animation if the user starts to enter their username or password.

Identifying running animations

You'll need to know when the user taps on either the username or password field. Add the following extension to the very bottom of **ViewController.swift**:

```
extension ViewController: UITextFieldDelegate {
  func textFieldDidBeginEditing(textField: UITextField) {
    print(info.layer.animationKeys())
  }
}
```

This will add a class extension to say `ViewController` conforms to the `UITextFieldDelegate` protocol. Separating protocols into their own extensions like this helps keep the file organized.

The one method you need to implement, `textFieldDidBeginEditing`, will be called when the user starts editing a text field. For now, you'll just print out a list of all the active animations running on the label.

Next, add the following code to the bottom of `viewDidAppear`:

```
username.delegate = self
password.delegate = self
```

This will make the class a delegate of both text fields.

Build and run your project; tap either the username or password field before the label animation completes and you should see the following output in your Xcode console:

Success! Once you know which animations are running, you can do several things with them:

1. Call `removeAllAnimations()` on the layer to stop all running animations or `removeAnimation(forKey:)` to remove just one.

2. Enumerate over the list of animations returned by `animationKeys()`. The animation objects are immutable, so you can't modify the animation while they're in progress.

3. Fetch an animation by key using `animationForKey(_:)`. As before, the returned animation object will be immutable.

To finish your "stop animation" effect, you'll cancel the animation that moves the label, but leave the fade animation running as it would look weird for the opacity of the label to jump directly to 1.0.

Add the following code to textFieldDidBeginEditing:

```
info.layer.removeAnimation(forKey: "infoappear")
```

This removes the slide-in animation and causes the info label to jump straight to the center of the screen — without affecting the fade-in animation.

Build and run your project one final time; tap either of the text fields and you'll see the instructions jump straight to the center of the screen and continue to fade in:

That's a wrap! You've learned about delegate methods, accessing animations by keys, and created your first composite layer animation as an added bonus! :]

Why not test your knowledge with the following challenge?

Challenge

In this challenge, you'll strengthen your knowledge of animation delegates and key-value coding of animation objects by replacing the existing cloud animation with layer animations.

Replace the `animate(cloud: UIImageView)` method with the following:

```
func animateCloud(layer: CALayer) {

  //1
  let cloudSpeed = 60.0 / Double(view.layer.frame.size.width)
  let duration: TimeInterval = Double(
    view.layer.frame.size.width - layer.frame.origin.x)
    * cloudSpeed

  //2
  let cloudMove = CABasicAnimation(keyPath: "position.x")
  cloudMove.duration = duration
  cloudMove.toValue = self.view.bounds.width +
    layer.bounds.width/2
  cloudMove.delegate = self
  cloudMove.setValue("cloud", forKey: "name")
  cloudMove.setValue(layer, forKey: "layer")
  layer.add(cloudMove, forKey: nil)
}
```

This method has a similar implementation to the one that animates the clouds using UIKit. In fact, the first few lines of part `//1` above are almost identical to the UIKit implementation.

In the second part of the above method, you create an instance of `CABasicAnimation` for the layer movement and set a name and layer on the animation.

Next, replace the calls in `viewDidAppear()` to `animateCloud()` with the following:

```
animateCloud(layer: cloud1.layer)
animateCloud(layer: cloud2.layer)
animateCloud(layer: cloud3.layer)
animateCloud(layer: cloud4.layer)
```

Your task now is to complete the animation by implementing the delegate code to reset each of the clouds.

You already know how to do this through `animationDidStop(_: finished:)`. Just follow these key points:

- Check if the animation name is `"cloud"`.

- If so, fetch the animation's layer from the `"layer"` key.

- Set the layer's `position.x` to `-layer.bounds.width/2`.

- Wait for half a second (use the `delay(seconds:)` function) and call `self.animateCloud()`, passing in the current layer.

Build and run your project; check that the clouds reappear once they've left the screen:

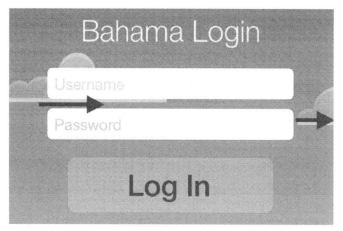

Congratulations — you've learned the basic layer animation techniques and are ready to move on to creating more complex animations. You'll learn about animation groups next in Chapter 10, "Groups and Advanced Timing".

Chapter 10: Groups and Advanced Timing

In the previous chapter you learned how to add multiple, independent animations to a single layer. But what if you want your animations to work synchronously and stay in step with each other? It's no fun having to fiddle with the math and timings of all the animations separately. That's where **animation groups** come in.

This chapter shows you how to group animations using `CAAnimationGroup`, which lets you add several animations to a group and adjust properties such as duration, delegate, and `timingFunction` all at once.

Grouping animations results in simplified code, and ensures that all your animations will synchronize as one, solid unit.

CAAnimationGroup

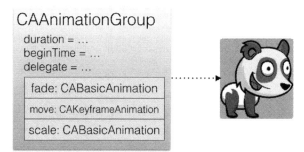

To start off, you'll extend your Bahama Air login screen using animation groups to add some new animation to the login button.

Open the starter project for this chapter, or carry on with your project from the previous chapter and challenge.

Open **ViewController.swift** and **remove** the following code from `viewWillAppear()`:

```
loginButton.center.y += 30.0
loginButton.alpha = 0.0
```

Then **remove** the following code from `viewDidAppear()`:

```
UIView.animate(withDuration: 0.5, delay: 0.5,
  usingSpringWithDamping: 0.5, initialSpringVelocity: 0,
  animations: {
    self.loginButton.center.y -= 30.0
    self.loginButton.alpha = 1.0
  },
  completion: nil
)
```

...and in its place add the following code:

```
let groupAnimation = CAAnimationGroup()
groupAnimation.beginTime = CACurrentMediaTime() + 0.5
groupAnimation.duration = 0.5
groupAnimation.fillMode = kCAFillModeBackwards
```

This code creates a new animation group for your use. `CAAnimationGroup` inherits from `CAAnimation`, so you can work with the same properties you already know and love such as `beginTime`, `duration`, `fillMode`, `delegate`, and `isRemovedOnCompletion`.

You'll add one final animation to the login button to scale, rotate, and fade it in with the end effect that the button falls neatly into place on the screen.

Add the first animation by adding the following code directly below the group animation code you just added:

```
let scaleDown = CABasicAnimation(keyPath: "transform.scale")
scaleDown.fromValue = 3.5
scaleDown.toValue = 1.0
```

In the code above you start with a very large version of the button and, over the course of the animation, shrink it to its normal size.

Here you specify only the fromValue and toValue, but you don't say what the duration of the animation should be nor do you set the fillMode of the animation. Where will those values come from?

You might have already guessed that since these values will be the same for all animations in the group, you'll set them on the group as a whole instead of on each animation separately.

Now add code for the next animation below the code you just added:

```
let rotate = CABasicAnimation(keyPath: "transform.rotation")
rotate.fromValue = .pi / 4.0
rotate.toValue = 0.0
```

This animation is similar to the previous one, but it animates the rotation component of the layer transform instead of the scale component. The animation starts with the layer rotated at a 45-degree angle and moves it to its normal orientation of zero degrees.

All that's left to add is the fade-in animation. Add the following code again below the lines you just added:

```
let fade = CABasicAnimation(keyPath: "opacity")
fade.fromValue = 0.0
fade.toValue = 1.0
```

This is the basic fade-in animation you've seen multiple times in this book.

Now add the code below to combine all animations and add them to the button:

```
groupAnimation.animations = [scaleDown, rotate, fade]
loginButton.layer.add(groupAnimation, forKey: nil)
```

To group animations, you simply add them to an array and assign that array as the value of the animations property of the group, just as you would with an ordinary CABasicAnimation.

Build and run your project to see the end result:

The button flies in and rotates as expected, but the animation looks stiff. In real life, objects tend to accelerate as they fall through space.

Fortunately, it's easy to add some realism to your animation. This is a great opportunity to learn about using easing with Core Animation.

Animation easing

You've already seen easing in action in the first chapters of this book that dealt with UIKit animations. Easing in layer animations is conceptually the same thing — only the syntax is different.

CAMediaTimingFunction has a few pre-defined easing functions, which you can use by name:

- kCAMediaTimingFunctionLinear runs the animation with an equal pace throughout its whole duration.

- kCAMediaTimingFunctionEaseIn alters the animation so it starts slower and finishes at a faster pace.

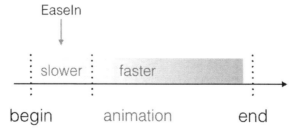

- kCAMediaTimingFunctionEaseOut produces the opposite effect of kCAMediaTimingFunctionEaseIn: the animations starts out faster and slows down as it finishes.

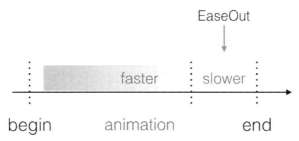

- `kCAMediaTimingFunctionEaseInEaseOut` slows the animation in the beginning and at the end, but increases the pace during the middle section.

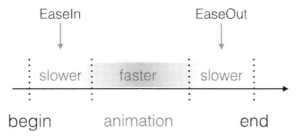

If you think about how objects accelerate as they fall through space, you'll see that you should use an ease-in animation that speeds up towards the end.

Find the piece of code in `viewDidAppear()` where you initialize `groupAnimation` and add the following line after that:

```
groupAnimation.timingFunction = CAMediaTimingFunction(
  name: kCAMediaTimingFunctionEaseIn)
```

This will set the animation easing on your animation group as a whole.

Build and run your project; the change is subtle, but the animation looks more realistic and snappier:

> **Note:** Although it's beyond the scope of this chapter, you can build your own custom easing function.
>
> Read up on the convenience initializer
> `CAMediaTimingFunction(controlPoints: _: _: _:)` in the Apple
> documentation or elsewhere on the web; this lets you define your easing function
> based on the control points of a cubic Bézier curve.

More timing options

The final section of this chapter explores four more animation properties that let you control the timing of your animation.

Repeating animations

`repeatCount` lets you repeat your animation a specified number of times.

To show how this works, you'll make the instructions fly onto the screen repeatedly instead of just once. Find the code in `viewDidAppear()` where you set the properties of the `flyLeft` animation such as duration, and set the number of animation repeats to 4:

```
flyLeft.repeatCount = 4
```

Build and run your project; you'll see the instructions fly in a total of four times, after which the label remains centered under the login button.

If you want to set the total repeat time in seconds, instead of setting the number of repeats, use the `repeatDuration` property instead of `repeatCount`.

However, the fact that the label flies off the screen each time it repeats looks a little weird. How could you create a fluid, reversing animation to make the label fly off the screen in the exact manner in which it entered?

It's far easier than you might think. Add the following code just after you set the `repeatCount`:

```
flyLeft.autoreverses = true
```

This will run your animation in reverse each time it completes, then run it in forward motion again.

Build and run your project; you'll see the label fly in, then out, then in again, and so forth:

That was easy and cool-looking, but there's still a little imperfection in your animation. The instructions animate four times, but the label then jumps straight to the center of the screen.

This is because a single animation cycle moves the label to the screen center and then out again. So when you run the animation four times, the final cycle ends with the label off the screen. This is why the label appears to jump to the center of the screen. You can't run *half* an animation cycle — or can you? :]

Change the `repeatCount` from 4 to 2.5 as shown below:

```
flyLeft.repeatCount = 2.5
```

Build and run your project now; you should see the animation finishes smoothly at the precise location you intended:

Changing the animation speed

Although they look nice, some of these animations feel a bit slow. You can control the speed of the animation independently of the duration by setting the `speed` property.

Still in the properties for `flyLeft`, add the following code after the line that sets the `autoreverses` property:

```
flyLeft.speed = 2.0
```

Even though the animation group duration is set to 5 seconds, the animation will complete in just 2.5 seconds since it runs at **double** the speed.

You can set the speed of an animation on its own, but you can also set the speed of a layer as well. The layer conforms to the same timing protocol as an animation: you simply set the speed of the layer to affect all animations you run on that layer.

Add the following code after the `flyLeft.speed` line you just added:

```
info.layer.speed = 2.0
```

Build and run your project; the `flyLeft` animation runs at double speed as before — but wait! The animation that moves the info label runs at *quadruple speed!* What's going on?

Lesson learned: speeds multiply hierarchically. First you set a speed of 2.0 on the info layer, and *then* you set the speed of `flyLeft` to 2.0 as well! You end up with the info layer running at 2.0 x 2.0 = 4.0 times the normal speed.

Just for fun, you can make everything on the screen run super fast by adjusting the speed property of the top-level view controller's layer. Add the following line underneath the line you just added:

```
view.layer.speed = 2.0
```

Build and run your project; you'll see that the form title, the text fields and even the clouds in the sky are double-stepping their way around the screen.

Due to the multiplication factor of animations, the fade animation on the info label runs at 4x speed, and the animation moving the info label across the screen runs at 8x speed! Wheeeee! :]

Now that you've had some fun with your project, **remove** all the repeating and speed adjustments as shown below:

```
flyLeft.repeatCount = 2.5
flyLeft.autoreverses = true
```

```
flyLeft.speed = 2.0
info.layer.speed = 2.0
view.layer.speed = 2.0
```

Playing with animation speeds, reversing and repeating was fun, but your user will likely not appreciate UI elements zipping around the screen like that! :]

But if you do need to adjust animation speeds locally, you can now do so on the animation level as well as for an entire layer.

Challenges

You learned quite a lot of new stuff in this chapter; so instead of having to solve a challenge on your own I'm giving you a free pass and walking you through a few more examples of what you learned above.

The challenge below is optional, but by working through it you'll get some more experience with animation groups — which is never a bad thing! :]

Challenge 1: Group animations for all form elements

In this challenge, you'll create a group of animations and run it on your form elements. Since this code will replace the existing form animations, the first thing you need to do is remove some existing code.

Delete the code that sets up the initial positions of the form heading and form fields, and then remove the code that animates the fields into the center of the screen.

In `viewWillAppear(_:)` create an animation group just like the one shown in this chapter that combines the following two animations:

• Fade from `0.25` to `1.0` opacity

• Move from the layer `position.x` from `-view.bounds.size.width/2` to `flyRight.toValue = view.bounds.size.width/2`

Add the two animations to an animation group and run that group on the form heading label and the two text field views.

Since you want your animation delegate method to kick in when the group animation completes, you'll need to set the delegate and keys on the animation group object rather than on the individual animations.

Don't forget to use setValue(_:forKey:) to set the **name** and **layer** keys on your animation before adding it to each of the text fields so your delegate methods get called correctly.

Further, you will need to adjust the beginTime parameter of your animation group object to give the correct delay to the different layers being animated as you did before.

Working through this challenge gave you some more valuable experience in working with groups and delegates. At this point you're ready to move on to the next chapter and add some bounciness to your layer animations.

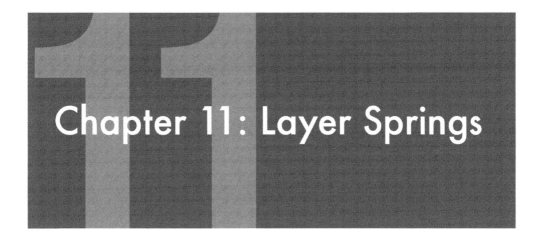

Chapter 11: Layer Springs

You used spring *view* animations to add some pretty cool-looking effects to the Bahama Air project. Now it's time to learn how to create spring animations for layers! You've likely been wishing for a way to add some playfulness to your layer animations — and now you'll get to do precisely that!

Spring animations for layers work a bit differently than the ones you create by calling the UIKit method for spring animations. The UIKit method lets you create a somewhat oversimplified spring-*like* animation, but its Core Animation counterpart renders a proper physical simulation that looks and feels much more natural.

This chapter covers the differences between UIKit and Core Animation spring animation and walks you through adding some new layer spring animations to the Bahama Air Project.

First though, you're going to *bounce* through a bit of theory! :]

Damped harmonic oscillators

Damped Harmonic What?

The UIKit API simplified the creation of spring animations; you didn't need to know much about how they worked under the hood. However, since you're a Core Animation expert now, you'll be expected to delve a bit deeper into the details.

Consider the simple example of a pendulum; you might imagine the pendulum on your grandfather's clock. It's too tall for the shelf, so has stood 90 years on the floor.

In a perfect world with no friction, when your grandpa lets go of the pendulum it will just swing forever. Tick, tock, tick, tock, tick, tock…:

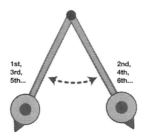

If grandpa were to attach a frictionless pen to the pendulum and slowly slide a sheet of paper underneath, he'd see a graph similar to the following:

This is an example of a **harmonic oscillator**: the pendulum moves back and forth (or *oscillates*) by equal amounts about its equilibrium point (the point where the pendulum sits when it's at rest). Without friction, the pendulum would keep swinging forever.

In the real world, however, the system loses energy due to friction and ultimately settles at its equilibrium point:

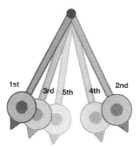

If grandpa slid a piece of paper underneath the pendulum now, the graph would look much like this:

This is a **damped** harmonic oscillator — there are forces acting against (or *damping)* the oscillation, so it slows down by a little bit each time until it comes to rest.

That wasn't so bad!

The length of time it takes the pendulum to settle down, and ultimately the way the graph of the oscillator looks, depends on the following parameters of the oscillating system:

- **damping**: This is due to air friction, mechanical friction and other external slowing forces acting on the system.

- **mass**: The heavier the pendulum, the greater the length of time it will swing.

- **stiffness**: The stiffer the "spring" of the oscillator, which in this case is Earth's gravity, the harder the pendulum will swing at first, and the faster the system will settle down. Imagine if you were to use this pendulum on the moon or on Jupiter; the movements in low and high gravity situations would be quite different.

- **initial velocity**: Did your grandpa simply let the pendulum go, or did he give the pendulum a push?

"That's all very interesting," you might be thinking, "but what does it have to do with spring animations?"

A great question, with a great answer! Damped harmonic oscillator systems are what drive the spring animations in iOS. The next section talks about this in more detail.

UIKit vs. Core Animation springs

You've likely noticed that a damped harmonic oscillator involves many more variables than does a simple UIKit spring animation.

When you use the spring-damping `animate` methods (with the `usingSpringWithDamping` and `initialSpringVelocity` parameters), the only spring-relevant parameters are the damping and the initial velocity.

UIKit adjusts all the other variables in a dynamic manner to make the system settle down in the given **duration**. That's why the UIKit spring animations sometimes feel a bit — well, *forced*. UIKit animations are just a bit too jumpy, and to a trained eye, a tad unnatural.

Luckily, Core Animation lets you create proper spring animations for your layer properties via the **CASpringAnimation** class. CASpringAnimation creates the spring animations for UIKit behind the scenes, but when you call it directly you can set the various variables of the system and let the animation settle down by itself. The drawback to this approach is that you can't tell the animation what its duration *should be*; that's determined by the system itself, given the variables you provide.

Since you know how damped harmonic oscillators work, it's no surprise that CASpringAnimation exposes the following properties:

- damping: The damping applied to the system

- mass: The mass of the weight in the system

- stiffness: The stiffness of the spring attached to the weight

- initialVelocity: The initial *push* applied to the weight.

If at any time you're wondering which variables you need to adjust to get your animation working the way you want, simply think back to the grandfather clock example, and that should get you straightened around.

That's enough prep for now — it's time to open up Xcode and lay down some spring animation code.

Creating your first layer spring animation

Open the starter project for this chapter, or alternatively if you worked through the project from the previous chapter you can pick up where you left off.

Run the project and watch for the scaling animation applied to the text fields when they reach their final destination:

This little scaling animation lets the user know the field is active and ready to be used. However, the animation ends somewhat abruptly. You can make it look much nicer by replacing the existing animation with a proper spring animation.

Open **ViewController.swift** and find `animationDidStop(_:finished:)`. The piece of code that creates the scale animation is as follows:

```
let pulse = CABasicAnimation(keyPath: "transform.scale")
pulse.fromValue = 1.25
pulse.toValue = 1.0
pulse.duration = 0.25
layer?.addAnimation(pulse, forKey: nil)
```

Since `CASpringAnimation` descends from `CABasicAnimation`, you only need to replace the class name and set the spring damping.

To do that, find the following line:

```
let pulse = CABasicAnimation(keyPath: "transform.scale")
```

…and replace it with the following:

```
let pulse = CASpringAnimation(keyPath: "transform.scale")
pulse.damping = 2.0
```

Run your project and enjoy your new spring animation!

Hold on — something's wrong with that animation. Run the project few more times and watch the animation closely; you'll notice the animation cuts off and jumps to its final frame at about `0.25` seconds in.

This is a case of your code doing precisely what you told it to do:

- You created a spring animation using a custom damping value and the defaults for all other system variables

- But you *also* told it to run for `0.25` seconds by setting its duration property.

The spring system can't settle within `0.25` seconds; the variables you provided mean the animation should run for a few seconds before it settles down.

Here's a visual demonstration of how you cut off the spring animation:

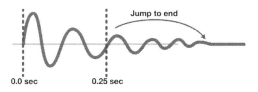

Fortunately, this is an easy fix. Once you set all system variables such as stiffness and damping, ask your `CASpringAnimation` how much time it will take to settle down and set that as the duration of the animation.

Replace `pulse.duration = 0.25` with the following:

```
pulse.duration = pulse.settlingDuration
```

`settlingDuration` estimates the time required for the system to settle; you can use that value to let Core Animation know how long the animation should remain on the screen.

Run your project again to enjoy smooth wobbly-bobbly animations:

It looks better, but *boy* does it run a long time. With the given parameters, the animation will take `1.93` seconds to settle down — that's way too long for an effect that's only meant to close off the preceding transition animation.

Think back to the pendulum example from the chapter's introduction: do you need *more* or *less* damping to decrease the animation's duration?

You're right — a greater damping value means the pendulum will settle faster. Change your animation's damping to `7.5` for a more subtle effect:

```
pulse.damping = 7.5
```

Run the project again; this time, the scaling effect is as *smooth as silk*.

Spring animation properties

That takes care of your first spring animation; all you had to do was adjust the damping and everything worked itself out.

But what about `stiffness`, `initialVelocity`, and `mass`?

`CASpringAnimation` comes with pre-defined values for all its springy properties:

- `damping`: `10.0`

- `mass`: `1.0`

- `stiffness`: `100.0`

- `initialVelocity`: `0.0`

In this section, you'll add input validation to the text fields and make the fields jump if the user enters too few characters. You'll use all four properties of `CASpringAnimation` to produce the precise effect you want.

Scroll to the very bottom of **ViewController.swift** and find the class extension that makes `ViewController` conform to the `UITextFieldDelegate` protocol.

Add to the `extension` body the following callback method:

```swift
func textFieldDidEndEditing(_ textField: UITextField) {
  guard let text = textField.text else { return }

  if text.characters.count < 5 {
    // add animations here
  }
}
```

The delegate method `textFieldDidEndEditing(_ textField:)` receives as a parameter the text field that just lost focus. In the code above you check whether the text value of that field is shorter than 5 characters; if so, you play an animation to attract the user's attention to that field.

Add the following code below the comment `// add animations here`:

```swift
let jump = CASpringAnimation(keyPath: "position.y")
jump.fromValue = textField.layer.position.y + 1.0
jump.toValue = textField.layer.position.y
jump.duration = jump.settlingDuration
textField.layer.add(jump, forKey: nil)
```

Run your project; click (or tap if on a device) inside the username text field, then immediately click (or tap) inside the password field.

This triggers `textFieldDidEndEditing(_ textField:)`, and since you didn't enter any text, the validation failure animation plays.

At present, the animation simply moves the field one point down and animates it one up back to its original location. That's not much fun — but you can easily fix that with your animation ninja skills!

Initial velocity

This property lets you specify the starting speed of the animation. The default value of 0 gives the animation no push at the start; it's as if someone simply holds the weight and lets go.

A positive value gives the animation a push in the direction of the equilibrium point, while a negative value starts the animation moving away from the equilibrium point.

Your jump animation should be quite visible, so give it a good push of 100.0 at the start. Add the following line just after the point where you initialize the animation object (the important thing is to add it **before** you calculate and set the duration):

```
jump.initialVelocity = 100.0
```

Check out your spring animation again:

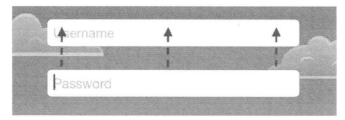

Even with a position delta of just 1 point, the field jumps much higher due to the extra push at the start. The field then oscillates a bit before settling down.

Mass

It looks better, but the jump animation settles a *bit* too fast. Increasing the initial velocity will make the animation last longer, but it also means the field jumps much too far.

What if you increase the *mass* of the attached weight instead, for an animation that lasts longer? Sounds good!

The default mass value is 1.0 (in your mind, you can choose pounds, kilograms, or any other measurement unit you fancy) and you can use any positive value that helps you achieve the desired effect.

For your current animation increase the mass to 10.0 like so:

```
let jump = CASpringAnimation(keyPath: "position.y")
jump.initialVelocity = 100.0
jump.mass = 10.0
```

Run your project; the change above increases the duration of your animation — but the extra mass means the text field jumps a little higher than planned.

No worries — you are still on the right path. Just couple more adjustments and you'll have this effect licked!

> **Note:** Adjusting the spring variables might not feel intuitive at the moment, but as you experiment further with these values you'll start to understand how to best achieve your desired effect.

Stiffness

The spring animation overshoots the target due to its high initial velocity and its extra mass. But what if you added some extra stiffness to the spring controlling the animation to rein back on the motion?

`stiffness` can take any positive value that you fancy: `0` creates a a very soft spring (bouncy bouncy), `100` is the default value (bouncy), and every increment above `100` makes the spring stiffer and stiffer (less bouncy bouncy).

In your animation, increase the stiffness to `1500` to restrain the jump to a sensible size; the new line of code is underlined below:

```
let jump = CASpringAnimation(keyPath: "position.y")
jump.initialVelocity = 100.0
jump.mass = 10.0
jump.stiffness = 1500.0
```

Run your project; the animation now jumps just the right distance and feels *tight*; this should definitely grab the attention of the user.

Damping

The animation looks great, but it does seem to go on a bit too long. You'll increase the system damping to make the animation settle faster.

The damping coefficient applied to the system can be any positive value; zero will make your animation oscillate forever. Increase the damping of your animation to `50.0`:

```
let jump = CASpringAnimation(keyPath: "position.y")
jump.initialVelocity = 100.0
jump.mass = 10.0
jump.stiffness = 1500.0
jump.damping = 50.0
```

Run the project now and enjoy a fine, subtle animation that attracts the user's attention without annoying them:

Specific layer properties

So far in this chapter you've created layer spring animations for the transform and position properties. Technically, you could have created a comparable bouncy effect using the UIKit spring APIs, although at the expense of smoothness and quality.

To wrap up with `CASpringAnimation`, you'll create a spring animation on a layer property that you *can't* create with view animations alone.

The validation animation is maybe a bit too subtle and smooth right now...

Make up your mind dude...

You'll add a not-so-subtle flashing red border around the text field that contains invalid input.

In `textFieldDidEndEditing(_ textField:)`, inside the `if` statement and just after you add the `jump` animation to the text field, add the following code to set a border on your text field:

```
textField.layer.borderWidth = 3.0
textField.layer.borderColor = UIColor.clear.cgColor
```

This code adds a transparent border around your text field. Next, you'll animate that border color.

Add the following code just below the line that sets a transparent color on the border:

```
let flash = CASpringAnimation(keyPath: "borderColor")
flash.damping = 7.0
flash.stiffness = 200.0
flash.fromValue = UIColor(red: 1.0, green: 0.27, blue: 0.0,
alpha: 1.0).cgColor
flash.toValue = UIColor.white.cgColor
flash.duration = flash.settlingDuration
textField.layer.add(flash, forKey: nil)
```

Here you create a spring animation with damping and stiffness values that flash the border in sync with the text field jumping.

A simple `CABasicAnimation` would have animated the border color from red to white. But because you've chosen a spring animation, the border color starts from red and oscillates a bit around the final white color.

Run the app to appreciate the end effect; the field border flashes a few times before it settles down and disappears:

And that ends your crash course on layer spring animations!

Challenges

You have a pretty solid understanding of layer spring animations by now, so I'll leave you to figure out the solution to this challenge on your own.

Challenge 1: Convert corner radius and background animations to springs

Your task is to revisit the code in both `tintBackgroundColor(layer:, toColor:)` and `roundCorners(layer:, toRadius:)`, replace the existing code with spring animations and configure the animations so that you can clearly see the rounded corners bounce without overdoing it.

Working through this challenge on your own will give you some time to experiment with the properties of `CASpringAnimation` and give you a feeling for what values work well.

When you've finished, you'll be ready to move on to the next chapter and tackle layer keyframe animations.

Chapter 12: Layer Keyframe Animations and Struct Properties

Keyframe animations on layers are a bit different than keyframe animations on a `UIView`. View keyframe animations are a simple way to combine independent simple animations together; they can animate different views and properties, and the animations can overlap or have gaps in between.

In contrast, `CAKeyframeAnimation` lets you animate a single property on a given layer. You can define different key points of the animation, but you can't have any gaps or overlaps in your animation. Even though that sounds restrictive at first, you can create some very compelling effects with `CAKeyframeAnimation`.

In this chapter, you'll create a number of layer keyframe animations, from the very basic to more advanced animations that simulate real-world collisions. In Chapter 15, "Stroke and Path Animations", you'll learn how to take layer animations even further and animate your layers along a given path.

For now, you'll walk before you run and create a funky wobbly effect for your first layer keyframe animation.

Introducing keyframe animations

Think for a moment how a basic animation works. Using `fromValue` and `toValue`, Core Animation progressively modifies a particular layer property between those values over a specified duration.

For instance, when you rotate a layer between 45° and −45° (or π/4 and −π/4 for you math types out there :]) you only need to specify those two values and the layer renders all intermediate values to complete the animation:

Instead of `fromValue` and `toValue`, `CAKeyframeAnimation` uses an array of values to animate through named `values`. The elements of `values` are the measured milestones of your animation. You'll also need to supply the time that the animation should reach each value's key point.

Take a look at the following simple layer keyframe animation example:

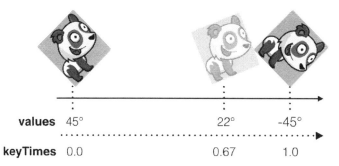

In the above animation, the layer rotates from 45° to −45°, but this time it has two separate stages: first, it rotates from 45° to 22° during the first two-thirds of the animation duration, and then it rotates all the way to −45° in the time remaining.

In essence, animating layers with keyframes requires you to provide key values for the property you're animating, along with a corresponding number of number of relative key times that progress between `0.0` and `1.0`.

Creating a layer keyframe animation

Open the starter project for this chapter, or alternatively if you worked through the project from the previous chapter you can pick up where you left off.

Open **ViewController.swift** and find `resetForm()`; this method executes when you finish animating the different login status messages from "Connecting" to "Authorizing" and so on. You'll animate the form title slightly on the faux failed authentication attempt to tell the user that that an error has occurred.

Add the following code to the end of `resetForm()`:

```
let wobble = `CAKeyframeAnimation`(keyPath:
"transform.rotation")
wobble.duration = 0.25
wobble.repeatCount = 4
wobble.values = [0.0, -.pi/4.0, 0.0, .pi/4.0, 0.0]
wobble.keyTimes = [0.0, 0.25, 0.5, 0.75, 1.0]
heading.layer.add(wobble, forKey: nil)
```

Here you create a new `CAKeyframeAnimation` in the same way you usually do for a `CABasicAnimation`: you specify a `keyPath`, set the animation's total duration and indicate how many times you want it to repeat.

Then you set up your animation values in the values array: you rotate the layer from 0° to −45° (equal to π/4), back to 0°, all the way to 45° and finally back to 0°. The animation starts and ends on the same value, which makes repeating it an easy task.

Finally, you set the key times for the values of the animation, making sure to set the start and end times to `0.0` and `1.0` respectively to avoid any jumps in your animation.

Build and run your project; tap on the login button, wait until the end of the sequence and you'll see the title wobble to alert the user that their login attempt failed:

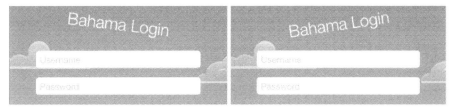

Keen-eyed readers have probably noticed that I haven't yet covered animations on `struct` properties. Most of the time, you can get away with animating a single component of a struct, such as the x component of a `CGPoint`, or the `rotation` component of a `CATransformation3D`, but you'll find out next that there's more to animating struct values than you might think at first.

Animating struct values

Struct instances are first-class citizens in Swift. In fact, there's very little difference syntactically between working with classes and structs.

However, Core Animation is an Objective-C framework built on C, which means that structs are handled *very* differently. Objective-C APIs like to deal with objects, so structs need some special handling.

This is why it's relatively easy to animate a layer property such as a color or a number, but it's not quite as easy to animate a struct property such as a `CGPoint`.

There are many animatable properties of `CALayer` that hold struct values, including position of type `CGPoint`, transform of type `CATransform3D`, and bounds of type `CGRect`. To help manage this, Cocoa includes the `NSValue` class, which "boxes in" or "wraps" a struct value as an object.

`NSValue` comes with a number of convenience initializers you can use for each struct you need to box, including the following:

```
init(cgPoint: CGPoint)
init(cgSize: CGSize)
init(cgRect rect: CGRect)
init(caTransform3D: CATransform3D)
```

How would you use these initializers to box your values? Here's what a sample position animation using `CGPoint` would look like:

```
let move = CABasicAnimation(keyPath: "position")
move.duration = 1.0
move.fromValue = NSValue(cgPoint: CGPoint(x: 100.0, y: 100.0))
move.toValue = NSValue(cgPoint: CGPoint(x: 200.0, y: 200.0))
```

If you try to assign a `CGPoint` directly to `fromValue` or `toValue` your animations will not work as you expect. Instead, you would box the `CGPoint` in an `NSValue` before assigning it to `fromValue` and `toValue`.

The same thing happens with keyframe animations: if you try to assign an array of `CGPoint` instances as the values of your animations the animations will not work since you have to use an array of boxed `CGPoint` `NSValues` instead.

The final section of this chapter will walk you through boxing your struct properties as you add the final layer keyframe animation involving, of all things, a hot-air balloon! :]

Intermediate keyframe animations

First you need to add the balloon image on screen. Open **ViewController.swift,** then add the following code to the bottom of `login()`:

```
let balloon = CALayer()
balloon.contents = UIImage(named: "balloon")!.cgImage
balloon.frame = CGRect(x: −50.0, y: 0.0, width:
50.0, height: 65.0)
view.layer.insertSublayer(balloon, below: username.layer)
```

In the code above, you create a new layer with the balloon image as its contents.

If you need to show an image on screen but don't need all the benefits of using a `UIView` (such as Auto Layout constraints, attaching gesture recognizers and so forth), you can simply use a `CALayer` like in the code example above.

You position the layer near the top left corner, just outside of the visible area of the screen. Finally, you insert the layer below the username field so the balloon appears behind all the other elements in your form.

Now you can create the animation in few familiar steps. Add the following code underneath the previous code:

```
let flight = CAKeyframeAnimation(keyPath: "position")
flight.duration = 12.0
```

Here you create a keyframe animation and set its duration to `12.0`, the approximate duration of the faux authentication process.

Next, add the following key value points and times:

```
flight.values = [
  CGPoint(x: -50.0, y: 0.0),
  CGPoint(x: view.frame.width + 50.0, y: 160.0),
  CGPoint(x: -50.0, y: loginButton.center.y)
].map { NSValue(cgPoint: $0) }

flight.keyTimes = [0.0, 0.5, 1.0]
```

Note how you use map to neatly convert an array of points into an array of points boxed as `NSValues`. Ain't Swift great? :]

This animates the balloon along the path that connects the three points you assigned to values, like so:

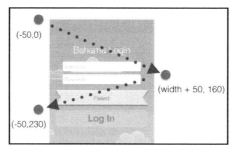

Add the final few following lines to run the animation and to set the final position of the balloon layer:

```
balloon.add(flight, forKey: nil)
balloon.position = CGPoint(x: -50.0, y: loginButton.center.y)
```

Build and run your project; watch as the balloon flies across the screen as soon as you tap the **Log In** button:

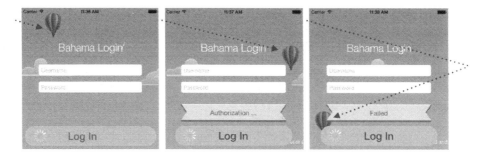

You can use the same technique to animate other struct properties such as `bounds`, `position`, and `transform`.

If you want to animate the balloon over a more complex set of points, such as a smooth curved path, stay tuned for Chapter 15, "Stroke and Path Animations" where you'll learn how to animate a layer over an arbitrary path using a special case of keyframe animation.

You've covered all of the chapters in this book that deal with basic layer animations; the next chapters will introduce you to some of the cool animations you can create using specialized layers.

Chapter 13: Shapes and Masks

This chapter marks a bit of a shift in this section of the book: not only are you going to start working with a different sample project, but you'll work with multi-layer effects, create layer animations that appear to interact physically with each other and morph between shapes as the animation runs.

If that sounds like a lot to take in, just think back to the great-looking animations you created in previous chapters with a relatively small bit of code!

The shapes in this chapter will be handled by `CAShapeLayer`, which is a `CALayer` sub-class that lets you draw various shapes on the screen, from the very simple to the very complex:

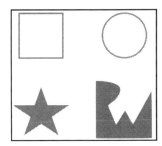

Instead of taking in drawing instructions, you give a the `CALayer` a `CGPath` to draw on screen. This comes in handy since Core Graphics already defines a very extensive API of drawing instructions for building `CGPath` shapes.

If you're more familiar with `UIBezierPath`, you can use that to define a shape and then use its `cgPath` property to get its Core Graphics representation. You will give that a try later in this very chapter.

After you create your desired shape you can set such properties on as the stroke color, fill color and stroke dash pattern.

Of course, by now you're likely asking "...but can I *animate* these properties?" Yes, you can:

- path: Morph the layer's shape into a different shape.

- fillColor: Change the fill tint of shape to a different color.

- lineDashPhase: Create a marquee or "marching ants" effect around your shape.

- lineWidth: Grow or shrink the size of the stroke line of your shape.

There are two more animatable properties that you can use when drawing shapes; you'll learn about these in Chapter 15: "Stroke and Path Animations."

The project for this chapter simulates the starting screen of a combat game that is searching for an online opponent. You'll simulate some online communication and add animations to show the communication state.

By the end of this chapter the project will look much like the screen below:

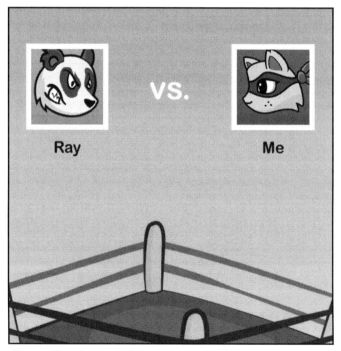

This chapter is designed to show you how to animate the new properties discussed above in the context of a common project you'd work on in real life. This will require a *bit* of extra work, but I know you'll enjoy the ride! :]

Finishing up the avatar view

Open the starter project for this chapter, select **Main.storyboard** and take a look at the user interface you'll be working with in this chapter:

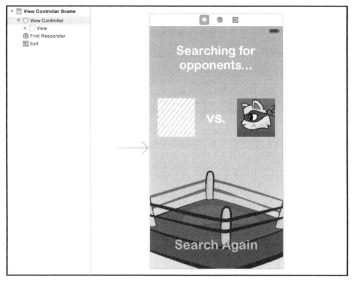

The project setup is fairly straightforward: a single view controller to display a nice background image, some labels, a "Search Again" button, and two avatar images, one of which will be empty until the app "finds" an opponent.

The two avatars are each an instance of the class `AvatarView`. In this section of the chapter, you'll quickly finish writing the class code while you learn how it `AvatarView` works.

Open **AvatarView.swift** and have a look at `didMoveToWindow()`, where you'll build up the following elements of the avatar view:

- `photoLayer`: The avatar's image layer.

- `circleLayer`: A shape layer for drawing a circle.

- `maskLayer`: Another shape layer for drawing a mask.

- `label`: A label to show the player's name.

You'll layer these on top of each other to build the composite avatar view as follows:

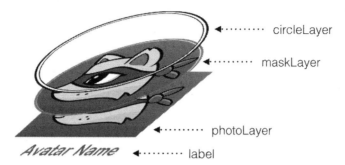

circleLayer

maskLayer

photoLayer

label

The above components already exist in the project, but haven't been added to the view — that's your first task. Add the following code to `didMoveToWindow()`:

```
photoLayer.mask = maskLayer
```

This simply masks the square image above with the circle-shaped mask in `maskLayer`.

Build and run your project to see how things look; you can also see the change right in the storyboard thanks to `@IBDesignable`:

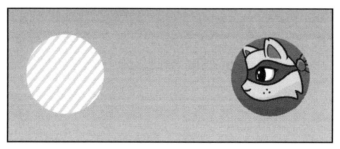

Now add the border layer to the avatar view's layer in `didMoveToWindow()`:

```
layer.addSublayer(circleLayer)
```

This adds the circular-shaped layer to the avatar, which frames it in nicely:

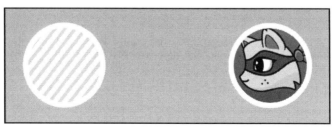

Both the mask layer and the frame layer are instances of `CAShapeLayer`; you'll make use of this fact when you animate them in the next section.

There's one more piece to add — the player name label. Add the following code to `didMoveToWindow()`:

```
addSubview(label)
```

This wraps up the avatar view like so:

Now you're ready to add some animations!

> **Note:** You may have noticed that the view doesn't look quite right in the storyboard. This is because a lot of the effects you've added extend outside the frame of the view and get clipped. Not to worry though: at actual runtime, the views will look correct.

Creating the bounce-off animation

The first animation you'll create will make it appear as if the two avatars are bouncing off each other while your project "searches" for an opponent.

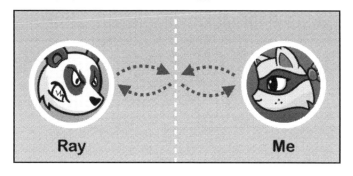

Open **ViewController.swift** and add the following line to `viewDidAppear()`:

```
searchForOpponent()
```

This method kicks off your searching-for-opponent animation.

Add the code below to `ViewController` to create the first iteration of this method:

```
func searchForOpponent() {
  let avatarSize = myAvatar.frame.size
  let bounceXOffset: CGFloat = avatarSize.width/1.9
  let morphSize = CGSize(
    width: avatarSize.width * 0.85,
    height: avatarSize.height * 1.1)
}
```

A bit of math is involved in this animation — but not too much! :]

First, you calculate the horizontal distance the avatars should move when they bounce towards each other and save that value in `bounceXOffset`. You'll use the morph size later to add an extra effect when the two avatars collide.

Now that you know the x-offset, you can calculate the locations to which the avatars should move.

Add the following code to `searchForOpponent()`:

```
let rightBouncePoint = CGPoint(
  x: view.frame.size.width/2.0 + bounceXOffset,
  y: myAvatar.center.y)

let leftBouncePoint = CGPoint(
  x: view.frame.size.width/2.0 - bounceXOffset,
  y: myAvatar.center.y)
```

When the avatars reach the right and left bounce points, respectively, they will just barely touch each other, at which point you'll animate them away from each other again.

Finally add the following code to `searchForOpponent()`:

```
myAvatar.bounceOff(point: rightBouncePoint,
  morphSize: morphSize)

opponentAvatar.bounceOff(point: leftBouncePoint,
  morphSize: morphSize)
```

`bounceOff(point: morphSize:)` doesn't yet exist; you'll add it in just a moment. It takes two parameters: the point to where the avatar should move and the size to which it should morph. That's all you need to create your animation.

Open **AvatarView.swift** and add the bounce method below:

```
func bounceOff(point: CGPoint, morphSize: CGSize) {
  let originalCenter = center

  UIView.animate(withDuration: animationDuration, delay: 0.0,
    usingSpringWithDamping: 0.8, initialSpringVelocity: 0.0,
    animations: {
      self.center = point
    },
    completion: {_ in
      //complete bounce to
    }
  )
}
```

In the above method, you first store the center coordinate of the avatar view; you'll need this later to animate the view back to its original location. Next, you use a spring animation to move the avatar view to the bouncePoint coordinate.

Now you need something to animate the avatar to its starting location. Add the following code to the end of `bounceOff(point: morphSize:)`:

```
UIView.animate(withDuration: animationDuration,
  delay: animationDuration, usingSpringWithDamping: 0.7,
  initialSpringVelocity: 1.0,
  animations: {
    self.center = originalCenter
  },
  completion: {_ in
    delay(seconds: 0.1) {
      self.bounceOffPoint(bouncePoint, morphSize: morphSize)
    }
  }
)
```

The above code uses another spring animation to move the avatar back to its original location. After a slight delay, you re-start the animation again from the completion closure.

Build and run your project to see how the bounce animation looks.

Note that when the avatars views touch they stay together for a short period, as if there's tension building between them. This short period is where you'll add the "squishing" effect using shape morphing techniques.

Morphing shapes

When the two avatars collide, they should squish a little in this perfectly-elastic collision. The view controller will pass in a morph size that makes the avatar image slightly taller and narrower for this effect:

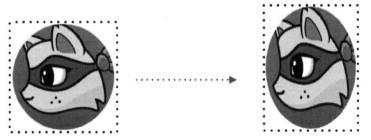

This will make it look like the avatars are pressing against each other when they meet in the middle of the screen.

The first thing to take care of is the frame to use for the morphing effect. And just to complicate things a little, the frame will be different for each avatar, depending on whether it animates from the left or the right.

Add the following code to the bottom of `bounceOff(point: morphSize:)`:

```
let morphedFrame = (originalCenter.x > point.x) ?

  CGRect(x: 0.0, y: bounds.height - morphSize.height,
    width: morphSize.width, height: morphSize.height):

  CGRect(x: bounds.width - morphSize.width,
    y: bounds.height - morphSize.height,
    width: morphSize.width, height: morphSize.height)
```

If the avatar animates from left to right, then the final position of the morphed avatar will touch the right edge of the original frame. It's the exact opposite for the avatar animating from right to left, as it will end up on the left edge of the original frame.

This means the avatar images end up touching slightly in the center of the screen, like so:

Finally you can add the shape-shifting animation code to the bottom of `bounceOff(point: morphSize:)`:

```
let morphAnimation = CABasicAnimation(keyPath: "path")
morphAnimation.duration = animationDuration
morphAnimation.toValue = UIBezierPath(ovalIn:
  morphedFrame).cgPath

morphAnimation.timingFunction = CAMediaTimingFunction(
  name: kCAMediaTimingFunctionEaseOut)
```

Here, you create a `CABasicAnimation` and set its `keyPath` as the path property. As with any other property layer animation, you only need to set the end value and Core Animation will render the intermediate states for you.

You then set the duration and use the class `UIBezierPath` to create an oval path for the effect. `UIBezierPath` is quite handy as it features a number of convenience initializer methods, including the one you used above which takes a `CGRect` and creates an oval path that fits into the rect.

Finally, you set the animation to ease-out which helps build the tension before the avatars bounce off.

That was a long haul, but all that's left is to add the animation to the avatar before you can see your crazy shape shifting in action!

Add the following line of code to the bottom of `bounceOff(point: morphSize:)`:

```
circleLayer.add(morphAnimation, forKey: nil)
```

Build and run your project to see the end result:

The avatar frames squish neatly against each other and then bounce off, like two angry battling amebae floating in the pre-historic sea!

The effect isn't quite complete, as only the frames morph, leaving the images underneath unchanged. Recall that you set the mask of the avatar image to be a `CAShapeLayer` — that's the same class as the avatar frame. So *theoretically* you could re-use the animation object on your frame for your mask.

Will theory work in practice? Give it a try, and add the following line to the bottom of `bounceOff(point: morphSize:)`:

```
maskLayer.add(morphAnimation, forKey: nil)
```

Build and run your project again; this time you should see both the frame and mask morph in perfect sync:

Awesome — you've just created a really nice-looking animation with only a bit of math and a few well-designed chunks of code! In the space of this chapter, you've learned how to create and animate shapes and how to use and animate shape layers as masks.

Challenges

The challenges in this chapter are optional, but I encourage you to work through them to practice your skills and add some real polish to your project. However if you're eager to start with gradient animations, then you can head straight on to the next chapter.

Challenge 1: Finish the communication state animations

For this challenge, you get a bit of a breather as you can simply follow along with the instructions below. Your task in this challenge is to add some status messages to show to the user as your faux "searching for an opponent" task progresses.

Open **ViewController.swift** and add the following code to the bottom of `searchForOpponent()`:

```
delay(seconds: 4.0, completion: foundOpponent)
```

The app will continue to "search" for four seconds before calling `foundOpponent()`, which will indicate to the player that the app has found an opponent.

Add the following method to the `ViewController` class:

```
func foundOpponent() {
   status.text = "Connecting..."

   opponentAvatar.image = UIImage(named: "avatar-2")
   opponentAvatar.name = "Ray"
}
```

Build and run your project and after about four seconds, you'll see the opponent's avatar appear:

Now that the app has found an opponent, it will start "connecting" the two players. All of this, of course, is just a simulation so you get to build a nice animation.

Add the following code to the bottom of `foundOpponent()`:

```
delay(seconds: 4.0, completion: connectedToOpponent)
```

This inserts another four-second delay after the app displays the opponent's avatar, after which you'll call the "connected state" method in the next code block.

Add the following new method to the class:

```
func connectedToOpponent() {
    myAvatar.shouldTransitionToFinishedState = true
    opponentAvatar.shouldTransitionToFinishedState = true
}
```

The above method sets `shouldTransitionToFinishedState` to true on both avatar views. This triggers a new animation that you will create in the next challenge, so for now nothing will happen.

Finally, you need to adjust the UI for the final state. Add the following code to the bottom of `connectedToOpponent()`:

```
delay(seconds: 1.0, completion: completed)
```

This code gives the animation a second to wrap up and then calls the final step in the sequence: `completed()`.

Add the final method sto the `ViewController` class:

```
func completed() {
    status.text = "Ready to play"
    UIView.animate(withDuration: 0.2) {
        self.vs.alpha = 1.0
        self.searchAgain.alpha = 1.0
    }
}
```

`completed()` sets the status message at the top of the screen to "Ready to play", then fades in the "vs." label and the "Search Again" button to restart the animation sequence. The button is already connected to `actionSearchAgain()` so you can tap it to restart the animations.

Build and run to see the entire sequence of animations:

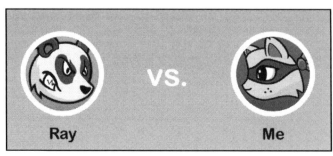

Challenge 2: Morph the avatars to squares

At this point the avatars just keep bouncing forever. Once the game is connected to an opponent, you'd like to stop the animation and reflect the state change in the UI.

In this challenge you are going to make use of the shouldTransitionToFinishedState property of the avatar class; when it's set to true you'll break the bounce animation and morph the avatars into a square shape.

Open **AvatarView.swift** and add a new variable called isSquare and set its initial value to false. Scroll to bounceOff(point: morphSize:) and find the animation completion block where there's a recursive call to bounceOff(point: morphSize:).

You'll need to wrap that call in a conditional so it only runs when isSquare is still false.

Next you'll run an extra animation while the avatars bounce off each other one last time.

Find the //complete bounce to comment and replace it with the following:

```
if self.shouldTransitionToFinishedState {
    self.animateToSquare()
}
```

Finally, add the animateToSquare() method to AvatarView and write the code to do the following:

1. Set isSquare to true.

2. Create a Bezier path with UIBezierPath(rect:) by using the avatar's bounds rectangle, and store the CGPath of this bezier path in a constant called squarePath.

3. Create a new layer animation with a keypath of path and set its duration to 0.25 seconds.

4. Set the fromValue of the animation to the circleLayer.path and the toValue to squarePath. This defines a morph animation from a circle to a square shape.

5. Add the animation to the circleLayer and then set its path property to the squarePath.

6. Similarly, add the animation to the mask layer as well and set its path property to squarePath.

Build and run your project; the final bounce will look much fancier. While the avatars touch for the last time they'll still look like this:

They bounce back to their starting point, morphing into squares for a *wow* effect:

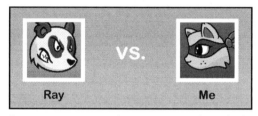

By now you know the basic animation techniques to work with shape layers and masks. You've likely already thought up many ways to apply shape animations in your own applications.

You continue to work with shapes and CAShapeLayer animations in Chapter 15, "Stroke and Path Animations". Head on to Chapter 14, "Gradient Animations" to learn how to add some really neat effects to your animations using animated gradients.

Chapter 14: Gradient Animations

A lot of the look and feel of iOS comes from very subtle animations in the UI. While it is no longer a part of iOS, one of the nicest was a simple little animation: the "slide to unlock" label on the lock screen. In this chapter you'll learn how to mimic this effect with a moving gradient and how to animate the colors and layout of those gradients:

Slide to reveal

You'll animate the gradient for a "Slide to reveal" label and then reveal a cool mystery effect when the user swipes over the label. You'll have to work through this chapter, however, to see what this cool effect is! :] As an extra bonus, you'll learn how to create a layer mask out of a piece of text and use it to mask a gradient.

Drawing your first gradient

Open the starter project for this chapter and select **Main.storyboard** to see how the UI looks at present:

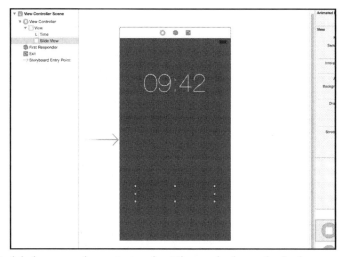

There's a static label on top that mimics the iPhone clock on the lock screen and another view near the bottom.

The bottom view is an instance of `AnimatedMaskLabel` that's included with the starter project. You'll work with this class throughout this chapter to add gradient animations.

Build and run your project; you'll see just the faux clock appear at the top of the screen:

You'll first draw the base gradient of `AnimatedMaskLabel`. Add the following code to **AnimatedMaskLabel.swift** inside the `gradientLayer` property code after the comment shown below:

```
// Configure the gradient here
gradientLayer.startPoint = CGPoint(x: 0.0, y: 0.5)
gradientLayer.endPoint = CGPoint(x: 1.0, y: 0.5)
```

This defines the orientation of the gradient and its start and end points.

Now add the following code to define the colors that build up the gradient after the code you just added:

```
let colors = [
   UIColor.black.cgColor,
   UIColor.white.cgColor,
   UIColor.black.cgColor
]
gradientLayer.colors = colors
```

The gradient above starts with a black color, blends to white, and finally blends back to black.

You can also specify where exactly in the gradient's frame these colors should appear. Add the following code below:

```
let locations: [NSNumber] = [
   0.25,
   0.5,
   0.75
]
gradientLayer.locations = locations
```

This sets up the gradient color milestones as follows:

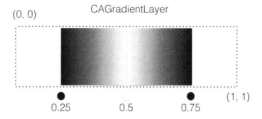

You can have as many key points and color milestones as you like, but the text gradient animation in this chapter only needs the simple black-white-black gradient shown above.

Add the following code to `layoutSubviews()` to give the gradient a frame:

```
gradientLayer.frame = bounds
```

All that you need to do now is add the gradient to the view's layer to see it in action. Add the line of code below to the end of `didMoveToWindow()`:

```
layer.addSublayer(gradientLayer)
```

Build and run your project; you should see the app display the exact gradient you're looking for:

That's a great start! Now you need to figure out how to animate this gradient.

Animating gradients

`CAGradientLayer` offers you four animatable properties along with the ones inherited from `CALayer`:

- `colors`: Animate the gradient's colors to give it a tint.

- `locations`: Animate the color milestone locations to make the colors move around inside the gradient.

- `startPoint` and `endPoint`: Animate the extents of the layout of the gradient.

In this section you'll animate locations to make the gradient "move".

Add the following code to the end of `didMoveToWindow()`:

```
let gradientAnimation = CABasicAnimation(keyPath: "locations")
gradientAnimation.fromValue = [0.0, 0.0, 0.25]
gradientAnimation.toValue = [0.75, 1.0, 1.0]
gradientAnimation.duration = 3.0
gradientAnimation.repeatCount = Float.infinity
```

In this layer animation, you begin by pushing the three color milestones to the left edge of the gradient's frame and end the animation with all three pushed towards the right edge:

The animation lasts 3 seconds and will repeat forever since you set `repeatCount` to `infinity`.

Finally, add the following line to the end of `didMoveToWindow()`:

```
gradientLayer.add(gradientAnimation, forKey: nil)
```

This will add the animation to the gradient layer. Build and run your project and you'll see the animation take shape:

This looks pretty nice, but the gradient is quite harsh, especially near the middle. No problem: just enlarge the gradient bounds and you'll get a much gentler gradient.

Find the line `gradientLayer.frame = bounds` in `layoutSubviews()` and replace it with the following code that sets a much larger frame for the gradient layer:

```
gradientLayer.frame = CGRect(
    x: -bounds.size.width,
    y: bounds.origin.y,
    width: 3 * bounds.size.width,
    height: bounds.size.height)
```

This sets the gradient frame to three times the width of the visible area. The animation enters the view, passes right through it, and exits out the right hand side:

Build and run your project to see what your changes look like:

That looks more like the smooth gradient you're going for. Now that you have the gradient, you'll need to create the text layers to use as a mask.

Creating a text mask

In this section you'll render the string stored in the text property of
AnimatedMaskLabel and use that to mask the gradient layer. Create a new constant
property inside the AnimatedMaskLabel class to hold the text attributes as follows:

```
let textAttributes: [String: AnyObject] = {
  let style = NSMutableParagraphStyle()
  style.alignment = .center
  return [
    NSFontAttributeName: UIFont(
      name: "HelveticaNeue-Thin",
      size: 28.0)!,
    NSParagraphStyleAttributeName: style
  ]
}()
```

Next you need to create a temporary graphic context in order to render the text as an
image. A natural place to do this is in the property observer for the text property. Add
the following code after the setNeedsDisplay() call:

```
let image = UIGraphicsImageRenderer(size: bounds.size)
  .image {
    _ in
    text.draw(in: bounds, withAttributes: textAttributes)
}
```

Here you use an image renderer to set up a context, draw to it, and get the results out as
a UIImage. Now you can use that image to create a mask on your gradient layer. To do
that, first create a layer out of the image as follows:

```
let maskLayer = CALayer()
maskLayer.backgroundColor = UIColor.clear.cgColor
maskLayer.frame = bounds.offsetBy(dx: bounds.size.width, dy: 0)
maskLayer.contents = image?.cgImage
```

You create `maskLayer` as an empty layer simply by using the default initializer of `CALayer`. You then set a fully transparent layer background since you're going to use the layer as a mask. Then you offset the layer frame by the width of the view; this way, the mask will show up in the center of the gradient. This is necessary as your "stretched" gradient is currently three times as wide as the visible view. Finally, you assign the image object directly to the contents property of the layer.

Add one more line to set the new layer as a mask for the gradient:

```
gradientLayer.mask = maskLayer
```

Build and run your project to see the fully developed animation in action:

Hey — that looks really slick! But you haven't yet discovered what's revealed when the user swipes across the label — and are you limited to a monochrome palette for your gradient? All will be revealed — as you work through the challenges below! :]

Challenges

I know the suspense is killing you; these two challenges will add a slide gesture recognizer to the label and add one additional color effect to the gradient animation.

Challenge 1: Slide to reveal gesture recognizer

Open **ViewController.swift** and add the following code to `viewDidLoad()`:

```
let swipe = UISwipeGestureRecognizer(target: self,
    action: #selector(ViewController.didSlide))
swipe.direction = .right
slideView.addGestureRecognizer(swipe)
```

This creates a slide-to-right gesture recognizer and attaches it to `slideView`. The recognizer will call `didSlide()` on `ViewController`.

`didSlide()` is already implemented for you, so all you need to do now is fire up the application and slide your finger over the animating label to reveal what lies beneath.

Challenge 2: Psychedelic gradient animations

In the final challenge of this chapter you'll experiment with adding more colors to the gradient and observe the effects.

If you'd like something to guide your exploration, try using the following list of colors for your gradient:

```
UIColor.yellow
UIColor.green
UIColor.orange
UIColor.cyan
UIColor.red
UIColor.yellow
```

You'll need to adjust the locations values as well to keep all of your colors in order. Start your animation with the following locations: `0.0, 0.0, 0.0, 0.0, 0.0` and `0.25`. Then animate the locations to: `0.65, 0.8, 0.85, 0.9, 0.95` and `1.0`.

Build and run your project; play around with the animation and the various parameters until you have it tuned it to your own design preferences:

This brings the chapter to a close; you've seen how easy it is to animate gradients as well as how to implement some advanced layer masking tricks with text layers.

The next chapter covers stroke animations for shapes, which is the final topic you'll cover in this section of the book on layer animations; you'll learn how to draw shapes interactively, and as a bonus, you'll cover advanced keyframe animations.

Chapter 15: Stroke and path animations

This chapter wraps up the layer animations section of this book; you'll learn about stroke and path animations as you add a cool pull-to-refresh animation to your existing Pack List project that entertains the user while the app pretends to fetch new data from the Internet:

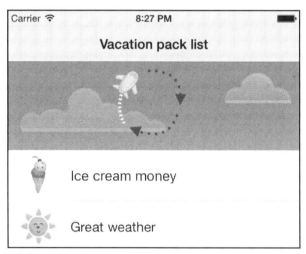

Along the way, you'll learn how to animate the drawing of shapes, and as a bonus, you'll look at a special kind of keyframe animation that you can use to move an object along any arbitrary path.

Creating interactive stroke animations

Open the starter project for this chapter, then build and run it to see how the UI looks:

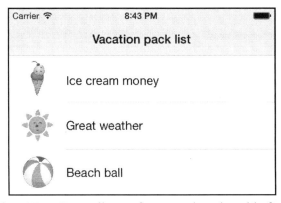

There's existing code in **ViewController.swift** to populate the table for you with a number of vacation items. Pull down the table and you'll see a refresh view appear at the top of the screen:

The refresh view stays visible for four seconds, then retracts. Your job here is to add an amusing animation to entertain users while they wait.

The refresh view already contains all the code for the pulling and releasing actions; you just need to worry about adding the animations.

> **Note:** The pull down to refresh code is based on one of our video tutorials. If you would like to know more about how it works check out the *Swift Scroll View School* video series at the following link: http://www.raywenderlich.com/video-tutorials.

The first step in building your animation is to create a circle shape. Open
RefreshView.swift and add the following code to init(frame:scrollView:):

```
ovalShapeLayer.strokeColor = UIColor.white.cgColor
ovalShapeLayer.fillColor = UIColor.clear.cgColor
ovalShapeLayer.lineWidth = 4.0
ovalShapeLayer.lineDashPattern = [2, 3]

let refreshRadius = frame.size.height/2 * 0.8

ovalShapeLayer.path = UIBezierPath(ovalIn: CGRect(
  x: frame.size.width/2 - refreshRadius,
  y: frame.size.height/2 - refreshRadius,
  width: 2 * refreshRadius,
  height: 2 * refreshRadius)
).cgPath

layer.addSublayer(ovalShapeLayer)
```

ovalShapeLayer is a property on RefreshView of type CAShapeLayer. You're already
quite familiar with shape layers; here you simply set the stroke and fill colors and set the
circle diameter to be 80% of the view height, which ensures a comfortable margin around
the shape.

There's one property in the code above that you haven't encountered yet:
lineDashPattern. This property lets you set a dash pattern for the shape stroke; you
simply you provide an array with the length of the dash and the length of the gap in
pixels.

Build and run your project to see how the circle looks:

That looks really nice — and it was easy to create. This will serve you well as a circular
progress bar.

In RefreshView, redrawFromProgress() is called whenever the user scrolls via
scrollViewDidScroll(_ scrollView:); this makes it a convenient place to update
the visuals of the progress bar.

Add the following code to `redrawFromProgress()`:

```
ovalShapeLayer.strokeEnd = progress
```

As progress increases from `0.0` to `1.0`, the stroke end of the shape moves forward towards the starting point of the stroke.

This is how the shape looks when progress is `0.25`:

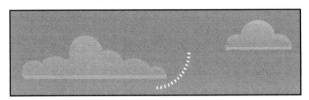

Here it is halfway around, at `0.5`:

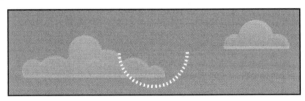

Build and run your project; drag the table view up and down to see the stroke length change.

Now you'll add a cool-looking airplane to the refresh control.

Scroll back to `init(frame:scrollView:)` and add the following code to the bottom of the initializer:

```
let airplaneImage = UIImage(named: "airplane.png")!
airplaneLayer.contents = airplaneImage.cgImage
airplaneLayer.bounds = CGRect(x: 0.0, y: 0.0,
  width: airplaneImage.size.width,
  height: airplaneImage.size.height)

airplaneLayer.position = CGPoint(
  x: frame.size.width/2 + frame.size.height/2 * 0.8,
  y: frame.size.height/2)

layer.addSublayer(airplaneLayer)
```

The code should look familiar. You've already done this few times in previous chapters. You simply load **airplane.png** and assign it as the contents of a layer on the screen, then position the airplane layer at the location where the circle starts drawing.

Build and run your project to see the airplane appear when you pull the table view down:

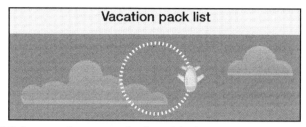

The plane should fade in as the user pulls the table down.

Add the following code to `init(frame:scrollView:)`:

```
airplaneLayer.opacity = 0.0
```

This makes the airplane completely transparent to start.

Now add the following code to `redrawFromProgress()` to progressively change the opacity of the airplane layer as the user pulls down:

```
airplaneLayer.opacity = Float(progress)
```

`opacity` is of type `Float` so you need to convert `progress` from a `CGFloat`.

Build and run your project; pull down the table and you should see the airplane appear gradually:

This wraps up the interactive animation part of this chapter. The next section walks you through animating a progress indicator to keep the users engaged while they wait for the faux refreshed data.

Animating both stroke ends

In this section, you'll animate *both* the `strokeStart` and `strokeEnd` properties to make the shape "run around".

You'll start the animation when the app starts to fetch the faux data. Add the following code to the end of `beginRefreshing()`:

```
let strokeStartAnimation = CABasicAnimation(
    keyPath: "strokeStart")
strokeStartAnimation.fromValue = -0.5
strokeStartAnimation.toValue = 1.0

let strokeEndAnimation = CABasicAnimation(
    keyPath: "strokeEnd")
strokeEndAnimation.fromValue = 0.0
strokeEndAnimation.toValue = 1.0
```

This code creates two animations: the first one animates `strokeStart` from -0.5 to 1.0. This is a simple and cheap animation trick; while the value animates from -0.5 to 0.0 nothing happens, as all negative values for these properties simply mean no part of the shape is visible.

This gives the second animation — the one on `strokeEnd` — a bit of a head start. This draws a small bit of the shape on the screen, until `strokeStart` catches up with `strokeEnd` at the end of the animation.

Add the following code the end of `beginRefreshing()` to run the two animations simultaneously:

```
let strokeAnimationGroup = CAAnimationGroup()
strokeAnimationGroup.duration = 1.5
strokeAnimationGroup.repeatDuration = 5.0
strokeAnimationGroup.animations =
    [strokeStartAnimation, strokeEndAnimation]
ovalShapeLayer.add(strokeAnimationGroup, forKey: nil)
```

In the code above, you create an animation group and repeat the animation five times. This should be long enough to keep the animation running while the refresh view is visible. Then you add both animations to the group and add the group to the progress bar.

Build and run your project; pull and release the table to see your animation in action:

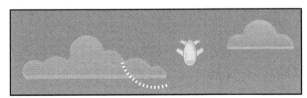

You've just created your own custom spinner! :] Although it looks pretty neat, you can make it even cooler with just a little effort - and some help from layer path animations!

Creating path keyframe animations

You saw how to animate a layer using a keyframe animation and the values property in Chapter 12, "Keyframe Animations and Struct Properties". to animate a layer along a path you do much the same thing but you assign a `CGPath` to the animation's path property instead.

Core Animation will then calculate the intermediate positions of the layer along the `CGPath` and animate it nicely over the animation's duration.

Add the following code to `beginRefreshing()`:

```
let flightAnimation = CAKeyframeAnimation(keyPath: "position")
flightAnimation.path = ovalShapeLayer.path
flightAnimation.calculationMode = kCAAnimationPaced
```

Here you `CAKeyframeAnimation` and, much like before, set the animated property to position. But this time you assign a value to path. In this case you can re-use the circular path of `ovalShapeLayer`.

Finally you set the animation `calculationMode` to a paced mode — this will make sure that the layer animates smoothly along the path.

`calculationMode` is yet another way you can control the timing of your animation. When you set that property to `kCAAnimationPaced` Core Animation animates your layer with a constant pace ignoring any key times you've set. This is very useful for producing smooth animations across an arbitrary path.

Another possible value to use is `kCAAnimationDiscrete`. This calculation mode makes Core Animation jump from key value to key value without any interpolation. Yes you got it right — Core Animation has a special mode to produce animations that don't animate anything. :]

Enough calculation mode fun — back to the task at hand.

Now you need to create a group out of this animation and run it on the airplane layer. You need the group later on as you'll add a second animation to complement the first.

Add the following code to `beginRefreshing()`:

```
let flightAnimationGroup = CAAnimationGroup()
flightAnimationGroup.duration = 1.5
flightAnimationGroup.repeatDuration = 5.0
flightAnimationGroup.animations = [flightAnimation]
airplaneLayer.add(flightAnimationGroup, forKey: nil)
```

In the code above, you create the group and give it the same duration and repeat count as the progress bar stroke animation. You then add `flightAnimation` as the only item in the group and add the group to the airplane layer.

Run the animation and check out the pilot's skills:

You've never seen an airshow like this one: the airplane performs loops in the sky and stays perfectly vertical! :] As amusing as this is, you should probably make the plane fly more naturally.

Note: `CAKeyframeAnimation` has a special property called `rotationMode`, which when set to `kCAAnimationRotateAuto` will automatically orient your layer in the direction it's moving. However, you'll create this effect manually in this chapter, as it's an easy task for simple, circular paths.

Insert the following new animation code **above** the line where you create `flightAnimationGroup`:

```
let airplaneOrientationAnimation = CABasicAnimation(keyPath:
"transform.rotation")
airplaneOrientationAnimation.fromValue = 0
airplaneOrientationAnimation.toValue = 2.0 * .pi
```

`airplaneOrientationAnimation` rotates the layer a full 360 degrees — from 0 to 2π — via its `transform`. In other words, the airplane image will rotate in a full circle around its center, and since you move the airplane layer along the circular path at the same time, the flight will end up looking natural.

Now you just need to add `airplaneOrientationAnimation` to the animation group.

Add the new animation to the array as shown below:

```
flightAnimationGroup.animations = [flightAnimation,
  airplaneOrientationAnimation]
```

Build and run your project and enjoy your completed pull-down-to-refresh control:

If you'd like to experiment with air acrobatics, you can try setting the rotation animation to go from 0 to 4π — good fun!

Keep in mind that you're not limited to simple paths such as squares or circles. You can feed just about any CGPath to your keyframe animation and send your layer along some extremely complicated paths.

If you're going to create more complex path animations and want to stay sane, you'd do well to keep in mind the note about rotationMode earlier in this chapter.

Section conclusion

This wraps up the basic layer animations section. You've been through a lot — and learned a ton of things along the way!

In this section of the book you covered:

• Basic movement, fading, rotation, and scaling animations

• Groups and keyframe animations

• Shapes, masks, and gradient animations

• Stroke and path animations

The next chapter will guide you through a totally new field of expertise — making some animation clones of your own!

Chapter 16: Replicating Animations

In this chapter you're going to try something completely new: using a container layer that lets you **replicate** animations.

Let me introduce you to my favorite layer class: CAReplicatorLayer.

The idea behind CAReplicatorLayer is simple. You create some content — it could be a shape, an image or anything else you can draw with layers — and CAReplicatorLayer makes copies of it on the screen, like so:

"Why would I need to clone shapes or images?" you would ask. And you would be right to ask that; it's not often you'd need the exact of anything cloned a number of times.

CAReplicatorLayer's superpowers come from the fact you can easily instruct it to make each clone slightly different from its ancestor.

For example, you could progressively change the tint of each copy. Your original layer could be magenta, while you progress the tint towards cyan as you create each copy.

Furthermore, you can apply a transform between copies; for example, you can apply a simple rotation transform between each copy to draw them in a circle, as shown below:

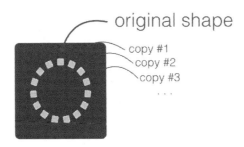

But the best feature of all is the ability to set an animation delay to follow each copy. When you set an `instanceDelay` of `0.2` seconds and add an animation to your original content, the first copy will animate with a delay of `0.2` seconds, the second copy will animate in `0.4` seconds, the third one in `0.6` seconds and so forth.

You can use this to create engaging and complex animations where you animate multiple elements in a synchronous manner.

In this chapter, you're going to work on a personal assistant app that will "listen" to your questions and answer back. As a wink to Apple's own personal assistant Siri, your project has been named Iris. :]

You're going to create two different replications. First, you'll create the visual feedback animation that plays while Iris talks, which will look much like a psychedelic sine wave:

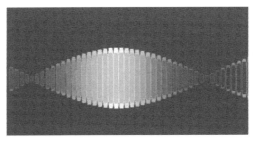

Then you'll use `CAReplicatorLayer` to create an interactive microphone-driven audio wave, which will provide visual feedback while the user speaks:

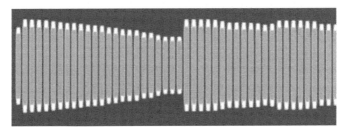

These two animations will introduce you to many features of `CAReplicatorLayer`. To cover every feature this layer offers would fill an entire book on its own! :]

But you don't need to listen to me yammer on about how much I like creating animations with `CAReplicatorLayer`; it's time to experience the magic for yourself.

Replicating like rabbits

Starter project overview

Launch the starter project for this chapter and open **Main.storyboard**. You'll notice that the project setup is quite straightforward:

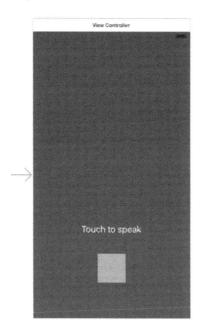

There is only a single view controller, which features a button and a label. The user asks their question while they hold down the button; when they release the button Iris will speak in response. The label will display the mic input levels and Iris' answer.

Open **ViewController.swift**; note the button events are already connected to actions. When the user touches down on the button, `actionStartMonitoring()` fires; when the user lifts their finger, `actionEndMonitoring()` fires.

Right now `ViewController` doesn't do much and simply calls `startSpeaking()` from within `actionEndMonitoring()` when the user lifts their finger.

The project features two more classes that are beyond the scope of this chapter, but they'll help you develop a fun and functional app while letting you focus on the animation parts. They are as follows:

- `Assistant`: The artificial intelligence assistant. It has a list of predefined amusing answers and speaks them in response to the user's questions.

- `MicMonitor`: Monitors the input levels on your iPhone's microphone and repeatedly calls a closure expression that you provide. This is where you have the chance to update the display.

Everything is ready for you to jump in and add some cool animations!

Setting up the replicator layer

Open **ViewController.swift** and add the following two properties:

```
let replicator = CAReplicatorLayer()
let dot = CALayer()
```

`dot` will be a simple shape drawn using the `CALayer` basic properties such as background and border color. `replicator` will help you get multiple dot copies on screen.

Next, add the following constants you'll need to create your animation:

```
let dotLength: CGFloat = 6.0
let dotOffset: CGFloat = 8.0
```

You'll use the first constant as the width and height of the `dot` layer, while the second constant holds the offset between each dot replication.

To finish off the setup, you'll have to add the replicator layer to the view controller's view. Add the following to `viewDidLoad()`:

```
replicator.frame = view.bounds
view.layer.addSublayer(replicator)
```

Here you make the replicator layer the same size as the view controller's view and add it as a sub-layer. If you were to run the project at this point, nothing would appear to have changed; that's because you didn't add any visible content to replicate.

The next step is to dress up the dot layer and add it to `replicator` in order to display the replications. Append the following to `viewDidLoad()`:

```
dot.frame = CGRect(
  x: replicator.frame.size.width - dotLength,
  y: replicator.position.y,
```

```
     width: dotLength, height: dotLength)

dot.backgroundColor = UIColor.lightGray.cgColor
dot.borderColor = UIColor(white: 1.0, alpha: 1.0).cgColor
dot.borderWidth = 0.5
dot.cornerRadius = 1.5
```

You first position the `dot` layer towards the right edge of the replicator and therefore, the right edge of the screen. Then you set the layer's background color and add a border. At this point the layer will look like the following:

To see it displayed on the screen, add the following:

```
replicator.addSublayer(dot)
```

This adds `dot` to `replicator`. Run your project and you'll see it show up:

So far so good. What you see is what you would expect from adding just about any layer to any other layer.

"But where's the magic you promised us?" you're asking. Hang tight — you're almost there! :]

You're going to work with three `CAReplicatorLayer` properties that will help you access that replication magic:

- `instanceCount`: Sets the number of copies you want

- `instanceTransform`: Sets the transform to apply between copies

- `instanceDelay`: Sets the animation delay between copies

You want the replication to fill the screen, so you'll have to divide the screen width by the offset between copies (dotOffset) to get the number of dots needed to fill up the width. This will give you more replications on iPhone 6 Plus and fewer on an iPhone 5.

Add the following line to viewDidLoad() to set the number of copies (including the original copy):

```
replicator.instanceCount = Int(view.frame.size.width /
  dotOffset)
```

On an iPhone 6 Plus instanceCount ends up as 51; on an iPhone 6 46, and on iPhone 4 and 5 series, 40.

Run the project again; hey, where are all the copies?

No, the photocopier isn't on the fritz again. :] All your copies of dot are there, but they're all on top of each other. You'll need to apply a transform to show them all.

Add the following to the end of viewDidLoad():

```
replicator.instanceTransform = CATransform3DMakeTranslation(
  -dotOffset, 0.0, 0.0)
```

In the code above, you first set a translation transform between each replication. You then take the negative value of dotOffset for the translation on the X axis because you want the copies to progress from right to left.

replicator will consider dot and subtract 8 points from its position; the first copy will appear at this point. The second copy will appear at another 8 points to the left and so forth.

Run your project; you'll see all copies line up in the middle of the screen, each replication translated 8 points from the previous one:

Your first replicated animation

To understand what `instanceDelay` does, you'll add a little test animation to `dot`. Add the following to the end of `viewDidLoad()`:

```
// This is a test animation, you're going to delete it
let move = CABasicAnimation(keyPath: "position.y")
move.fromValue = dot.position.y
move.toValue = dot.position.y - 50.0
move.duration = 1.0
move.repeatCount = 10
dot.add(move, forKey: nil)
// This is the end of the code you're going to delete
```

This animation simply moves `dot` up 50 points and repeats that action 10 times. Run the project and you'll see all clones obediently moving across the screen like so many synchronized kill-bots.

Next you'll add a bit of delay to the animation. Insert the following line of code:

```
replicator.instanceDelay = 0.02
```

Run your project once more and observe how all copies follow the original dot animation, but only after an ever-increasing delay:

Now that you have the basics covered, it's time to move on to cooler animations.

Before you go on, **delete** the test animation you just added (use the comments above as a guide); you're going to create much better animations in its place.

Replicating multiple animations

`CAReplicatorLayer` replicates the content and animations you create in the manner you instruct. But it's up to you to come up with some cool animations that would look even *cooler* when replicated.

In this section, you'll work on the animation that plays while Iris speaks. To do this, you'll combine a number of simple animations with different delays to produce the final effect.

Scale animation

First you'll continuously scale the dot layer up and down to produce a wave of dots.

Find `startSpeaking()` and add the following scale animation:

```
let scale = CABasicAnimation(keyPath: "transform")
scale.fromValue = NSValue(caTransform3D: CATransform3DIdentity)
scale.toValue = NSValue(caTransform3D:
  CATransform3DMakeScale(1.4, 15, 1.0))
scale.duration = 0.33
scale.repeatCount = .infinity
scale.autoreverses = true
scale.timingFunction = CAMediaTimingFunction(name:
  kCAMediaTimingFunctionEaseOut)
dot.add(scale, forKey: "dotScale")
```

This is a simple layer animation like the many others in this section of the book. You scale the dot layer vertically 15-fold and run the animation continuously back and forth.

Run the project and tap the gray button; this calls `actionStartMonitoring()`, `actionEndMonitoring()` and finally your code in `startSpeaking()`. You should see your original dot layer animate and all copies follow with their respective delays:

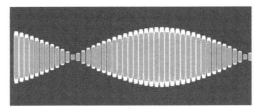

Congrats — you're off to a great start with `CAReplicatorLayer`!

> **Note:** For some extra-curricular fun, try changing the timing function of the animation to see what other cool waveforms you can create.

Opacity animation

Next you'll make the original dot layer fade in and out. This will make the wave some dimension and change the alpha as it grows and shrinks to simulate light conditions. It will look much like a spinning twisty ribbon candy:

Add the following fade animation to `startSpeaking()`:

```
let fade = CABasicAnimation(keyPath: "opacity")
fade.fromValue = 1.0
fade.toValue = 0.2
fade.duration = 0.33
fade.beginTime = CACurrentMediaTime() + 0.33
fade.repeatCount = .infinity
fade.autoreverses = true
fade.timingFunction = CAMediaTimingFunction(name:
  kCAMediaTimingFunctionEaseOut)
dot.add(fade, forKey: "dotOpacity")
```

You fade the dot layer from opacity `1.0` to `0.2` over the duration of the scale animation. This time around, you start the animation with a delay of `0.33` seconds; this starts the fade-out effect when the wave it at its fullest.

Run your project and enjoy the new effect as the two animations run simultaneously:

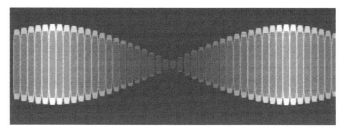

Tint animation

If you push your imagination (and squint a little) you can imagine the wave twisting around and around on your screen. That impression would be a lot more clear if you animated its tint, as if the wave had a different color on each side.

This should be an easy enough task – all you have to do is animate the background color of `dot`.

Add a third animation to `startSpeaking()`:

```
let tint = CABasicAnimation(keyPath: "backgroundColor")
tint.fromValue = UIColor.magenta.cgColor
tint.toValue = UIColor.cyan.cgColor
tint.duration = 0.66
tint.beginTime = CACurrentMediaTime() + 0.28
tint.fillMode = kCAFillModeBackwards
tint.repeatCount = Float.infinity
tint.autoreverses = true
tint.timingFunction = CAMediaTimingFunction(name:
  kCAMediaTimingFunctionEaseInEaseOut)
dot.add(tint, forKey: "dotColor")
```

This animation changes the dot's tint from magenta to cyan and back. You use a duration of `0.66` seconds; this is twice the frequency of the scaling animation and gives the impression that the color changes every time the wave "twists".

You also give the animation a delay of `0.28` seconds; this makes the color tint animation start just before the "twist" occurs in the wave. This subtle effect provides a hint of the next color just before the wave "twists" as if there's a bit of reflection going on.

Run the project to check out the new effect:

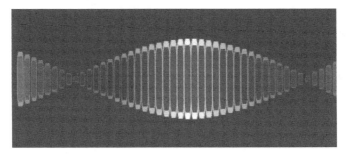

Animating CAReplicatorLayer properties

So far you've created a pretty dazzling effect by animating the content in your replicator layer. But since `CAReplicatorLayer` is a layer itself, you can animate a number of its own properties too.

You can animate `CAReplicatorLayer`'s basic properties like `position`, `backgroundColor` or `cornerRadius` but, you can create some interesting effects by animating some of the special properties in this layer that aren't present in other layers.

The animatable properties unique to `CAReplicatorLayer` include the following:

- `instanceDelay`: Animate the amount of delay between instances
- `instanceTransform`: Change the transform between replications on the fly
- `instanceColor`: Change the blend color used for all instances
- `instanceRedOffset`, `instanceGreenOffset`, `instanceBlueOffset`: Apply a delta to apply to each instance color component
- `instanceAlphaOffset`: Change the opacity delta applied to each instance

In this section, you'll animate the instance transform to make the speech wave even *more* psychedelic!

Add one more animation to the end of startSpeaking():

```
let initialRotation = CABasicAnimation(keyPath:
  "instanceTransform.rotation")
initialRotation.fromValue = 0.0
initialRotation.toValue   = 0.01
initialRotation.duration = 0.33
initialRotation.isRemovedOnCompletion = false
initialRotation.fillMode = kCAFillModeForwards
initialRotation.timingFunction = CAMediaTimingFunction(name:
  kCAMediaTimingFunctionEaseOut)
replicator.add(initialRotation, forKey: "initialRotation")
```

This animation affects just the rotation component of the instance transform; that is, it preserves the translation component you set for the instances in viewDidLoad() and only animates the rotation.

You animate the rotation between instances from 0.0 radians to 0.01 radians. Each replication will appear slightly rotated compared to its neighbor.

Run your project; enjoy your replicating animations on a totally new level — or should I say *curve*? :]

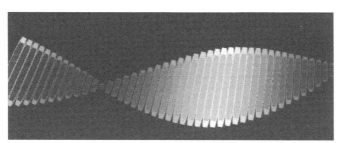

The instanceRotation animation above looks nice — but when I say *psychedelic*, I mean *PSYCHEDELIC!* What if you were to combine the effect of all running replication animations AND twist and spin the wave at the same time?

Add the animation below to complete the effect:

```
let rotation = CABasicAnimation(keyPath:
  "instanceTransform.rotation")
rotation.fromValue = 0.01
rotation.toValue   = -0.01
rotation.duration = 0.99
rotation.beginTime = CACurrentMediaTime() + 0.33
rotation.repeatCount = .infinity
rotation.autoreverses = true
```

```
rotation.timingFunction = CAMediaTimingFunction(name:
    kCAMediaTimingFunctionEaseInEaseOut)
replicator.add(rotation, forKey: "replicatorRotation")
```

Here, you run a second animation on instanceTransform.rotation that starts once the first animation has finished. You then animate the transform rotation from 0.01 radians (the final value of the first animation) to −0.01 radians and back.

This gives the speech animation a final, crazy boost:

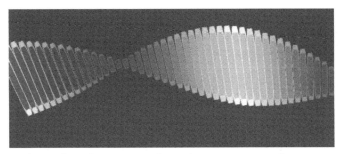

This is an outstanding (if not hypnosis-inducing) animation, and you created it by combining just a few select animations. The trick is to know which properties to animate and how to select the correct delays and durations to get the effect you're looking for.

> **Note:** Personally, I think the effect looks best if I rotate my head 45 degrees right. But be careful not to watch it too long - it could make you dizzy! :]

All that's left is to give your not-so-helpful assistant, Iris, the ability to listen and to respond.

First you'll give the power of speech to Iris. The starter project class named Assistant will help you do that. Add the following to the top of startSpeaking():

```
meterLabel.text = assistant.randomAnswer()
assistant.speak(meterLabel.text!, completion: endSpeaking)
speakButton.isHidden = true
```

You first get a random answer from the Assistant class and visualize it via the meterLabel. Then you call speak(_:completion:) on assistant; passing in endSpeaking() as into the completion parameter to be called when speaking is finished.

Next you'll add the code in endSpeaking() that removes all running animations and gracefully returns the wave to its initial state.

Insert the following into `endSpeaking()`:

```
replicator.removeAllAnimations()
```

This removes the animations on `instanceTransform` of `replicator`.

Next you need to animate the `dot` layer back to its original scale. Add:

```
let scale = CABasicAnimation(keyPath: "transform")
scale.toValue = NSValue(caTransform3D: CATransform3DIdentity)
scale.duration = 0.33
scale.isRemovedOnCompletion = false
scale.fillMode = kCAFillModeForwards
dot.add(scale, forKey: nil)
```

For this animation you don't specify a `fromValue`; this means that Core Animation will start the animation from the current value and animate the transform to `CATransform3DIdentiy`.

This is necessary because at any given time each of the replicated instances has a different transform. Omitting `fromValue` animates each replication from its current scale to the animation's final value.

Finally, add the following code to remove the rest of the currently running animations from `dot` and reset the speak button state:

```
dot.removeAnimation(forKey: "dotColor")
dot.removeAnimation(forKey: "dotOpacity")
dot.backgroundColor = UIColor.lightGray.cgColor
speakButton.isHidden = false
```

Run the project again; this time, Iris will speak a random answer right back at you!

When Iris is done speaking, the wave will gracefully animate back to its initial state:

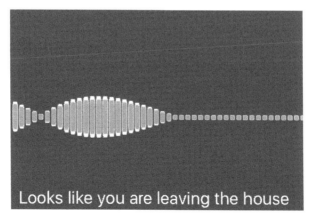

Interactive replication animations

Right now you need to press the speak button each time to see and hear Iris' answer. But you don't get to actually *ask* her anything, which, to be honest, is the really fun part.

In this final section you'll create an animation that displays the microphone input while you ask Iris your questions.

Note: In case the microphone in the iOS simulator does not work for you use a physical device to test your app in this part of the chapter.

Add the following to `actionStartMonitoring()`:

```
dot.backgroundColor = UIColor.green.cgColor
monitor.startMonitoringWithHandler {level in
  self.meterLabel.text = String(format: "%.2f db", level)
}
```

The above method fires when the user presses on the speak button. To indicate the app is "listening", you change the dot layer color to green. Then you call `startMonitoringWithHandler()` on the monitor instance.

Note: The `MicMonitor` class is pretty simple – peek inside **MicMonitor.swift** if you're interested to see how it gets the microphone levels.

The closure block you provide as a parameter executes repeatedly and gets the current microphone level as a parameter.

Run the app and hold the button; speak to the device and you'll see the current mic levels displayed. If iOS prompts you for microphone access, simply tap OK on the system alert:

So far so good; all you need now is to use the level variable to animate the replicator content accordingly.

First of all, you'll need to normalize the mic level to something you can use for your animations. level has a value in the rage of –160.0 db to 0.0 db, –160.0 db being the quietest and 0.0 db meaning extremely loud sound.

Add an extra line of code to the handler block to convert the level value to something useful and store it in scaleFactor so that the complete block looks like this:

```
monitor.startMonitoringWithHandler {level in
    self.meterLabel.text = String(format: "%.2f db", level)
    let scaleFactor = max(0.2, CGFloat(level) + 50) / 2
}
```

scaleFactor will store values between 0.1 and 25.0. You can use this to scale dot to a reasonable size to represent the microphone input levels.

Add the following instance property to the ViewController class:

```
var lastTransformScale: CGFloat = 0.0
```

For the scaling animation, you'll need to save the last scaled value to this property. Since you'll constantly overwrite the running scale animation, you need to keep track of the last value the layer was supposed to scale to.

Now jump back to the microphone handler closure and add to it the following code, which animates from the last transform to the new one you calculated from the current microphone levels:

```
let scale = CABasicAnimation(keyPath: "transform.scale.y")
scale.fromValue = self.lastTransformScale
scale.toValue = scaleFactor
scale.duration = 0.1
scale.isRemovedOnCompletion = false
scale.fillMode = kCAFillModeForwards
self.dot.add(scale, forKey: nil)
```

This layer animation runs only on the y-axis of the scale component of the dot layer transform. You animate the scale from the last value used to the current scaleFactor.

Finally, still inside the handler, add the following code to save the current scaleFactor value for the next handler call:

```
self.lastTransformScale = scaleFactor
```

This code ought to bring the replicator layer to life. Run the project, hold the button and speak. You'll see an actual audio wave show up on screen, all handled by the replicator layer while you simply animate the original dot layer:

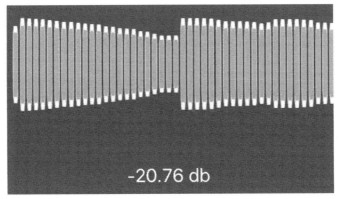

But when you let go of the speak button, the result is somewhat baffling:

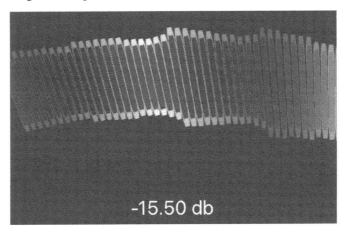

Aha — you need to reset the animations and stop monitoring the microphone. You can take care of that in `actionEndMonitoring()`.

Insert the following at the top of that method:

```
monitor.stopMonitoring()
dot.removeAllAnimations()
```

Here you disable the microphone monitor by calling `stopMonitoring()` and removing all animations running on the `dotlayer`. This way the app can move on and display the Iris animation.

Give the app a try. Isn't talking to Iris a lot of fun? :]

The microphone input animation ends somewhat abruptly, but you'll get to fix that in the challenges below.

Challenges

Challenge 1: Smooth the transition between microphone input and Iris animations

Your first challenge is to not just remove the two animations running on the `dot` layer by calling `dot.removeAllAnimations()`, but to animate the wave back to a state suitable for the next animation to be run.

Take this challenge in three steps:

- First, delete the line where you remove the running animations on dot from `actionEndMonitoring()`.

- Then, in its place, animate the scale of dot back to a value of 1.0 on the y-axis. Leave the animation on the screen to wait for the Iris animation to start — don't remove it when it's done.

- Finally, add another animation that changes the dot tint from green to magenta. For this animation, use a `fillMode` of `kCAFillModeBackwards` — without it, the replicator layer will reset the tint to the final value retroactively.

Mind the durations of these two new animations. They should finish before the Iris animation starts.

When you've completed this challenge, the two animations should blend nicely into each other like so:

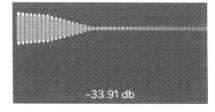

Section IV: View Controller Transition Animations

By now you know how to create a wide range of beautiful animations for your apps. You've experimented with moving, scaling and fading views, animating different types of layers – and a whole lot more.

It's time to learn how to use these animation techniques in the broader context of app navigation and layout. You've animated multiple views and layers already, but now take a bigger-picture perspective and think about animating entire view controllers!

One of the most recognizable animations of iOS is a new view controller being pushed onto the navigation stack, as shown below:

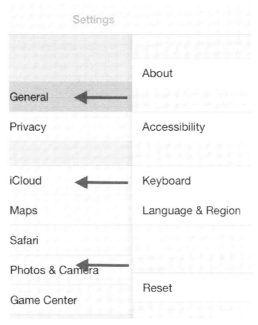

Since iOS 7, Apple added a bit of flair to that animation by adding a bit of lag before the old navigation controller starts moving away under the new one. It's a great effect – but when you're trying to build your own brand image, custom transition animations can be a big help.

In this section, you'll learn how to use animations to create your own custom view controller transitions.

You'll work on two projects in this section. In Chapter 17, you'll add transition animations to the Beginner Cook app:

- **Chapter 17, Custom Presentation Controller & Device Orientation Animations** – Learn how to present view controllers via custom animated transitions – and as a bonus, you'll create an animated transition to handle device orientation changes.

The project used in Chapters 18 and 19 – Logo Reveal – will help you learn how to create custom navigation controller transitions, including a cool effect where it appears that a logo grows to reveal the content of the next screen, like so:

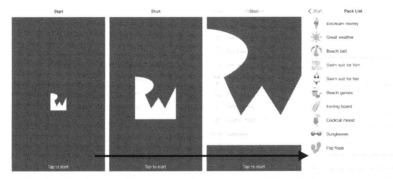

- **Chapter 18, UINavigationController Custom Transition Animations** – You'll build upon your skills with presenting view controllers and develop a really neat reveal transition for a navigation controller app.

- **Chapter 19, Interactive UINavigationController Transitions** – You'll continue on with the Logo Reveal project and make the reveal transition interactive: the user will be able to scrub back and forth through the animated transition!

Implementing custom view controller transitions takes some coding, but the results are lots of fun to look at and use. Custom transitions are an important animation technique that really makes an app stand out!

Chapter 17: Presentation Controller & Orientation Animations

Whether you're presenting the camera view controller, the address book, or one of your own custom-designed modal screens, you call the same UIKit method every time: present(_:animated:completion:). This method "gives up" the current screen to another view controller.

The default presentation animation simply slides the new view up to cover the current one. The illustration below shows a "New Contact" view controller sliding up over the list of contacts:

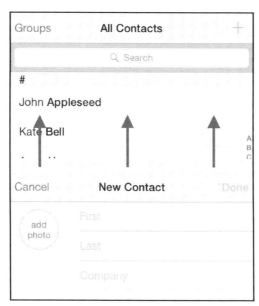

In this chapter, you'll create your own custom presentation controller animations to replace the default one and liven up this chapter's project.

Looking through the starter project

Open the starter project for this chapter, an app called Beginner Cook. Select **Main.storyboard** to begin the tour:

The first view controller (ViewController) contains the app's title and main description as well as a scroll view at the bottom, which shows the list of available herbs.

The main view controller presents HerbDetailsViewController whenever the user taps one of the images in the list; this view controller sports a background, a title, a description and some buttons to credit the image owner.

There's already enough code in **ViewController.swift** and **HerbDetailsViewController.swift** to support the basic application. Build and run the project to see how the app looks and feels:

Tap on one of the herb images, and the details screen comes up via the standard vertical cover transition. That might be OK for your garden-variety app, but your herbs deserve better!

Your job is to add some custom presentation controller animations to your app to make it blossom! You'll replace the current stock animation with one that expands the tapped herb image to a full-screen view like so:

Roll up your sleeves, put your developer apron on and get ready for the inner workings of custom presentation controllers!

Behind the scenes of custom transitions

UIKit lets you customize your view controller's presentation via the delegate pattern; you simply make your main view controller (or another class you create specifically for that purpose) adopt `UIViewControllerTransitioningDelegate`.

Every time you present a new view controller, UIKit asks its delegate whether or not it should use a custom transition. Here's what the first step of the custom transitioning dance looks like:

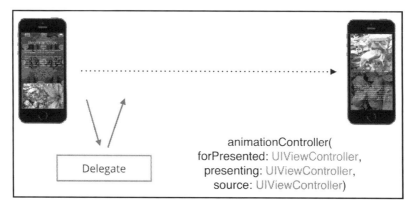

UIKit calls `animationController(forPresented:presenting:source:)` to see if a `UIViewControllerAnimatedTransitioning` is returned. If that method returns `nil`, UIKit uses the built-in transition. If UIKit receives a `UIViewControllerAnimatedTransitioning` object instead, then UIKit uses that object as the animation controller for the transition.

There are a few more steps in the dance before UIKit can use the custom animation controller:

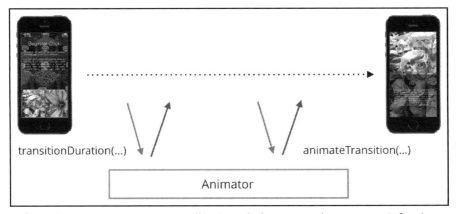

UIKit first asks your animation controller (simply known as the **animator**) for the transition duration in seconds, then calls `animateTransition(using:)` on it. This is when your custom animation gets to take center stage.

In `animateTransition(using:)`, you have access to both the current view controller on the screen as well as the new view controller to be presented. You can fade, scale, rotate and manipulate the existing view and the new view however you like.

Now that you've learned a bit about how custom presentation controllers work, you can start to create your own.

Implementing transition delegates

Since the delegate's task is to manage the animator object that performs the actual animations, you'll first have to create a stub for the animator class before you can write the delegate code.

From Xcode's main menu select **File\New\File...** and choose the template **iOS\Source\Cocoa Touch Class**.

Set the new class name to **PopAnimator**, make sure Swift is selected, and make it a subclass of **NSObject**.

Open **PopAnimator.swift** and update the class definition to make it conform to the
`UIViewControllerAnimatedTransitioning` protocol as follows:

```
class PopAnimator: NSObject,
  UIViewControllerAnimatedTransitioning {

}
```

You'll see some complaints from Xcode since you haven't implemented the required
delegate methods yet, so you'll stub those out next.

Add the following method to the class:

```
func transitionDuration(using transitionContext:
  UIViewControllerContextTransitioning?) -> TimeInterval {
    return 0
}
```

The `0` value above is just a placeholder value for the duration; you'll replace this later
with a real value as you work through the project.

Now add the following method stub to the class:

```
func animateTransition(using transitionContext:
  UIViewControllerContextTransitioning) {

}
```

The above stub will hold your animation code; adding it should have cleared the
remaining errors in Xcode.

Now that you have the basic animator class, you can move on to implementing the
delegate methods on the view controller side.

Open **ViewController.swift** and add the following extension to the end of the file:

```
extension ViewController: UIViewControllerTransitioningDelegate
{

}
```

This code indicates the view controller conforms to the transitioning delegate protocol.
You'll add some methods here in a moment.

Find `didTapImageView(_:)` in the main body of the class. Near the bottom of that
method you'll see the code that presents the details view controller. `herbDetails` is the
instance of the new view controller; you'll need to set its transitioning delegate to the
main controller.

Add the following code right before the last line of the method that calls present(...):

```
// ...
present(herbDetails, animated: true, completion: nil)
herbDetails.transitioningDelegate = self // Add this line
```

Now UIKit will ask ViewController for an animator object every time you present the details view controller on the screen. However, you still haven't implemented any of the UIViewControllerTransitioningDelegate methods, so UIKit will still use the default transition.

The next step is to actually create your animator object and return it to UIKit when requested. Add the following new property to ViewController:

```
let transition = PopAnimator()
```

This is the instance of PopAnimator that will drive your animated view controller transitions. You only need one instance of PopAnimator since you can continue to use the same object each time you present a view controller, as the transitions are the same every time.

Now add the first delegate method to the extension in ViewController:

```
func animationController(forPresented presented:
UIViewController, presenting: UIViewController, source:
UIViewController) -> UIViewControllerAnimatedTransitioning? {
  return transition
}
```

This method takes a few parameters that let you make an informed decision whether or not you want to return a custom animation. In this chapter you'll always return your single instance of PopAnimator since you have only one presentation transition.

You've already added the delegate method for presenting view controllers, but how will you deal with dismissing one?

Add the following delegate method to handle this:

```
func animationController(forDismissed dismissed:
UIViewController) -> UIViewControllerAnimatedTransitioning? {
  return nil
}
```

The above method does essentially the same thing as the previous one: you check which view controller was dismissed and decide whether to return nil and use the default animation, or return a custom transition animator and use that instead. At the moment you return nil, as you aren't going to implement the dismissal animation until later.

You finally have a custom animator to take care of your custom transitions. But does it work?

Build and run your project and tap one of the herb images:

Nothing happens. Why? You have a custom animator to drive the transition, but... oh, wait, you haven't added any code to the animator class! :] You'll take care of that in the next section.

Creating your transition animator

Open **PopAnimator.swift**; this is where you'll add the code to transition between the two view controllers.

First, add the following properties to this class:

```
let duration = 1.0
var presenting = true
var originFrame = CGRect.zero
```

You'll use duration in several places, such as when you tell UIKit how long the transition will take and when you create the constituent animations.

You also define presenting to tell the animator class whether you are presenting or dismissing a view controller. You want to keep track of this because typically, you'll run the animation forward to present and in reverse to dismiss.

Finally, you will use originFrame to store the original frame rect of the image the user taps — you will need that to animate from the original frame to a full screen image and vice versa. Keep an eye out for originFrame later on when you fetch the currently selected image and pass its frame to the animator instance.

Now you can move on to the UIViewControllerAnimatedTransitioning methods.

Replace the code inside transitionDuration() with the following:

```
return duration
```

Reusing the duration property lets you easily experiment with the transition animation. You can simply modify the value of the property to make the transition run faster or slower.

Setting your transition's context

It's time to add some magic to animateTransition. This method has one parameter of type UIViewControllerContextTransitioning, which gives you access to the parameters and view controllers of the transition.

Before you start working on the code itself, it's important to understand what the animation context actually *is*.

When the transition between the two view controllers begins, the existing view is added to a transition container view and the new view controller's view is created but not yet visible, as illustrated below:

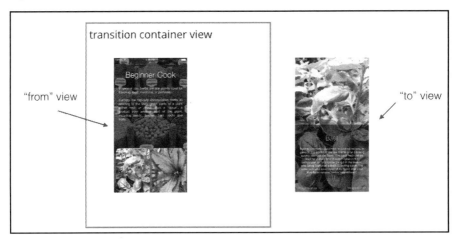

Therefore your task is to add the new view to the transition container within animateTransition(), "animate in" its appearance, and "animate out" the old view if required.

By default, the old view is removed from the transition container when the transition animation is done.

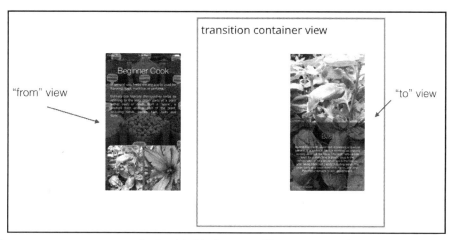

Before you get too many cooks in this kitchen, you'll create a simple transition animation to see how it works before implementing a much cooler, albeit more complicated, transition.

Adding a fade transition

You'll start with a simple fade transition to get a feel for custom transitions. Add the following code to animateTransition():

```
let containerView = transitionContext.containerView

let toView = transitionContext.view(forKey: .to)!
```

First, you get the container view where your animations will take place, and then you fetch the new view and store it in toView.

The transition context object has two very handy methods that give you access to the transition players:

- view(forKey:): This lets you access the views of the "old" and "new" view controllers via the arguments UITransitionContextViewKey.from or UITransitionContextViewKey.to respectively.

- viewController(forKey:): This lets you access the "old and "new" view controllers via the argumentsUITransitionContextViewControllerKey.from or UITransitionContextViewControllerKey.to respectively.

At this point, you have both the container view and the view to be presented. Next you need to add the view to be presented as a child to the container view and animate it in some way.

Add the following to `animateTransition()`:

```
containerView.addSubview(toView)
toView.alpha = 0.0
UIView.animate(withDuration: duration,
  animations: {
    toView.alpha = 1.0
  },
  completion: { _ in
    transitionContext.completeTransition(true)
  }
)
```

Note that you call `completeTransition()` on the transition context in the animation completion block; this tells UIKit that your transition animations are done and that UIKit is free to wrap up the view controller transition.

Build and run your project; tap one of the herbs in the list and you'll see the herb overview fade in over the main view controller:

The transition is acceptable and you've seen what to do in `animateTransition` — but you're going to add something even better!

Adding a pop transition

You're going to structure the code for the new transition slightly differently, so replace all the code in `animateTransition()` with the following:

```
let containerView = transitionContext.containerView
let toView = transitionContext.view(forKey: .to)!
let herbView = presenting ? toView :
  transitionContext.view(forKey: .from)!
```

`containerView` is where your animations will live, while `toView` is the new view to present. If you're presenting, `herbView` is just the `toView`; otherwise it will be fetched from the context. For both presenting and dismissing, `herbView` will always be the view that you animate. When you present the details controller view, it will grow to take up the entire screen. When dismissed, it will shrink to the image's original frame.

Add the following to `animateTransition()`:

```
let initialFrame = presenting ? originFrame : herbView.frame
let finalFrame = presenting ? herbView.frame : originFrame

let xScaleFactor = presenting ?

  initialFrame.width / finalFrame.width :
  finalFrame.width / initialFrame.width

let yScaleFactor = presenting ?

  initialFrame.height / finalFrame.height :
  finalFrame.height / initialFrame.height
```

In the code above, you detect the initial and final animation frames and then calculate the scale factor you need to apply on each axis as you animate between each view.

Now you need to carefully position the new view so it appears exactly above the tapped image; this will make it look like the tapped image expands to fill the screen.

Add the following to `animateTransition()`:

```
let scaleTransform = CGAffineTransform(scaleX: xScaleFactor,
                                       y: yScaleFactor)

if presenting {
  herbView.transform = scaleTransform
  herbView.center = CGPoint(
    x: initialFrame.midX,
    y: initialFrame.midY)
  herbView.clipsToBounds = true
}
```

When presenting the new view, you set its scale and position so it exactly matches the size and location of the initial frame.

Now add the final bits of code to `animateTransition()`:

```
containerView.addSubview(toView)
containerView.bringSubview(toFront: herbView)

UIView.animate(withDuration: duration, delay:0.0,
  usingSpringWithDamping: 0.4, initialSpringVelocity: 0.0,
  animations: {
    herbView.transform = self.presenting ?
      CGAffineTransform.identity : scaleTransform
    herbView.center = CGPoint(x: finalFrame.midX, y:
finalFrame.midY)
  },
  completion:{_ in
    transitionContext.completeTransition(true)
  }
)
```

This will first add `toView` to the container. Next, you need to make sure the `herbView` is on top since that's the only view you're animating. Remember that when dismissing, `toView` is the original view so in the first line, you'll be adding it *on top* of everything else, and your animation will be hidden away unless you bring herbView to the front.

Then, you can kick off the animations. using a spring animation here will give it a bit of bounce.

Inside the `animations` expression, you change the transform and position of `herbView`. When presenting, you're going from the small size at the bottom to the full screen so the target transform is just the identity transform. When dismissing, you animate it to scale down to match the original image size.

At this point, you've set the stage by positioning the new view controller over the tapped image, you've animated between the initial and final frames, and finally, you've called `completeTransition()` to hand things back to UIKit. It's time to see your code in action!

Build and run your project; tap the first herb image to see your view controller transition in action.

Well, it's not perfect, but once you take care of a few rough edges your animation will be exactly what you wanted!

Currently your animation starts from the top-left corner; that's because the default value of `originFrame` has the origin at (0, 0) – and you never set it to any other value.

Open **ViewController.swift** and add the following code to the top of `animationController(forPresented:)`:

```
transition.originFrame =
selectedImage!.superview!.convert(selectedImage!.frame, to: nil)

transition.presenting = true
selectedImage!.isHidden = true
```

This sets the `originFrame` of the transition to the frame of `selectedImage`, which is the image view you last tapped. Then you set presenting to true and hide the tapped image during the animation.

Build and run your project again; tap different herbs in the list and see how your transition looks for each.

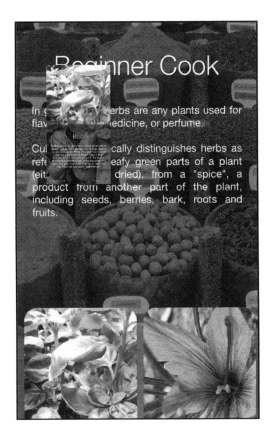

Adding a dismiss transition

All that's left to do is dismiss the details controller. You've actually done most of the work in the animator already — the transition animation code does the logic juggling to set the proper initial and final frames, so you're most of the way to playing the animation both forwards and backwards. Sweet! :]

Open **ViewController.swift** and replace the body of `animationController(forDismissed:)` with the following:

```
transition.presenting = false
return transition
```

This tells your animator object that you're dismissing a view controller so the animation code will run in the correct direction.

Build and run the project to see the result. Tap on an herb and then tap anywhere on screen to dismiss it.

The transition animation looks great, but notice the herb you picked has disappeared from the scroll view! You'll need to make sure the tapped image re-appears when you dismiss the details screen.

Open **PopAnimator.swift** and add a new closure property to the class:

```
var dismissCompletion: (()->Void)?
```

This will let you pass in some code to run when the dismiss transition completes.

Next, find `animateTransition()` and add the following code to the completion handler in the call to `animateWithDuration()`, right before the call to `completeTransition()`:

```
if !self.presenting {
  self.dismissCompletion?()
}
```

This code executes `dismissCompletion` once the dismiss animation has finished — which is the perfect spot to show the original image.

Open **ViewController.swift** and add the following code to `viewDidLoad()`:

```
transition.dismissCompletion = {
  self.selectedImage!.isHidden = false
}
```

This code displays the original image to replace the herb details view controller once the transition animation completes.

Build and run your app to enjoy the transition animations both ways, now that the herbs aren't getting lost along the way!

The transition animation still looks a bit rough around the edges but you'll finish it on your own in this chapter's challenges.

Before you get to the challenges though, there's one more animation topic to deal with: view transitions for managing changes to device orientation.

Device orientation transition

> **Note:** This section of the chapter is optional; if you're not interested in learning how to handle changes in device orientation in your view controllers, skip ahead directly to the challenges.

You can think of device orientation changes as a presentation transition from a view controller to itself, just at a different size.

`viewWillTransition(to size:coordinator:)`, introduced in iOS 8, gives you a simple and straightforward way to handle device orientation changes. You don't need to build separate portrait or landscape layouts; instead, you just need to react to the change to the view controller view's size.

Open **ViewController.swift** and add the following stub for
`viewWillTransition(to:with:)`:

```
override func viewWillTransition(to size: CGSize, with
coordinator: UIViewControllerTransitionCoordinator) {
  super.viewWillTransition(to: size, with: coordinator)

}
```

The first parameter (`size`) tells you what size your view controller is transitioning to. The second parameter (`coordinator`) is the transition coordinator object, which gives you access to a number of the transition's properties.

All you need to do in this app is reduce the alpha of the app's background image to improve the readability of the text when the device is in landscape mode.

Add the following code to `viewWillTransitionToSize`:

```
coordinator.animate(
  alongsideTransition: {context in
    self.bgImage.alpha = (size.width>size.height) ? 0.25 : 0.55
  },
  completion: nil
)
```

`animate(alongsideTransition:)` lets you specify your own custom animations to execute in parallel with the rotation animation that UIKit performs by default when you change the orientation.

Your animation closure will receive a transitioning context, just like the one you used when presenting a view controller. In this case, you don't have "from" and "to" view controllers since they're the same, but instead you can fetch properties such as the transition duration.

Inside the animation closure you check if the width of the target size is bigger than the height; if so, you reduce the alpha value of the background image to `0.25`. This makes the background fade out when transitioning to landscape mode and fade in to `0.55` alpha when transitioning to portrait orientation.

Build and run your app; rotate the device (or press Cmd + left arrow if testing in the iPhone Simulator) to see your alpha animation in action.

You can clearly see the background dim when you rotate the screen to a landscape mode. This makes the longer lines of text easier to read.

However if you tap on a herb image you will notice that animation is somewhat messy.

This happens because the screen has a landscape orientation, but the images still have portrait dimensions. Therefore the transition between the original image and the image stretched to fill up the screen is not fluid.

Not to fear — you can use your new friend `viewWillTransition(to:with:)` to fix this problem too.

There is an instance method on `ViewController` called `positionListItems()` that sizes and positions the herb images. This method is called from `viewDidLoad()` when your app first starts.

Add a call to this method inside the `animate(alongsideTransition:)` animation block you added last, just after you set the `alpha`:

```
self.positionListItems()
```

This will animate the size and position of the herb images while the device rotates. As soon as the screen finishes re-orientating the herb images will also have resized:

And since those images will now have a landscape layout also your transition animation will work just fine. Give it a try!

That's it for this chapter; take a look at the challenges below where you'll polish some of the remaining rough edges of your transition animations.

Challenges

There are two tiny imperfections in your presentation animation: you can see the detail view text up to the very last moment when it just disappears; in addition, the initial herb images have rounded corners, which makes the animation look jumpy at the end.

Challenge 1: Smooth the transition animation

Your first task is to fade the contents of the herb details view in or out as appropriate while transitioning. This corrects that awkward moment when the text of the detail view just disappears as it's dismissed.

Take a look at the storyboard file; you'll see the details controller already has all of its text views added to a main view connected to the `containerView` outlet.

All you need to do is fade `containerView` in or out while the transition animation takes place.

There are three steps in the solution to this challenge:

- Get a reference to the `HerbDetailsViewController` using the transition context's `viewController(forKey:)` method. Remember that the key will be different depending on whether you are presenting or dismissing and that you'll need to cast the result as `HerbViewController`. The two keys to choose from are `UITransitionContextViewControllerKey.to` and `UITransitionContextViewControllerKey.from`.

- Before you start the animation (the one animation already in `animateTranstion`), set the `alpha` of `containerView` to zero; it's an outlet property of `HerbDetailsViewController`. You only need to do this when you're presenting the view controller, not when dismissing it since it will be visible already when dismissing.

- Set the alpha of `containerView` in your animation closure — where you animate `herbView` – to fully opaque (`1.0`) when you're presenting and fully transparent (`0.0`) when you're dismissing.

To check the result of your changes more closely, you can increase the transition duration to `10` seconds and observe the animation in detail (or use **Debug/Toggle Slow Animations in Frontmost App** from the iOS Simulator main menu).

Challenge 2: Animate the corner radius

Finally you'll animate the corner radius of the details view so that it matches the rounded corners of the herb images in the main view controller.

At the end of `animateTransition()` create and run a layer animation to change the corner radius of `herbView`'s layer. Animate `herbView.layer.cornerRadius` from `20.0/xScaleFactor` to `0.0` if presenting, and vice versa if dismissing. You need to take the scale factor into account because you're also transforming the view. Set the duration of the animation to `duration / 2` so that it has finished before the springing starts, otherwise it will look quite strange!

That wraps up presentation controller animations. Next up, navigation controller animations. You'll notice a lot of similarities between the two, so put the herbs aside and dive right in!

Chapter 18:
UINavigationController
Custom Transition Animations

UINavigationController is one of the few built-in app navigation solutions available in iOS. You've likely used navigation controllers in your own projects – and you've certainly used them as you've worked through this book.

Pushing a new view controller onto the navigation stack or popping one off gives you sleek animation with no work on your part. A new screen comes from the right and pushes away the old one with a slight lag:

The above screenshot shows how iOS pushes a new view controller onto the navigation stack in the Settings app: The new view slides in from the right to cover the old view and the new title fades in while the old title titles fades from view.

The navigation paradigm in iOS has become old hat to users, as the same animations have been used for many years. This frees you to embellish your navigation controller transitions without throwing the user off.

In much the same way you built custom presenting view controllers in the previous chapter, you can build custom transitions to push and pop new view controllers.

You'll be working with the Logo Reveal project. In this chapter, you'll add a custom transparent view that gives the user a glimpse of the content hidden behind:

If you worked through the previous chapter, you'll find that custom navigation controller transitions feel quite similar to presenting view controllers.

Introducing Logo Reveal

Open the starter project for this chapter and select **Main.storyboard**. You'll see the project has been created from the standard Master Detail app template. It features a navigation controller, master view controller, and a detail view controller like so:

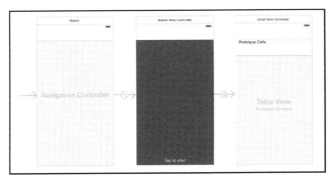

The navigation's already been hooked up for you so you can focus on customizing your navigation controllers.

Build and run your project; tap anywhere on the default screen (`MasterViewController`) to present the vacation packing list (`DetailViewController`):

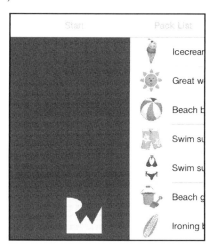

Custom navigation transitions

UIKit lets you customize navigation transitions via the delegate pattern in almost the same way you do for presenting view controllers.

You'll make your `MasterViewController` class adopt the `UINavigationControllerDelegate` protocol and set it to be the delegate to your navigation controller. Each time you push a view controller onto the navigation stack, the navigation controller will ask its delegate whether it should use the built-in transition or a custom one, as illustrated below:

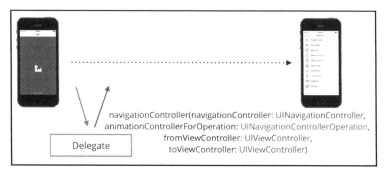

When you push or pop a view controller, the navigation controller asks its delegate to provide an animation controller for that operation.

If you return `nil` from that delegate method, the navigation controller will use the default transition. However, if you return an object, the navigation controller will use this instead as a custom transition animation controller. Yup — this sounds a *lot* like the previous chapter, doesn't it?

The animation controller should adopt the same `UIViewControllerAnimatedTransitioning` protocol you worked with in the previous chapter. Once you provide an animation controller object (or animator), the navigation controller will call the following methods on it:

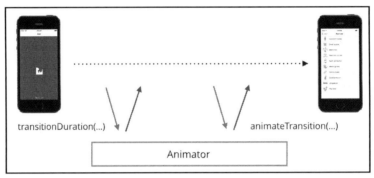

First, the navigation controller calls `transitionDuration()` to find out how long the transition will last; it then calls `animateTransition()`, which is where your custom transition animation code will live.

The navigation controller delegate

Before you can implement the delegate methods, you'll need to create the basic skeleton of the animator class.

From Xcode's main menu select **File\New\File…** and choose the template **iOS\Source\Cocoa Touch Class**.

Set the new class name to **RevealAnimator** and make it a subclass of **NSObject**.

Make the new class comply with the `UIViewControllerAnimatedTransitioning` protocol like so:

```
class RevealAnimator: NSObject,
  UIViewControllerAnimatedTransitioning {

}
```

Now you need to implement the two required
`UIViewControllerAnimatedTransitioning` methods to resolve Xcode's error
messages.

Add the following properties to the class:

```
let animationDuration = 2.0
var operation: UINavigationControllerOperation = .push
```

Your animation will last two seconds. That's a long time in the UI navigation world, but
it will let you see your animation in minute, excruciating detail. `operation` is a property
of type `UINavigationControllerOperation` that tells whether you're pushing or
popping a view controller.

Now add the following two `UIViewControllerAnimatedTransitioning` methods to
the class:

```
func transitionDuration(using transitionContext:
UIViewControllerContextTransitioning?) -> TimeInterval {
  return animationDuration
}

func animateTransition(using transitionContext:
UIViewControllerContextTransitioning) {

}
```

`transitionDuration()` simply returns the animation duration in seconds, while
`animateTransition()` is the future home for your custom animations. You'll populate
`animateTransition()` once you finish setting up your navigation controller delegate.

All your Xcode errors should have resolved by this point. Open
MasterViewController.swift, which will serve as your navigation controller delegate.

Add the code below to the bottom of the file, outside of the class definition:

```
extension MasterViewController: UINavigationControllerDelegate {

}
```

This adopts the `UIViewNavigationControllerDelegate` protocol in a new extension;
this view controller can now serve as the navigation controller delegate.

You'll need to set the navigation controller's delegate early in the view controller lifecycle,
before you invoke any segues or push something onto the stack.

Add the following code to `viewDidLoad()`:

```
navigationController?.delegate = self
```

Your next task is to create an instance of `RevealAnimator` and pass it to the navigation controller when asked for an animation controller.

Add the following property to `MasterViewController`:

```
let transition = RevealAnimator()
```

This is the animator you'll use for pushing and popping view controllers.

Now that you have your animator, add the following method to the class extension:

```
func navigationController(_
  navigationController: UINavigationController,
  animationControllerFor
  operation: UINavigationControllerOperation,
  from fromVC: UIViewController,
  to toVC: UIViewController) ->
  UIViewControllerAnimatedTransitioning? {
  transition.operation = operation
  return transition
}
```

That's one monster of a method name, but if you cut through the noise you'll see that it boils down to the following parameters:

- `navigationController`: This helps to distinguish between navigation controllers in the event your object is a delegate of more than one navigation controller; this isn't likely, but you still need to protect against the possibility.

- `operation`: This is a `UINavigationControllerOperation` value, either `.push` or `.pop`.

- `fromVC`: This is the view controller currently visible on the screen; it's usually the last view controller in the navigation stack.

- `toVC`: This is the view controller you'll transition to.

If you support different transitions for different view controllers, this is where you'll choose what kind of animator object to return. To keep things simple in this project, you'll always return your `RevealAnimator` object after you set the animator's operation property to indicate either a push or pop transition.

Build and run your project; tap the first view controller and you'll see the navigation bar animate over two seconds.

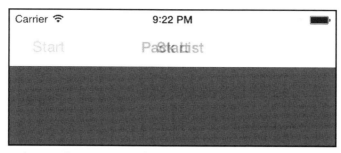

Note that the update to the navigation bar lasts for the duration you specified in
RevealAnimator – but at this point nothing else will happen. Your animator takes
control of the transition, but since you didn't write any code in animateTransition(),
no animation of the content takes place.

However, at least this indicates that the navigation controller is calling through to your
custom transition properly. Now it's time to get animating!

Adding a custom reveal animation

The plan for your custom transition animation is relatively simple. You'll simply animate
a mask on DetailViewController to make it look like the transparent part of the RW
logo reveals the contents of the underlying view controller.

You'll have to juggle layers and some animation tasks, but it's nothing you haven't done
so far in the book. Creating the transition animation will be an easy feat for an
animation pro like you! :]

Open **RevealAnimator.swift** and add the following property:

```
weak var storedContext: UIViewControllerContextTransitioning?
```

Since you're going to create some layer animations for your transition, you'll need to
store the animation context somewhere until the animation ends and the delegate
method animationDidStop(_:finished:) executes. At that point, you'll call
completeTransition() from within animationDidStop() to wrap up the transition.

Add the following code to animateTransition() to store the transition context for
later use:

```
storedContext = transitionContext
```

Note: If you skipped ahead, you can learn more detail on how you fetch transition view controllers from the context and animation container views in Chapter 17, "Custom Presentation Controller & Device Orientation Animations".

Now add the following initial transition code to `animateTransition()`:

```
let fromVC = transitionContext.viewController(forKey:
  .from) as! MasterViewController
let toVC = transitionContext.viewController(forKey:
  .to) as! DetailViewController

transitionContext.containerView.addSubview(toVC.view)
toVC.view.frame = transitionContext.finalFrame(for: toVC)
```

Since you'll work on the push transition initially, you can make an assumption about the identity of the "from" and "to" view controllers of the transition.

First, you fetch the "from" view controller (`fromVC`) and cast it to a `MasterViewController`; you then fetch `toVC` as a `DetailViewController`.

Finally, you simply add `toVC.view` to the transition container view and set its `frame` to the "final" frame within the `transitionContext`. This places the vacation packing list in its final location over the main screen.

Now you're going to create the reveal animation. The secret to a reveal animation is to have an object — in your case, the RW logo — grow to cover the entire area of the screen.

This sounds like a job for a scale transformation! Add the following to `animateTransition()`:

```
let animation = CABasicAnimation(keyPath: "transform")
animation.fromValue =
  NSValue(caTransform3D: CATransform3DIdentity)
animation.toValue =
  NSValue(caTransform3D:
  CATransform3DConcat(
    CATransform3DMakeTranslation(0.0, -10.0, 0.0),
    CATransform3DMakeScale(150.0, 150.0, 1.0)
  )
)
```

This animation grows the logo 150 times in size and moves it up a little at the same time. Why? The logo is uneven in shape and you want the view controller behind to show through the "hole" of the RW shape. Moving it up a little bit means the bottom of the zoomed image will cover the screen much faster.

The image below shows how your zoom animation will work:

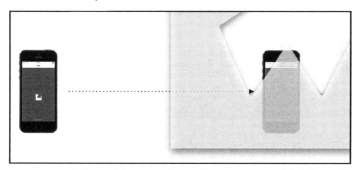

If you used a symmetrical shape like a circle or ellipse, you wouldn't have this problem, but your animation wouldn't be nearly as cool. :]

Now add the following lines to `animateTransition()` to refine the animation a bit:

```
animation.duration = animationDuration
animation.delegate = self
animation.fillMode = kCAFillModeForwards
animation.isRemovedOnCompletion = false
animation.timingFunction = CAMediaTimingFunction(name:
  kCAMediaTimingFunctionEaseIn)
```

First, you set the duration of the animation to match the transition duration. You then set the animator as the delegate and configure the animation model to leave the animation on screen; this avoids glitches when the transition wraps up since the RW logo will be hidden away anyway. Finally, you add easing to make the reveal effect accelerate over time.

Since `RevealAnimator` is not currently an animation delegate so jump to the top of the file and add the `CAAnimationDelegate` protocol to the class definition like so:

```
class RevealAnimator: NSObject,
UIViewControllerAnimatedTransitioning, CAAnimationDelegate {
  ...
}
```

This should clear the error you currently had in Xcode.

Your animation is complete — but to which layer should it be applied?

Add the following code to the end of `animateTransition(using:)`:

```
let maskLayer: CAShapeLayer = RWLogoLayer.logoLayer()
maskLayer.position = fromVC.logo.position
toVC.view.layer.mask = maskLayer
maskLayer.add(animation, forKey: nil)
```

This creates a `CAShapeLayer` to be applied to the `DestinationViewController`. The `maskLayer` is positioned in the same location as the "RW" logo on the `MasterViewController`. Then you simply set `maskLayer` as the mask of the view controller's view.

You then add the animation to the mask layer — which means you can test out the current state of your transition.

Build and run your project to see how things look so far:

Not bad, not bad; your reveal is running, but the animation is somewhat clunky and you can't go back to the main screen once you push the pack list on top. Time to fix those issues!

Taking care of the rough edges

You likely noticed you can still see the original logo behind the zooming reveal logo. The easiest way to handle this is to run the reveal animation on the original logo as well. You already have the animation, so it's no matter to reuse it. This will make the original logo grow with the mask, matching its shape exactly so it won't be in the way.

Add the following to `animateTransition()`:

```
fromVC.logo.add(animation, forKey: nil)
```

Build and run your project again to verify that the original logo is no longer hanging around:

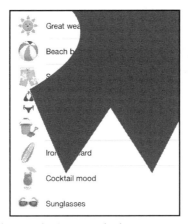

Now, a slightly harder problem: What's up with the navigation not working any more after the first push transition?

If you take a look at what you've done so far, you'll see that you never really wrap up the transition. You planned to call `completeTransition()` when the animation ended — but never got around to implementing that code.

`RevealAnimator` is set as the delegate of your reveal animation. Therefore, you need to override `animationDidStop(_:finished:)` and complete the transition within that method.

Add the following code to `RevealAnimator`:

```
func animationDidStop(_ anim: CAAnimation, finished flag: Bool)
{
  if let context = storedContext {
    context.completeTransition(!context.transitionWasCancelled)
    //reset logo
  }
  storedContext = nil
}
```

Here you check whether you have a stored transition context; if so, you call `completeTransition()` on it. This passes the ball back to the navigation controller to wrap up with the transition on UIKit's side.

At the end of the method, you simply set the reference to the transition context to `nil`.

Since the reveal animation won't be removed automagically upon completion, you'll need to handle things yourself.

Replace the `//reset logo` comment, located in `animationDidStop()`, with the following:

```
let fromVC = context.viewController(forKey: .from)
  as! MasterViewController

fromVC.logo.removeAllAnimations()
```

Since the only time you need to mask the contents of the view controller is during push transitions, you can safely remove the mask once the view controller finishes transitioning.

Add the following code right after `removeAllAnimations` in `animationDidStop()`:

```
let toVC = context.viewController(forKey: .to)
  as! DetailViewController
toVC.view.layer.mask = nil
```

This will remove the mask after the view has appeared and the transition is complete.

That should do it. Build and run your project; push the packing list view controller onto the screen, then tap **Start** to return to the original view. The proof that you're calling your custom transition is shown by the following spectacular crash:

```
func animateTransition(transitionContext: UIViewControllerContextTransitioning) {
    storedContext = transitionContext

    let fromVC = transitionContext.viewControllerForKey(UITransitionContextFromViewControllerKey) as MasterViewController
                                                            Thread 1: EXC_BREAKPOINT (code=EXC_I386_BPT, s
    let toVC = transitionContext.viewControllerForKey(UITransitionContextToViewControllerKey) as DetailViewController

    transitionContext.containerView().addSubview(toVC.view)
```

You're trying to cast the "from" view controller to a `MasterViewController` instance – which is true only for the push transition, but not for the pop transition. Whoops.

Open **RevealAnimator.swift** and find `animateTransition()`. You'll need to wrap most of the code here in a conditional. Add the following line just **after** the first line where you set `storedContext`:

```
if operation == .push {
```

Then, scroll all the way to the end of the method and add a closing brace for the `if` at the very end of the method.

The condition checks whether you're dealing with a push transition before you try to cast it. This should take care of that crashing piece of code.

Build and run to try it out again. Your push transition is working, but your pop transition won't do anything yet since you don't have any code in `animateTransition()` to handle it.

This is where you get to flex your ninja coding muscles; you'll create the pop transition on your own in the Challenges section below – and add a bit of elegance to the reveal animation along the way.

Challenges

Challenge 1: Fade in the new view controller

Right now the transition looks like a sharp cutout; the contents of the new view controller are visible instantly and make the whole animation look a bit clunky.

Your challenge is to fade in the new view controller as the reveal animation runs.

To do this, create a fade in `CABasicAnimation` and add it to the layer of `toVC.view`. Use the same transition duration for this new animation and set fromValue and `toValue` to animate from fully transparent to fully opaque.

Call your new animation just after the point where you add the reveal animation to both the logo and the mask layers.

When you are finished, your transition should look like the following:

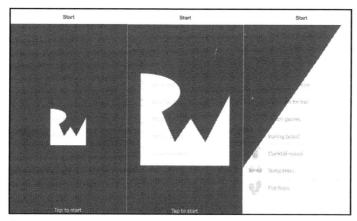

It appears as if your cutout becomes progressively more transparent as it grows; this gives the transition a mysterious effect.

Challenge 2: Add pop transition

To create a pop transition, you'll simply add a complementary else branch to the if statement inside `animateTransition()` of `RevealAnimator`. Inside the else branch you can add any animations you want, but don't forget to call `completeTransition()` when you're finished.

Here's how to create a simple shrink transition:

- Add an else branch to the if inside `animateTransition()`.

- Fetch the "from" and "to" views using the `viewForKey` method on the context. Because you're not doing anything with the properties of the view controller this time, you can just fetch the views alone.

- Work with the transition `containerView` and insert the toView **below** fromView. Tip: use `insertSubview(_:belowSubview:_)`.

- Use an animation to scale `fromView` to `0.01`. Don't use `0.0` for scaling — this will confuse UIKit. For this animation you can use an ordinary view animation – there's no need to create a layer animation.

- When the animation finishes, call `completeTransition()` on the transition context just as you did before.

This will result in the following tasteful shrinking transition:

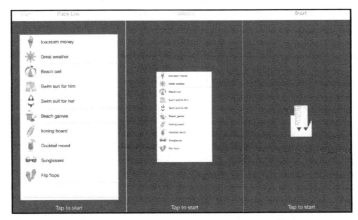

As you might have guessed, you can create custom transitions for `UITabBarController` too. You won't cover them here, but they work in a similar way to navigation controller transitions so you can easily figure them out based on what you've learned so far.

The next chapter takes transitions to the next level, and shows you how to let your user *interact* with the transitions themselves!

Chapter 19: Interactive UINavigationController Transitions

The reveal transition you created in the previous chapter looks pretty neat, but custom animations are only half the story. You've been sheltered from the truth, dear friend, but no more; as your reward for making your way to the end of this book, you're about to become privy to the secrets of the iOS ancients.

Not only can you create a custom animation for your transition — you can also make it *interactive* and respond to the actions of the user. Typically, you'd drive this action through a pan gesture, which is the approach you're going to take in this chapter.

When you're done, your users will be able to scrub back and forth through the reveal transition by sliding their finger across the screen. How cool would that be?

Yeah, I thought you'd be interested! :] Read on to see how it's done!

Creating an interactive transition

When your navigation controller asks its delegate for an animation controller, two things can happen. You can return `nil`, in which case the navigation controller runs the standard transition animation. You know that much already.

However — if you *do* return an animation controller, then the navigation controller asks its delegate for an interaction controller like so:

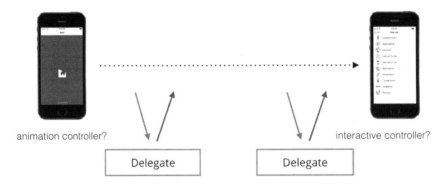

The interaction controller moves the transition along based on the user's actions, instead of simply animating the changes from start to finish. The interaction controller does not necessarily need to be a separate class from the animation controller; in fact, performing some tasks is a little easier when both controllers are in the same class. You just need to make sure that said class conforms to both `UIViewControllerAnimatedTransitioning` and `UIViewControllerInteractiveTransitioning`.

`UIViewControllerInteractiveTransitioning` has only one required method — `startInteractiveTransition(_:)` — that takes a transitioning context as its parameter. The interaction controller then regularly calls `updateInteractiveTransition(_:)` to move the transition along. To begin, you'll need to change how you handle your user input.

Handling the pan gesture

First of all, the tap gesture recognizer in `MasterViewController` just won't cut it anymore. A tap happens momentarily and then it's gone; you can't track its progress and use it to drive a transition. On the other hand, a pan gesture has clear states for the starting, progressing, and ending phases of the transition.

Open the starter project for this chapter; alternatively, you can use your completed project (including the challenges) from the previous chapter.

Open **Main.storyboard**; go to the master view controller and change the text of the label towards the bottom of the screen to "**Slide to start**" like so:

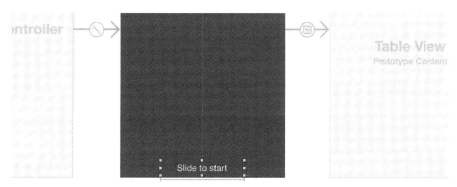

This will reflect the action you expect from the user.

Next, open **MasterViewController.swift** and **remove** the following code from viewDidAppear(_:):

```
let tap = UITapGestureRecognizer(target: self, action:
  #selector(didTap))
view.addGestureRecognizer(tap)
```

In its place, insert the following pan recognizer code:

```
let pan = UIPanGestureRecognizer(target: self,
    action: #selector(didPan))
view.addGestureRecognizer(pan)
```

As the user pans across the screen, the recognizer invokes didPan() on your MasterViewController class.

To get rid of the error, showing right now in Xcode, add an empty didPan method to MasterViewController:

```
func didPan(recognizer: UIPanGestureRecognizer) {
}
```

You'll need to modify your RevealAnimator class quite a bit to handle the new, interactive transition; you'll take care of this in the next section.

Using interactive animator classes

To manage your transition, you'll use one of Apple's built-in interactive animator classes: UIPercentDrivenInteractiveTransition. This class conforms to UIViewControllerInteractiveTransitioning and lets you get and set your transition's progress as a value representing the percentage complete.

This makes your life a little easier, as you can use this class to adjust the percentComplete property accordingly and call **update()** to set the current visible progress of the transition. This will skip through the transition animation to the point that corresponds to the calculated transition progress. You'll learn more about how UIPercentDrivenInteractiveTransition works as you work through the rest of this chapter.

Open **RevealAnimator.swift** and update the class definition at the top of the file as follows:

```
class RevealAnimator: UIPercentDrivenInteractiveTransition,
    UIViewControllerAnimatedTransitioning, CAAnimationDelegate {
```

Note that UIPercentDrivenInteractiveTransition is a class and not a protocol like the rest so it needs to be in first position. Now RevealAnimator inherits from UIPercentDrivenInteractiveTransition.

Next, add the following property to tell the animator whether or not it should drive the transition in an interactive fashion:

```
var interactive = false
```

Now add the following method to RevealAnimator:

```
func handlePan(recognizer: UIPanGestureRecognizer) {

}
```

When the user pans across the screen, you'll pass the recognizer to handlePan() in RevealAnimator, at which point you'll update the current progress of the transition. You'll populate handlePan() in just a bit, but first you'll need to set up the gesture handling.

Open **MasterViewController.swift** and add the following delegate method to provide an interaction controller to the MasterViewController extension in that file:

```
func navigationController(_
    navigationController: UINavigationController,
```

```
  interactionControllerFor animationController:
  UIViewControllerAnimatedTransitioning) ->
  UIViewControllerInteractiveTransitioning? {
  if !transition.interactive {
    return nil
  }
  return transition
}
```

You only return an interaction controller when you want the transition to be interactive. For example, in your Logo Reveal project the reveal transition is interactive, but the custom pop transition will remain as-is.

Now you need to hook up your pan gesture recognizer to the interaction controller. Find `didPan(recognizer:)` in `MasterViewController` and replace with:

```
func didPan(recognizer: UIPanGestureRecognizer) {
  switch recognizer.state {
  case .began:
    transition.interactive = true
    performSegue(withIdentifier: "details", sender: nil)
  default:
    transition.handlePan(recognizer: recognizer)
  }
}
```

As the pan gesture starts, you ensure `interactive` is set to `true` and then begin the segue to the next view controller. Performing the segue kicks off the transition as detailed in the previous chapter; the delegate methods you've added return transition for the animation controller *and* for the interaction controller.

In all cases, if the gesture has already started you simply hand things over to the interaction controller as illustrated below:

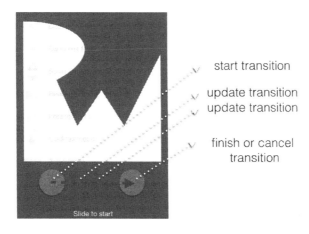

Calculating your animation's progress

The most important bit of your pan gesture handler is to figure out how far along the transition should be.

Open **RevealAnimator.swift** and add the following code to handlePan():

```
let translation = recognizer.translation(in:
  recognizer.view!.superview!)
var progress: CGFloat = abs(translation.x / 200.0)
progress = min(max(progress, 0.01), 0.99)
```

First, you get the translation from the pan gesture recognizer; the translation lets you know how many points the user moved their finger/stylus/appendage/whatever on both the X and Y axes. Logically, the further the user pans from the initial location, the greater the progress of the transition.

To calculate the current progress, you take the translation on the X axis and divide it by 200 points. For example, if the user's finger is 100 points away from the initial pan location, the transition will be 50% complete. 200 points is a bit of an arbitrary number, but it's a good starting point for the total distance the user needs to pan to complete the transition. You shouldn't care whether the user pans to the right or to the left - that's why you use abs() to get the absolute value of the pan distance.

Finally, you cap the progress variable between 0.01 and 0.99; my testing shows that interaction controllers behave better if you don't let the user finish or revert the transition from the pan gesture alone.

Now that you know the progress of the transition animation, you can update the transition animation as well.

Add the following code to handlePan():

```
switch recognizer.state {
  case .changed:
    update(progress)
  default:
    break
}
```

update() is a method from UIPercentDrivenInteractiveTransition which sets the current progress of the transition animation.

As the user pans across the screen, the gesture recognizer repeatedly calls didPan() in MasterViewController, which in turn forwards the recognizer to handlePan() in RevealAnimator.

Build and run your project; pan across the screen to see what your transition looks like:

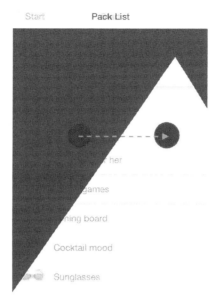

Since your transition isn't quite complete, the whole navigation breaks as soon as you lift your finger. However, you can see that the reveal animation followed your pan gesture – you're getting close to completing your interactive transition!

`updateInteractiveTransition()` smoothly handled your transition's progress and displayed the correct frame of the transition animation for you; your code didn't need to lift a finger. :] It's sometimes surprising to see how advanced some of Apple's UI features can be right out of the box!

All that's left is to handle the end state of your interactive transition.

Handling early termination

Here you face a totally new problem: the user might lift their finger before they've panned **200** points on the X axis. This leaves the transition in an unfinished state.

Luckily, `UIPercentDrivenInteractiveTransition` gives you a couple of methods for free that you can use to revert, or complete, the transition depending on the user's actions.

Add the following two cases inside the switch statement you added above, just before the default case:

```
case .cancelled, .ended:
  let transitionLayer = storedContext!.containerView.layer
  transitionLayer.beginTime = CACurrentMediaTime()
  if progress < 0.5 {
    cancel()
    transitionLayer.speed = -1.0
  } else {
    transitionLayer.speed = 1.0
    finish()
  }
```

The .cancelled and .ended cases are effectively the same thing as far as your project is concerned. Before doing anything else, you fetch the layer of the containerView for the transition and set its beginTime to the current Core Animation time.

If the user panned far enough before they released, you fully present the new view controller; if not, you simply roll back the animation progress. In both cases, you set the completion speed to make the animation run in the correct direction.

> **Note:** Setting the time and speed is a workaround for what seems like a UIKit bug; if you *don't* use layer animations in the transition, you don't have to set the layer's begin time and the completion speed.

If the user pans through less than **50%** of the required distance, you call cancel() — an inherited method — to animate the transition back to its initial state. If the user pans through more than **50%** of the distance, you call finish(), which plays the animation the rest of the way through. These two states are illustrated below:

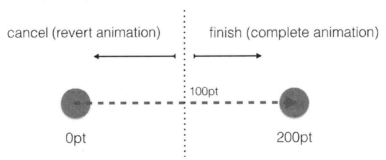

Build and run the app, and try panning part way and most of the way to see the difference.

Did you notice that when you panned through the reveal animation, you couldn't go *back* to the list? That's because you set interactive to true in `handlePan()`, and you never reset it to false! Therefore, when you pop the view controller, you return an interaction controller from the delegate method that's never updated — and your pop transition gets stuck at `0%` progress.

The correct spot to reset the interactive property is when the pan gesture ends.

Add the following code to the `.ended` case:

```
interactive = false
```

This should let you pop back to the initial screen.

Build and run again, and you should be able to move back and forth.

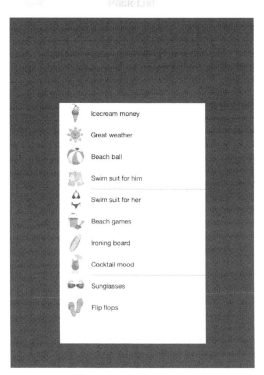

You've completed your Logo Reveal project. `RevealAnimator` is now performing two *different* transition animations, including one that's interactive! Great job!

This wraps up the section on view controller transitions. Congratulations on working through this section; these transition APIs are not easy to learn, but all the effort has been worth it.

Challenges

Challenge 1: Make the pop transition interactive

The final challenge is a bit more difficult than usual, but by now you're an animation ninja, and I know you can handle anything I throw at you!

Your task in this challenge is to make the pop transition interactive. That's not as easy as it sounds, as you'll need to change code in a number of places throughout the project.

The challenge directions below are just broad strokes, so you'll need to plan your approach before you start coding.

First, in `DetailViewController`; make a weak property to hold the animator and fetch the animator object from `MasterViewController`. You can access `MasterViewController` from the navigation controller stack.

Once you do that, add a pan gesture handler to `DetailViewController`. Your handler should be almost identical to the method in `MasterViewController` with one small difference: it should pop the current view controller rather than invoke a segue.

At this point the custom pop transition should be mostly functional. You are using view animations for your pop transition, but view animations don't need `beginTime` or `completionSpeed` to be adjusted. Ensure you don't modify these properties when the animator operation is `.pop`.

You'll end up with a cool interactive pop transition — and don't forget to make sure that tapping the **Back** button in the navigation bar still works! :]

Section V: Animations with UIViewPropertyAnimator

`UIViewPropertyAnimator` is a class introduced in iOS10, which helps developers create interactive, interruptible view animations.

Since you made it this far through the book (huge congrats btw), you already know how to make use of most that Core Animation has to offer. And since all APIs in UIKit just wrap that lower level functionality, there will not be many surprises for you when looking at `UIViewPropertyAnimator`.

This class, however, does make some certain types of view animations a little easier to create so it is definitely worth looking into.

Most notably when you run animations via an animator you have the possibility to adjust those animations on the fly - you can pause, stop, reverse, and alter the speed of animations that are already running.

As said, you could do everything mentioned above by using a combination of layer and view animations but `UIViewPropertyAnimator` wraps a number of APIs together conveniently in the same class, which is a bit easier to use.

Further, this new class completely replaces neither the `UIView.animate(withDuration...)` set of APIs nor the animations you create with using `CAAnimation` so chances are you will still need to often use those in conjunction with `UIViewPropertyAnimator` animations.

> **Note:** `UIViewPropertyAnimator` was introduced in iOS10 and as some new APIs are, they're not completely polished yet. Depending on how you use it, you might experience a variety of issues.

In this section of the book you are going to work on bug project featuring plenty of different view animations, which you are going to implement by using `UIViewPropertyAnimator`.

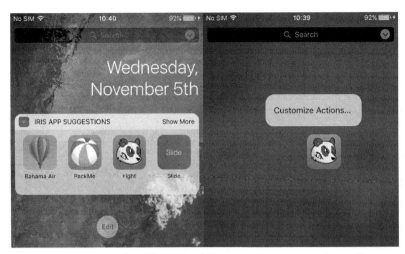

- **Chapter 20, Getting started with UIViewPropertyAnimator** – Learn how to create basic view animations and keyframe animations. You'll look into using custom timing that goes beyond the built-in easing curves.

- **Chapter 21, Intermediate animations with UIViewPropertyAnimator** – In this chapter you are going to learn about using animators with Auto Layout. Further you will learn how to reverse animations or make additive animations for smoother changes along the way.

- **Chapter 22, Interactive animations with UIViewPropertyAnimator** – Learn how to drive your animations interactively based on user's input. For extra fun you'll look into both basic and keyframe animations interactivity.

- **Chapter 23, UIViewPropertyAnimator View Controller Transitions** – Create custom View Controller transitions using a `UIViewPropertyAnimator` to drive the transition animations. You will create both static and interactive transitions.

After working through all these chapters you will definitely be at home with using `UIViewPropertyAnimator` for all kind of animations in your apps!

Chapter 20: Getting Started with UIViewPropertyAnimator

`UIViewPropertyAnimator` was introduced in iOS10 and addressed the need to be able to create easily interactive, interruptible, and/or reversible view animations.

Before iOS10, the only option to create view-based animations was the `UIView.animate(withDuration:...)` set of APIs, which did not provide any means for developers to pause or stop already running animations. Further, to reverse, speed up, or slow an animation, developers had to use layer-based `CAAnimation` animations.

`UIViewPropertyAnimator` makes creating all of the above a bit easier since it's a class that lets you keep hold of running animations, lets you adjust the currently running ones and provides you with detailed information about the current state of an animation.

`UIViewPropertyAnimator` is a big step away from the pre-iOS 10 "fire-and-forget" animations. That being said, `UIView.animate(withDuration:...)` APIs still do play a big role in creating iOS animations; these APIs are simple and easy to use, and often times you really just want to start a short fade-out or a simple move and you really don't need to interrupt or reverse those. In these cases using `UIView.animate(withDuration:...)` is just fine.

Further, `UIViewPropertyAnimator` does not implement everything that `UIView.animate(withDuration:...)` has to offer, so sometimes you will still need to fall back on the old APIs.

But enough about which API is better or newer... let's have a look what `UIViewPropertyAnimator` is all about.

Basic animations

Open and run the starter project for this chapter. You should see a screen similar to the lock screen in iOS. The initial view controller displays a search bar, a single widget, and an edit button at the bottom:

Some of the app's functionality that doesn't have to do with animations is already implemented for you. For example, if you tap on **Show More**, you will see the widget expand and show more items. If you tap on **Edit** you will see another view controller pop up for editing the widget list.

Of course, the app is just a simulation of the lock screen in iOS. It doesn't actually perform any actions, and is set up specially for you to play with some `UIViewPropertyAnimator` animations. Let's go!

First, you are going to create a very simple animation starting when the app initially opens up. Open **LockScreenViewController.swift** and add a new `viewWillAppear(_:)` method to that view controller:

```
override func viewWillAppear(_ animated: Bool) {
    tableView.transform = CGAffineTransform(scaleX: 0.67, y: 0.67)
    tableView.alpha = 0
}
```

The table view in `LockScreenViewController` displays the widgets on that screen, so in order to create a simple scale and fade view animation transition, you first scale the whole table view down and make it transparent.

If you run the project right now you will see the date and some empty space below:

Next, create an animator when the view controller's view appears on screen. Add the following to `LockScreenViewController`:

```
override func viewDidAppear(_ animated: Bool) {
    let scale = UIViewPropertyAnimator(duration: 0.33,
        curve: .easeIn)
}
```

Here, you use one of the convenience initializers of `UIViewPropertyAnimator`. You are going to try all of them, but you'll start with the simplest one: `UIViewPropertyAnimator(duration:, curve:)`.

This initializer makes an animator instance and sets the animation's total duration and timing curve. The latter parameter is of type `UIViewAnimationCurve`, and this is an enum with the following curve-based options:

- `easeInOut`

- `easeIn`

- easeOut

- linear

These match the timing options that you've used with the
UIView.animate(withDuration:...) APIs, and they produce similar results.

Now that you've created an animator object, let's have a look at what can you do with it.

Adding animations

Add the animation code to viewDidAppear(_:):

```
scale.addAnimations {
  self.tableView.alpha = 1.0
}
```

You use addAnimations to add blocks of code, which perform the desired animations
just like you do with UIView.animate(withDuration:...). The difference when
using an animator is that you can add multiple animation blocks. For example, you can
include logic to conditionally add more or fewer animations to the same animator.

Besides being able to conditionally build up complex animations, you can also add
animations with different delays. There is a version of addAnimations which takes the
following two parameters:

- animation, which is the block with animations to perform,

- and delayFactor, which is the delay before the animations start.

Notice that the latter parameter isn't called delay, but specifically: delayFactor. This is
because you don't provide an absolute value in seconds, but rather a factor (between 0.0
and 1.0) of the animator's **remaining** duration.

Add a second animation to the same animator with some delay:

```
scale.addAnimations({
  self.tableView.transform = CGAffineTransform.identity
}, delayFactor: 0.33)
```

To figure out the actual delay in seconds, take delayFactor and multiply it by the
remaining duration of the animator. Since you haven't yet started the animations, the
remaining duration is equal to the **total duration**.

So in the case above:

```
delayFactor(0.33) * remainingDuration(=duration 0.33) = delay of
0.11 seconds
```

Why isn't that second parameter just a simple value in seconds?

Well, imagine your animator is already running, and you decide to add some new animations to it mid-way. In this case the **remaining duration** will not be equal to the **total duration**, since some time has already passed since you starter the animations.

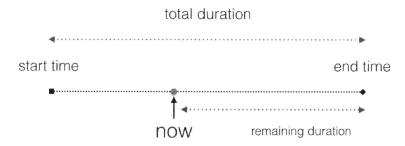

In this situation, `delayFactor` will let you schedule an animation with delay based on the remaining available time. Further, this ensures you cannot set a delay longer than the remaining running time.

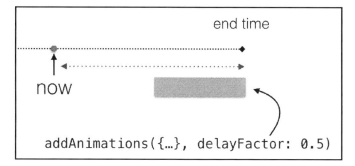

Adding completions

Now add a completion block, just like you're used to with `UIView.animate(withDuration:...)`:

```
scale.addCompletion {_ in
  print("ready")
}
```

In this simple example, you are only printing to the console, but you can do literally anything you wish; clean up some temporary views, reset the position of visual elements you moved around, and so on.

As with addAnimations(_:), you can call addCompletion(_:) several times to add more completion handlers. These will be executed one after another and in the order you added them to the animator.

Last but not least, you need to **start the animator**.

Before you call startAnimations(), nothing will happen on screen, so keep in mind while getting accustomed with UIViewPropertyAnimator that if you don't see your animations on screen, you probably have forgotten to start them.

Add at the end of viewWillAppear(_:):

```
scale.startAnimation()
```

Run the project now and enjoy a smooth transition animation when the app pops up on the screen:

Abstracting animations away

You've probably already noticed that just like layer animations, animations with UIViewPropertyAnimator add quite a bit of code.

Working with an object that isn't "fire-and-forget" makes it really easy to extract some of your animation code into a separate class. Since you are going to create plenty of animations for the project in this section of the book, you'll extract most of them in a separate file.

Create a new file called **AnimatorFactory.swift** and replace its default contents with:

```
import UIKit

class AnimatorFactory {
}
```

Then add a method, which includes the animation code you just wrote, but instead of running the animations by default, returns the animator as the result:

```
static func scaleUp(view: UIView) -> UIViewPropertyAnimator {
  let scale = UIViewPropertyAnimator(duration: 0.33,
    curve: .easeIn)
  scale.addAnimations {
    view.alpha = 1.0
  }
  scale.addAnimations({
    view.transform = CGAffineTransform.identity
  }, delayFactor: 0.33)
  scale.addCompletion {_ in
    print("ready")
  }
  return scale
}
```

That method takes a view as its parameter and creates all animations on that view. Finally it returns the ready-to-go animator.

Switch to **LockScreenViewController.swift** and replace `viewDidAppear(_:)` with:

```
override func viewDidAppear(_ animated: Bool) {
  AnimatorFactory.scaleUp(view: tableView)
    .startAnimation()
}
```

That's much nicer, shorter, and cleaner!

By the end of this section, you will really appreciate `AnimatorFactory` since it's going to remove a lot of code from your view controller.

> **Note:** In your own projects, you might want to prefer to use an enumeration or a struct to access your abstracted animators. In this book, you're going to use static class methods for brevity.

Running animators

You better run!
And never come to
these whereabouts again!

Joke aside, at this point you might be asking yourself *"What's the point of creating an animator object if its only purpose is to be started right away?"*

That is a good question!

Should you need a single block of animations that you run and don't need to alter anymore, go ahead and use `UIView.animate(withDuration:...)`. The tipping point in your decision on which API to use depends whether you want to simply run an animation — or run it and *eventually* interact with it later on.

What if you **do** want to use a `UIViewPropertyAnimator`, but you still have just one block of animations and completion, and want to run it right away? Isn't there a more streamlined way to create such animations?

Why, yes there is! I'm glad you asked. This is the very reason this section of the chapter is called *running animators*. There's a class method on `UIViewPropertyAnimator` that creates an animator and starts it right away for you.

Next you will fade in a blur layer (`blurView`) while the user is using the search bar, and fade it out when the user is done searching.

Open **LockScreenViewController.swift** and add a new method to the `LockScreenViewController` class:

```swift
func toggleBlur(_ blurred: Bool) {
  UIViewPropertyAnimator.runningPropertyAnimator(
    withDuration: 0.5, delay: 0.1, options: [.curveEaseOut],
    animations: {
      self.blurView.alpha = blurred ? 1 : 0
    },
    completion: nil
  )
}
```

In `toggleBlur(_:)` you use `UIViewPropertyAnimator.runningPropertyAnimator(withDuration:delay:options:animations:completion )` to create an animator that is already running.

You have certainly noticed that `UIViewPropertyAnimator.runningPropertyAnimator(withDuration:...)` takes exactly the same parameters as `UIView.animate(withDuration:...)` to make it easier for you to use this new API.

Even though it looks like this might be a "fire-and-forget" kind of API, please note that it actually *does* return an animator instance. So you can add more animations, more completion blocks, and generally interact with the animations that are currently running.

Now let's see what that fade animation looks like. `LockScreenViewController` is already set as the delegate of the search bar, so you simply need to implement the required methods to trigger the animation at the correct times.

Add a new `LockScreenViewController` extension:

```
extension LockScreenViewController: UISearchBarDelegate {

  func searchBarTextDidBeginEditing(_ searchBar: UISearchBar) {
    toggleBlur(true)
  }

  func searchBarTextDidEndEditing(_ searchBar: UISearchBar) {
    toggleBlur(false)
  }
}
```

When the users taps on the search field you fade in the blur, and fade it out when the user has finished using the search bar. To give the user more ways to cancel the search, add these two methods:

```
func searchBarResultsListButtonClicked(_ searchBar: UISearchBar)
{
  searchBar.resignFirstResponder()
}

func searchBar(_ searchBar: UISearchBar, textDidChange
searchText: String) {
  if searchText.isEmpty {
    searchBar.resignFirstResponder()
  }
}
```

This will allow the user to dismiss the search by tapping on the right hand side button or by deleting their search query. Run the app now and tap in the search bar text field.

You'll see the widgets disappear under a blur effect view. When you tap the button on the right side of the search bar, the blur view fades back out.

Basic keyframe animations

Earlier you learned how to add more animation blocks to the same animator and make them start with a given delay factor. This is handy, but it doesn't do quite the same thing as you're used to with using view keyframe animations.

The `UIView.animateKeyframes` API is very powerful as it allows you to group animations in any way, with any kind of delay and duration.

Prepare for some good news!

You can actually use `UIView.animate` and `UIView.animateKeyframes` from within your `UIViewPropertyAnimator` animation blocks.

So in the event you would like to create a complex keyframe animation but still realize the benefits of creating an animator, like being able to pause or reverse, you can!

In this section of the chapter, you are going to create a simple jiggle keyframe animation. You'll play that animation on any icon the user taps to give them a little visual tap feedback:

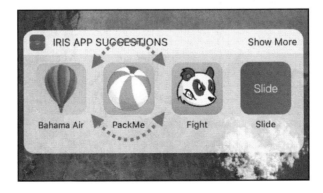

Switch to **AnimatorFactory.swift** and add a new method:

```
static func jiggle(view: UIView) -> UIViewPropertyAnimator {
  return UIViewPropertyAnimator.runningPropertyAnimator(
    withDuration: 0.33, delay: 0, animations: {

    },
    completion: {_ in

    }
  )
}
```

Your jiggle animator will run for **0.33** seconds, but still doesn't really do much. Add the following **inside** the `animations` block:

```
UIView.animateKeyframes(withDuration: 1, delay: 0,
  animations: {

    UIView.addKeyframe(withRelativeStartTime: 0.0,
      relativeDuration: 0.25) {
      view.transform = CGAffineTransform(rotationAngle: -.pi/8)
    }
    UIView.addKeyframe(withRelativeStartTime: 0.25,
      relativeDuration: 0.75) {
      view.transform = CGAffineTransform(rotationAngle: +.pi/8)
    }
    UIView.addKeyframe(withRelativeStartTime: 0.75,
      relativeDuration: 1.0) {
      view.transform = CGAffineTransform.identity
    }
  },
  completion: nil
)
```

This code defines a view keyframe animation much like the ones you've created while working through Chapter 5, "Keyframe Animations".

The first keyframe rotates the given view to the left, the second rotates it to the right, and finally the third one brings it back home — er, I mean resets its `transform`.

To make sure the icon remains in its initial position even if the animation was interrupted, add this in the completion block:

```
view.transform = .identity
```

There isn't an obvious way to interrupt the animation, but since you are using an animator, there's always the possibility to add the code to pause or stop that particular animator later on.

There's quite a difference between how you think about your animations now, as compared to the `UIView.animate(withDuration:...)` family of APIs. When using an animator, your animation can always end up completing successfully or being stopped mid-way, or even completing not at its end state, but at its starting state if it was reversed during execution.

Next, since the animation is finalized, you can use the `jiggle(view:)` method to get the keyframes animator and run it on some views.

Open **IconCell.swift** (the file is located in the Widget sub-folder). This is the custom collection cell class that displays each of the icons in the widget view:

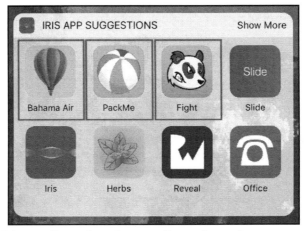

Whenever one of those cells is selected, you will run the jiggle animator on its image to give the user a bit of touch feedback.

Add a new convenience method on the cell to start an animator on its image:

```
func iconJiggle() {
  AnimatorFactory.jiggle(view: icon)
}
```

Now Xcode complains that your `AnimatorFactory.jiggle` method returns a result, but you don't use it in any way. Luckily that's an easy problem to fix.

Switch to **AnimatorFactory.swift** and add the following to the line before `static func jiggle(view: UIView) -> UIViewPropertyAnimator` a `@discardableResult` attribute, so that Xcode knows that you might choose to ignore the result of the method:

```
@discardableResult
static func jiggle(view: UIView) -> UIViewPropertyAnimator
```

Do not remove the return type altogether — you will use the result of that method later on.

To finally run the animation, open **WidgetView.swift** and find
`collectionView(collectionView:didSelectItemAt:)`. This is the collection view delegate method called when the user taps on a collection view cell. Append the following to it:

```
if let cell = collectionView.cellForItem(at: indexPath) as?
IconCell {
  cell.iconJiggle()
}
```

Run the app one more time and try tapping on some icons; you will see them shortly jump under your finger:

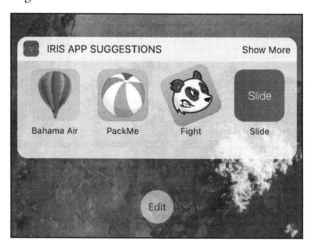

> **Note:** There currently isn't a way to make the animator animation repeat, if you happened to be wondering.

With this animation, you've concluded the basics tour. Hopefully you've learned some of the benefits of using `UIViewPropertyAnimator` over the older APIs.

What you covered, however, is but a small fraction of what `UIViewPropertyAnimator` can do. In the next chapters, you will look into more interesting ways to set your animations' timing, interactivity, and power view controller transitions.

Challenges

You already know some of the basics about working with `UIViewPropertyAnimator`, but there's much more to learn in the next three chapters. In this chapter's challenge section, take the time to reflect on what you've learned and experience your first encounter with property animator's state.

Challenge 1: Extract blur animation into factory

To practice abstracting animations one more time, extract the blur animation from `toggleBlur(_:)` into a static method on `AnimatorFactory`.

This time, the static factory method should take two parameters: the view to animate and whether to animate to a fully transparent or fully opaque state.

In the end, you should be able to easily toggle the visibility of `blurView` by using this one-liner:

```
func toggleBlur(_ blurred: Bool) {
  AnimatorFactory.fade(view: blurView, visible: blurred)
}
```

Do you appreciate how easy it is to abstract and re-use animations with `UIViewPropertyAnimator`? I know I certainly do!

Challenge 2: Prevent overlapping animations

In this challenge, you will learn how to check if an animator is currently executing its animations.

If you tap repeatedly on the same icon, you will see that it jumps back to its initial state on each tap and the animations look choppy.

Right now, you simply ignore the result of `AnimatorFactory.jiggle` — but what if you didn't? If you actually get hold of the animator object and use it to check if there's a currently active jiggle animation, you can prevent further taps on that same icon.

First, add an optional property called `animator` to the `IconCell` class.

Next, instead of discarding the result of `AnimatorFactory.jiggle`, store it in `animator`. Now each time the user taps the icon, you can check if there's an animation already running on the icon.

At the beginning of `iconJiggle()` check if `animator` is set, and if so, check if its `isRunning` property is `true`. `isRunning` tells you if the animator is currently running its animations — i.e., it has been already started but it hasn't completed yet.

If there's a running animator, all that is left to do is return out of `iconJiggle()` without creating a new animation. This will fix your problem and the users can tap as many times on the icon as they wish.

Up next – even more complex animations with `UIViewPropertyAnimator`!

Chapter 21: Intermediate Animations with UIViewPropertyAnimator

You've already tried some animations with `UIViewPropertyAnimator`, and have started improving the Widgets project user experience by adding delightful animations to the interface. You've also looked into creating basic and keyframe animations and saw that using the `UIViewPropertyAnimator` class isn't difficult at all!

More importantly you've tackled some issues that aren't as straightforward when using the `UIView.animate(withDuration:...)` set of APIs — for example, checking if an animation is currently running, conditionally adding animations and completions, and abstracting animations into standalone classes.

If you successfully completed the challenges from the previous chapter, just re-open the project and keep working on it. Otherwise, you can use the starter project provided for this chapter:

Let's see how you can give your animations this extra *something* by using custom timings!

Custom animation timing

Throughout this book, you've been using the four built-in curves: linear, ease in, ease out, and ease in out. By now there isn't much left to say about those that hasn't been said already, so through most of this chapter you are going to focus on custom curves. If by any chance, you skipped over the earlier chapters where built-in curves are explained, have a quick detour to Chapter 1, "Getting Started with View Animations" and search for the **Animation Easing** section.

Assuming you have a solid grasp of what the four built-in curves are, let's have a look at using one in an animation.

Built-in timing curves

Currently, when you activate the search bar you fade in a blur view on top of the widgets. In this example, you are going to remove that fade animation and animate the blur effect itself.

Open **LockScreenViewController.swift** and add a new method to the class:

```swift
func blurAnimations(_ blurred: Bool) -> () -> Void {
  return {

  }
}
```

This is a method that will return a prepared animations block, which you can add to an animator later on. Depending on the parameter value, the animations in the block will either remove or create the blur effect in `blurView`.

First let's add the code to create the animations. Insert in between the braces:

```swift
self.blurView.effect = blurred ?
  UIBlurEffect(style: .dark) : nil
self.tableView.transform = blurred ?
  CGAffineTransform(scaleX: 0.75, y: 0.75) : .identity
self.tableView.alpha = blurred ? 0.33 : 1.0
```

Setting the `effect` property on `blurView` to either `nil` or a blur effect will spawn an animation. Furthermore, you adjust the visibility and transform of the table view, that contains the widgets.

Great! Now the completed method looks like this:

```swift
func blurAnimations(_ blurred: Bool) -> () -> Void {
  return {
```

```
      self.blurView.effect =
        blurred ? UIBlurEffect(style: .dark) : nil
      self.tableView.transform = blurred ?
        CGAffineTransform(scaleX: 0.75, y: 0.75) : .identity
      self.tableView.alpha = blurred ? 0.33 : 1.0
    }
  }
```

You can use this to produce two different animations depending on the current state of the screen.

Next you will need to adjust the UI. Scroll to `viewDidLoad()` and **remove** these two lines:

```
blurView.effect = UIBlurEffect(style: .dark)
blurView.alpha = 0
```

These are the lines that set the effect up, but you don't need them anymore since you are going to use the new effect-based animations.

Speaking of which, replace the contents of `toggleBlur(_:)` with:

```
func toggleBlur(_ blurred: Bool) {
  UIViewPropertyAnimator(duration: 0.55, curve: .easeOut,
    animations: blurAnimations(blurred))
    .startAnimation()
}
```

Note that the **curve** parameter is of type `UIViewAnimationCurve`. This enumeration includes the four built-in curve types: `.linear`, `.easeIn`, `.easeOut`, and `easeInOut`.

Give the new animation a try; tap into the search bar and you will see the blur effect gradually appear on screen:

Notice how the blur doesn't simply fade in or out, but it actually interpolates the **amount** of blur in the effect view.

Now you can try different timing curves like `.easeIn` or `.linear` to see how they alter the animation.

Custom Bézier curves

Sometimes when you would like to be very specific about the timing of your animations, using these curves to simply "slow down at start" or "slow down about the end" isn't enough.

Earlier in the book you learned that you can create a custom `CAMediaTimingFunction` and give your layer animations custom timings. However, this was mentioned briefly in a note and you didn't have the chance to look more into that.

In this section, you are going to learn what Bézier curves are and how to use them to design your own custom animation timings. The good news is since `UIViewPropertyAnimator` uses layer animations behind the scenes, you can go back and apply what you master in this chapter to your layer animations as well.

But first — what *are* Bézier curves?

> **Note:** If you already have a solid understanding of Bézier curves, skip over this rather simple explanation of the mechanics behind them.

Let's start with something simple – a line. It's pretty neat, because all you need to draw a line on screen are the coordinates of the two points that define it; the start (A) and the end (B):

The handy aspect of being able to describe a shape on screen so precisely is that you can also apply transforms to it: you can scale the line up, you can move it, and rotate it too. All thanks to those two points in a coordinate system. Further, you can persist lines to disk and load them back, because you can describe them with numbers, and you know how to persist those!

Now let's look at curves. Curves are much more interesting than lines, because they can draw *anything* on screen. For example:

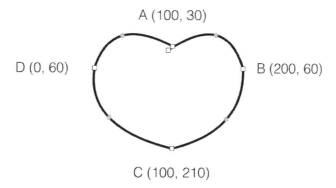

What you see above are four curves put together; their ends meet at the points where you see the little white squares. The interesting thing to note in the picture are the little green circles. After you look at the picture for a while you will notice that the circles "kind of define" where each one of the curves bends.

So curves are not random. They also have some specifics just like lines, which can help you define them via coordinates. You can then get all the benefits of coordinates like persisting them, transforming them, etc.

You define a curve by adding control points to lines. Let's add one control point to the line we had before:

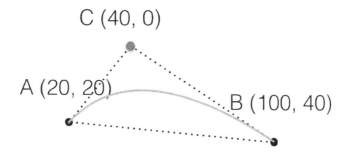

You can imagine the curve being drawn by a pencil attached to a line, whose start point moves along the line AC, and its end point moves along the line CB:

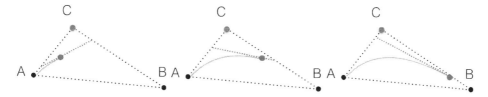

Bézier curves with one control point are called quadratic. You are, however, more interested in cubic Bézier curves — those have two control points.

You can also use cubic curves to describe animation timing. In fact, the built-in curves you've been using are also cubic curves that have been predefined for you.

Core Animation uses cubic curves that always start at coordinate (0, 0), which represents the beginning of the animation duration. Naturally the end point of these timing curves is always (1, 1) — the end of the duration and progress of the animation.

Let's have a look at an ease-in curve:

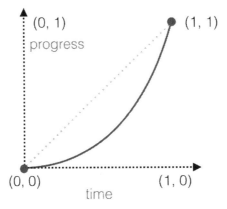

As the time passes (moving left-to-right horizontally across the coordinate space), the curve makes very little progress on the vertical axis, Then about half way through the animation duration, progress speeds up and catches up with time so they both reach (1, 1) by the end of the animation.

It all makes sense now, right?

Can you guess which one below is an ease-out and which one is an ease-in-out curve?

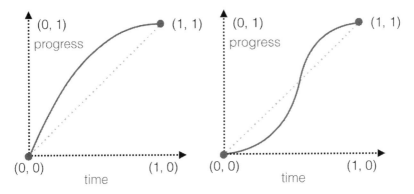

Now that you understand how Bézier curves work, the only remaining question is how to visually design some curves and get the control points' coordinates so you can use them for an iOS animation.

> Note: Open a web browser and visit **http://cubic-bezier.com**. This is a handy web site by computer science researcher and speaker Lea Verou. It allows you to drag around the two control points of a cubic Bézier and see an instant animation preview.

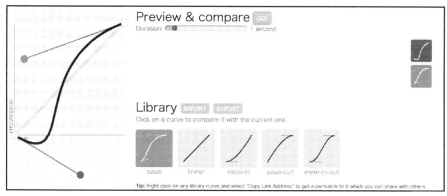

I encourage you to play around until you have a good idea how different timing curves affect animation timing.

Next you'll move on to adding a custom timing animation to the Widgets project.

Open **LockScreenViewController.swift** and replace the existing animation in `toggleBlur()` with:

```swift
func toggleBlur(_ blurred: Bool) {
  UIViewPropertyAnimator(duration: 0.55,
    controlPoint1: CGPoint(x: 0.57, y: -0.4),
    controlPoint2: CGPoint(x: 0.96, y: 0.87),
    animations: blurAnimations(blurred))
    .startAnimation()
}
```

This is the second convenience initializer of the `UIViewPropertyAnimator` class. Besides the duration and animations block, it takes two control points as parameters. These help you define your custom cubic curve.

Wait a second! One of those points above has a negative coordinate!

Indeed! Since you're anyways doing a custom timing curve, why not do something exotic?

You can drag the control points so they pull the curve into the space defining negative values for the progress axis. The effect is rather amusing: If you're moving a view in the right direction from point **A** to point **B**, it'll first take a "step back" leftwards, and then continue in the correct direction towards point **B**.

In the case of your blur and scale animations, the table view will actually first scale *up* a bit before scaling down. Doing this adds a bit of "elasticity" to your animation.

Be careful though: If you overdo it, this will create a rather comical effect on your animation :].

Spring Animations

There is another convenience initializer — `UIViewPropertyAnimator(duration:dampingRatio:animations:)` — for defining spring driven animations.

This will produce the same animation as `UIView`'s `animate(withDuration: delay: usingSpringWithDamping: initialSpringVelocity: options: animations: completion:)` with an initial velocity of `0`.

Like the `UIView` method, this API creates spring animations *backwards* as discussed in Chapter 11. You provide the duration you'd like to have for your animation, and UIKit calculates all aspects of the spring that would give you that duration. You know that doesn't give as good a spring effect as doing the calculation properly. Luckily, there is a better way of creating spring animations with `UIViewPropertyAnimator`, coming up next :]

Custom timing providers

Meet the fourth and last initializer you're going to cover here:
`UIViewPropertyAnimator(duration:timingParameters:)`.

This time, you can create a whole new object that could provide any timing data for your animations! You can use one of the UIKit objects that let you define custom cubic or spring based timings, but you can also roll out your own.

You'll see how to create a custom spring animation before moving on to the next section in this chapter where you'll create some spring animations in practice.

The second parameter named `timingParameters` is of type `UITimingCurveProvider` — a protocol defined by UIKit. There two classes in UIKit that conform to that protocol: `UICubicTimingParameters` and `UISpringTimingParameters`.

Let's look at `UISpringTimingParameters`.

Providing damping and velocity

Even if you're using a custom timing provider, you can still chose to go the easy way and provide just the damping ratio and initial velocity as you do when using the convenience initializer. The code would look like this:

```
let spring = UISpringTimingParameters(dampingRatio:0.5,
   initialVelocity: CGVector(dx: 1.0, dy: 0.2))

let animator = UIViewPropertyAnimator(duration: 1.0,
   timingParameters: spring)
```

The `spring` parameter represents the configuration of your spring, and you provide it to your `animator` object to use for the timing of your animations. This would still calculate the spring "backwards" as discussed earlier.

Note how initial velocity is a vector type. UIKit will apply a two-dimensional initial velocity at the start, in case you are animating the position or size of any of your views. If you're animating `alpha` or a single axis of your view's location, UIKit will consider only the `dx` property of your initial velocity vector.

`initialVelocity` is also an optional parameter so if you don't need to set a velocity at all, simply provide a damping ratio.

Custom springs

If you would like to be more specific about your spring, you can use a different initializer on `UISpringTimingParameters` that lets you specify the spring's mass, stiffness, and damping, much like you did for your layer animations earlier in the book.

The code to configure a custom spring is thus:

```
let spring = UISpringTimingParameters(mass: 10.0,
    stiffness: 5.0, damping: 30,
    initialVelocity: CGVector(dx: 1.0, dy: 0.2))

let animator = UIViewPropertyAnimator(duration: 1.0, t
    imingParameters: spring)
```

If you need a quick refresher on how all those parameters work, take a quick detour to Chapter 11 "Layer Springs".

In the next section you will try some of those custom timing animations.

Auto Layout animations

Phew! That was a rather lengthy theoretical part of the chapter, so I'm sure you're excited to write some code and give few animations a try.

You became proficient in Auto Layout animations in Chapter 7, "Animating Constraints", so it won't come as a surprise to you that in the next part you are going to be animating some constraints.

Layout constraint animations with `UIViewPropertyAnimator` are very similar to how you create them with `UIView.animate(withDuration:...)`. The trick was to update a constraint, and then call `layoutIfNeeded()` from within an animations block.

Let's try the same with `UIViewPropertyAnimator`.

Open **AnimatorFactory.swift** and add a new factory method:

```
@discardableResult
static func animateConstraint(view: UIView, constraint:
    NSLayoutConstraint, by: CGFloat) -> UIViewPropertyAnimator {

}
```

In this method, you are going to animate a change to a constraint's `constant` and then call `layoutIfNeeded()` on the provided view.

What is this animation going to look like? No idea! It really depends what kind of constraint you provide to the method. If you give it a trailing space constraint, it will move the view horizontally; if you provide it with a height constraint, the view will scale up or down.

Inside the method create an animator:

```
let spring = UISpringTimingParameters(dampingRatio: 0.2)
let animator = UIViewPropertyAnimator(duration: 2.0,
  timingParameters: spring)

animator.addAnimations {
  constraint.constant += by
  view.layoutIfNeeded()
}
return animator
```

You use the simple convenience spring initializer, then you simply change the constraint and trigger an Auto Layout pass.

Now switch to **LockScreenViewController.swift** and add to `viewWillAppear(_:)`:

```
dateTopConstraint.constant -= 100
view.layoutIfNeeded()
```

This will move the date label up by 100 points like so:

Next, trigger an animation to move the label (and all other views attached to it) down to its original location.

Append the following to `viewDidAppear(_:)`:

```
AnimatorFactory.animateConstraint(view: view,
  constraint: dateTopConstraint, by: 100)
  .startAnimation()
```

Run the app and check out the resulting animation! Since you are moving down all views *and* scaling up your table view, this results in a rather complex yet smooth transition:

The animation looks a bit excessive though. The first couple of times, it looks nice, but if your users see this bouncy transition multiple times every day they are certainly going to hate your app.

This is a nice reminder that UI spring animations should be all about *moderation*.

Switch back to **AnimatorFactory.swift** and change the parameters of your spring animation. Set `dampingRatio` to **0.55**, and `duration` to **1.0**. This should make the animation more subtle yet still playful.

Next, you'll explore a different situation when you will animate constraints. Currently, when you tap on **Show More** the widget changes its Height constraint and reloads the top table view contents to resize the widget.

In the next animation, you are going to animate the cell height change.

Open the **WidgetCell.swift** file and find `toggleShowMore(_:)`. You can peek inside to see the current code that changes the cell height and reloads the parent table view.

Remove all the code within `toggleShowMore(_:)` and replace it with:

```
self.showsMore = !self.showsMore
```

First let's define the animations you'd like to run. Append to `toggleShowMore(_:)`:

```
let animations = {
    self.widgetHeight.constant = self.showsMore ? 230 : 130
    if let tableView = self.tableView {
```

```
        tableView.beginUpdates()
        tableView.endUpdates()
        tableView.layoutIfNeeded()
    }
}
```

In this piece of code, you perform a little trick. First you change the constraint as usual, but then you call `beginUpdates()` and `endUpdates()` on the table view. Doing this will ask all cells about their height and adjust the layout as needed. If any of your cells says it wants to be higher or shorter, UIKit will adjust its frame accordingly.

At the end of the block, you call `layoutIfNeeded()` to ensure the layout change will happen inside the animations block.

Now let's create the animator. Add to the end of `toggleShowMore(_:)`:

```
let spring = UISpringTimingParameters(mass: 30, stiffness: 1000,
    damping: 300, initialVelocity: CGVector(dx: 5, dy: 0))

toggleHeightAnimator = UIViewPropertyAnimator(duration: 0.0,
timingParameters: spring)
toggleHeightAnimator?.addAnimations(animations)
toggleHeightAnimator?.startAnimation()
```

The view already features a property called `toggleHeightAnimator`, so you simply create a spring configuration and store the new animator in that property. Note that in this case you define all of the spring properties, so the duration that you pass to the property animator is ignored. The spring itself determines how long the animation takes to run.

Run the app, tap Show More, and enjoy a smooth spring-driven animation:

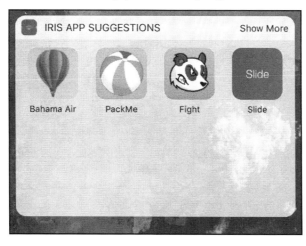

At the bottom of the method, add the following code that reloads the icons in the widget:

```
widgetView.expanded = showsMore
widgetView.reload()
```

This code triggers `reloadData()` on the collection view and that reloads all icons. Try the animation again and this time you see a different number of icons depending on the widget height:

Built-in view transitions

To finish up this animation, you'll have a look at using the built-in view transitions with `UIViewPropertyAnimator`.

In Chapter 3, "Transitions", you learned about the built-in view transitions you can use in iOS. Now you are going to use a cross-fade to change the title of the widget button from **Show More** to **Show Less** and vice versa.

Inside `toggleShowMore(_:)` add this code after you define your `animations` block (but before you define your animator):

```
let textTransition = {
  UIView.transition(with: sender, duration: 0.25,
    options: .transitionCrossDissolve,
    animations: {
      sender.setTitle(
        self.showsMore ? "Show Less" : "Show More",
        for: .normal)
    },
    completion: nil
  )
}
```

You define a view transition, and inside its `animations` block, you alter the button title depending whether the widget is currently expanded or not.

So how do you add this transition to your animator? Just as you would with any other animations block!

Find the spot where you add `animations` to your animator and add `textTransition` as well with a `0.5` delay factor. The final code should look like this:

```
toggleHeightAnimator?.addAnimations(animations)
toggleHeightAnimator?.addAnimations(textTransition, delayFactor:
0.5)
toggleHeightAnimator?.startAnimation()
```

This will change the button title with a nice cross-fade effect:

You're starting to push `UIViewPropertyAnimator` to its limits! Before you move on to the next chapter and interactive animations, make sure to look into this chapter's challenge, which will introduce you to creative additive animations with `UIViewPropertyAnimator`.

Challenges

Challenge 1: Additive animations

When using `UIView.animate(withDuration:...)`, adding animations to the same view property happens additively.

For example, if you are moving a view across the screen from point **A** to **B**, and change your mind mid-way about the end point and decide to send the view over to point **C** instead, it will not just break off the movement at the current point and move directly towards the new end point.

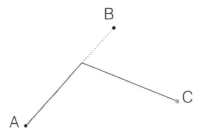

UIKit is smarter than that, so by default it will try to "ease" your view into its new trajectory. The actual movement will look something like this:

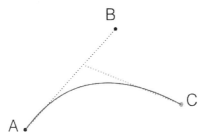

The animations aren't replaced at the time you add changes, but are combined so that the changes happen additively.

Consider your widget height animation: You have a little issue when the user quickly taps again on the Show More button. The animation ends up in the desired state, but there's a jump mid-way, not a smooth transition.

For this challenge, if the menu state is switched again in `toggleShowMore(_:)` before the previous animation completes, then instead of creating a new animator you should "add" animations to the existing `toggleHeightAnimator`.

- Check if `toggleHeightAnimator` is currently running using `isRunning`.

- If the animator has already been created, simply add the new animation!

When you're done with this challenge, move on to the next chapter to learn how to add interactivity to your property animator animations.

Chapter 22: Interactive Animations with UIViewPropertyAnimator

You've already covered a lot of the `UIViewPropertyAnimator` APIs such as basic animations, custom timings and springs, and abstracting of animations. But you haven't yet looked into what makes this class really interesting compared to the old style "fire-and-forget" APIs.

`UIView.animate(withDuration:...)` offers a way to animate views on screen, but once you've defined the desired end state, the animations are sent off for rendering and control is out of your hands.

But what if you wanted to interact with the animations? Or to create animations, which aren't static but are driven by user gestures or microphone input like you did in the part of the book covering layer animations?

This is where `UIViewPropertyAnimator` really comes through in regard to animating views. The animations created with this class are fully interactive: you can start, pause them, and alter their speed. Finally you can simply "scrub-through" the animation by directly setting the current progress.

Since `UIViewPropertyAnimator` can drive both preset animations and interactive animations, things get a bit complicated when it comes to telling what state an animator is currently. The next part of the chapter will teach you how to deal with animator state.

If you have completed the challenge in the previous chapter, just keep working on your Xcode project; if you skipped over the challenge, open the starter project provided for this chapter.

You should have the project featuring different animations which kick in when you enter text in the search bar, tap on an icon, or expand the widget view.

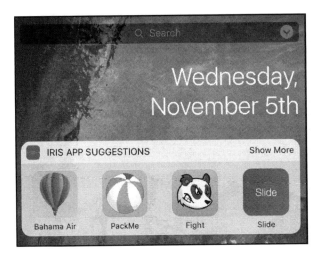

An animation state machine

Besides taking care of your animations, `UIViewPropertyAnimator` exhibits behaviors of a state machine, and can give you information about many different aspects of the current state of your animations.

You can check if an animation has started, if it has been paused or completely stopped, or whether the animation has been reversed. And finally, you can check where the animation "completed", such as at the desired end state, from the beginning, or somewhere in between.

There are three properties on `UIViewPropertyAnimator` that help you figure out the current state:

The `isRunning` property (read-only) tells you if the animator's animations are currently in motion. The property is `false` by default and becomes `true` when `startAnimation()` is called. It becomes `false` again if you pause or stop the animations, or your animations complete naturally.

The `isReversed` property is by default `false` since you always start your animations in forward direction, i.e. your animation plays from its start state to its end state. If you change this property to `true`, the animation will reverse direction and play back to its initial state.

Note: It would make sense to be able to change the value of isReversed as many times as you want, but in reality on iOS 10 you can do that only once. Once you reverse the animation direction, trying to change the value of isReversed again will not affect the animation anymore.

The state property (read-only) determines whether the animator is active and currently animating, or in some other passive state.

By default, state is inactive. This usually means you've just created the animator and haven't called any methods on it yet. Please note that this is not the same as having isRunning set to false: isRunning is really only concerned with animations being played, while when state is inactive that really means that the animator hasn't done anything much yet.

state becomes active when you either:

• Call startAnimation() to start your animations

• Call pauseAnimation() without even starting your animations first,

• Set the fractionComplete property to "rewind" the animation to a certain position.

Once your animations complete naturally, state switches back to inactive.

If you call stopAnimation() on your animator, it will set its state property to stopped. In this state, the only thing you could do is either abandon the animator altogether or call finishAnimation(at:) to complete the animations and bring the animator back to the inactive state.

As you probably figured out, UIViewPropertyAnimator can only switch between states in a certain sequence. It can't go straight from inactive to stopped, nor from stopped to active.

If you're in doubt, you can always come back to this part of the chapter and consult the state flow diagram below:

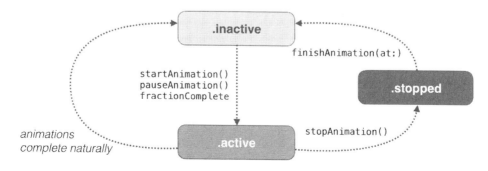

Don't worry if managing the state with `UIViewPropertyAnimator` sounds a bit complicated at first. Should you call a method you're not allowed to call in the current state, your app will immediately crash so you will have the chance to figure out where you went wrong.

Interactive 3D touch animation

In this part of the chapter, you are going to create an interactive animation similar to the 3D touch interaction on your iPhone home screen:

> **Note:** For this section, you'll need either a 3D touch compatible iOS device, or a Force Touch trackpad for the simulator.

As you continue to press on a home screen icon, you'll see the animation interactively progress under your finger; the background gets more and more blurred, and there's a light blur frame growing out of the icon.

These two animations tell the user they are working through a gesture and gives them feedback about their progress through that animation. When you've pressed hard enough, the icon frame detaches from the icon and becomes a menu:

It's a neat little interactive animation, which you will get to reproduce in this chapter.

> **Note:** You are not going to learn the details about handling 3D touch with
> `UIPreviewInteractionDelegate`, since the chapter is about creating
> animations. If you want to learn more about `UIPreviewInteractionDelegate`,
> check out our *iOS10 by Tutorials* book on raywenderlich.com.

Open **WidgetView.swift** and find the extension on `WidgetView` that conforms to
`UIPreviewInteractionDelegate`. These are the delegate methods that UIKit calls
when the user is pressing on your widget view.

In order to get you started developing the animation itself, the
`UIPreviewInteractionDelegate` methods have already been wired to call relevant
methods on `LockScreenViewController`.

What the code in `WidgetView` does is as follows:

- Call `LockScreenViewController.startPreview(for:)` when the 3D touch starts.

- Call `LockScreenViewController.updatePreview(percent:)` repeatedly while the
  user presses harder (or softer).

- Call `LockScreenViewController.finishPreview()` when the peek interaction has
  finished successfully.

- Finally, call `LockScreenViewController.cancelPreview()` if the user lifted their
  finger without completing the preview gesture.

Without further ado, let's get to coding!

Open **LockScreenViewController.swift** and add these three properties, which you will
need in order to create the peek interaction:

```
var startFrame: CGRect?
var previewView: UIView?
var previewAnimator: UIViewPropertyAnimator?
```

You will use `startFrame` to track where the animation started. `previewView` will be a
snapshot view of your icon; you'll use it temporarily during the animation.

The `previewAnimator` will be the interactive animator driving the preview animation.

Add one more property to hold the blur effect to display the icon frame (as in the
screenshots above):

```
let previewEffectView = IconEffectView(blur: .extraLight)
```

IconEffectView is a custom class included with the starter project. It's a simple blur view which contains a single label. You're going to use it to mock the menu that pops out of the pressed icon like so:

Scroll down to extension LockScreenViewController: WidgetsOwnerProtocol and insert a new method inside:

```
func startPreview(for forView: UIView) {
  previewView?.removeFromSuperview()
  previewView = forView.snapshotView(afterScreenUpdates: false)
  view.insertSubview(previewView!, aboveSubview: blurView)
}
```

As you saw previously, WidgetView calls startPreview(for:) whenever the user starts pressing on an icon. The forView parameter is the collection cell image that the user began the gesture on.

First you remove any existing previewView view, just in case to make sure you don't leave artifacts on screen. Then you make a snapshot of the collection view icon and finally add it onscreen just above the blur effect view.

> **Note:** In iOS 10, snapshotView(afterScreenUpdates:) does not seem to be working correctly in the Simulator. Therefore you will need to work through this part of the chapter **on your device.**

You can run the app right now and start pressing on an icon. You will see a copy of the icon popup at the top left corner!

Of course the icon isn't covering the existing one because you haven't set its position. Let's keep on building the animation:

```
previewView?.frame = forView.convert(forView.bounds, to: view)
startFrame = previewView?.frame
addEffectView(below: previewView!)
```

You set the correct position on the icon copy so that it covers completely the existing icon. Then you store that start location and size for future reference in `startFrame`. Finally you call `addEffectView(below:)` to add the blur frame below the icon snapshot.

Add the implementation of `addEffectView(below:)` to `LockScreenViewController` using the snippet below to insert the effect below the icon snapshot:

```
func addEffectView(below forView: UIView) {
  previewEffectView.removeFromSuperview()
  previewEffectView.frame = forView.frame

  forView.superview?.insertSubview(previewEffectView,
    belowSubview: forView)
}
```

This completes the setup stage of the animation. Congrats for making it through!

Next switch to **AnimatorFactory.swift** to create the animation itself. Add the following method to `AnimatorFactory`:

```
static func grow(view: UIVisualEffectView,
  blurView: UIVisualEffectView) -> UIViewPropertyAnimator {

  // 1
  view.contentView.alpha = 0
  view.transform = .identity

  // 2
  let animator = UIViewPropertyAnimator(
    duration: 0.5, curve: .easeIn)

  return animator
}
```

Your new factory method takes two parameters:

- `view`: The view to animate

- `blurView` The blur background that will animate alongside the primary animation.

It then performs the following actions:

1. First, it baselines the current state of the view by fading out the view contents — that's the label saying "Customize Actions..." — and resetting the transform on the view.

2. Then a new animator is created with `0.5` seconds duration and an ease-in timing curve.

Now, just before the line `return animator`, you can add the animations and completions for this animator. To do that, insert the following:

```
// 3
animator.addAnimations {
  blurView.effect = UIBlurEffect(style: UIBlurEffectStyle.dark)
  view.transform = CGAffineTransform(scaleX: 1.5, y: 1.5)
}

// 4
animator.addCompletion { _ in
  blurView.effect = UIBlurEffect(style: UIBlurEffectStyle.dark)
}
```

3. In the animation added here, setting the `effect` property on your blur view will create a nice blur transition. You've already done this in previous chapters, but this time the blur will happen interactively depending on how hard the user is pressing the screen. Finally, the blur is scaled up on the icon frame by simply adjusting its `transform` property.

4. The completion method explicitly sets the final state of the blur view. In iOS 10, these interactive animations with `UIViewPropertyAnimator` are sometimes a bit buggy, so as soon as your animations complete, UIKit will call your completion and the code in it will make sure you're leaving the UI in the condition you want.

You're almost ready with your grow animation. You just need to scrub through it interactively as the user presses on the icon.

Go back to **LockScreenViewController.swift** and append the following to `startPreview()`:

```
previewAnimator = AnimatorFactory.grow(view: previewEffectView,
  blurView: blurView)
```

Note how this time, unlike in the previous chapters, you create and configure your animator — but you don't start the animations. This time, you'll drive the animation progress interactively based on the 3D touch input.

To progress through the animation, implement the `updatePreview(percent:)` method. This is the one `WidgetView` will repeatedly call with the current touch force:

```swift
func updatePreview(percent: CGFloat) {
  previewAnimator?.fractionComplete =
    max(0.01, min(0.99, percent))
}
```

The important aspect to understand is that you restrict `fractionComplete` in the range `0.01` and `0.99`. If you set the `fractionComplete` to `0.0` or `1.0`, the animator will complete and you don't want that to happen inside `updatePreview`. You will finish or cancel the animation from the designated methods.

You can give your interactive animation a try right now!

Run the app and start gently pressing on one of the icons. When you start pressing, you will see the blur frame starting to "grow out" of the icon. The blur effect appears subtly in the background:

When you press harder and harder, the frame keeps growing and the blur becomes more prominent:

As soon as you apply enough force to complete the preview gesture, you will feel the haptic feedback under your finger and the animation will stop in this state.

Why does the animation stop? No, it's not your fault — the peek gesture completes, and once it does that, it just stops sending updates; that is, it stops calling your updatePreview(percent:) method.

Next, you will implement the methods to cancel or complete the interaction.

You will (surprise!) need more animators. Open **AnimatorFactory.swift** and add an animator, which undoes everything your "grow" animator does.

One situation where you'll need this animator is when the user cancels the gesture. Another is at the very end of a successful interaction when you need to clean up the UI.

Add the new factory method:

```
static func reset(frame: CGRect, view: UIVisualEffectView,
    blurView: UIVisualEffectView) -> UIViewPropertyAnimator {

  return UIViewPropertyAnimator(duration: 0.5,
    dampingRatio: 0.7) {

    view.transform = .identity
    view.frame = frame
    view.contentView.alpha = 0

    blurView.effect = nil
  }
}
```

This method takes in the starting frame of the original animation, the view to animate, and the background blurView. The animation block resets all properties in the state before the interaction started.

Switch back to **LockScreenViewController.swift** and add a new method inside the WidgetsOwnerProtocol extension:

```
func cancelPreview() {
  if let previewAnimator = previewAnimator {
    previewAnimator.isReversed = true
    previewAnimator.startAnimation()
```

```
      }
    }
```

This is the method that `WidgetView` will call if the user abruptly lifts their finger, or if a FaceTime calls pops on screen, and cancels the ongoing gesture.

So far you haven't started your animator at all. You have been repeatedly setting `fractionComplete` and this drove the animations interactively.

However, once the user cancels the interaction, you can't keep driving the animation interactively because you have no more input. Instead, you play back the animation to its initial state by setting `isReversed` to `true`, and calling `startAnimation()`. Now **this** is something you can't do with `UIView.animate(withDuration:...)`!

Give the interaction another try. Press through half of the animation and then let go to test `cancelPreview()`.

The animation correctly plays back when you lift your finger but in the end the dark blur reappears abruptly.

The issue is rooted in your grow animator's code. Switch back to **AnimatorFactory.swift** and look at the code in `grow(view: UIVisualEffectView, blurView: UIVisualEffectView)` — more specifically, this part:

```
animator.addCompletion { _ in
  blurView.effect = UIBlurEffect(style: .dark)
}
```

Now that the animation can play either forwards or backwards, you need to take care of this in your completion block.

The parameter that `addCompletion()`'s closure takes is of type `UIViewAnimatingPosition`. Its value can be either `.start`, `.end`, or `.current`.

If your animation completed naturally, or otherwise reached its end state, you will get the .end value in your completion closure. If you reversed the animation, it will complete at the .start position. Finally, if you stop your animation mid-way and finish it right there, your completion block will get the .current value.

So, to handle the possibility of completing or canceling the preview gesture, remove the existing completion block and replace it with this:

```
animator.addCompletion { position in
  switch position {
  case .start:
    blurView.effect = nil
  case .end:
    blurView.effect = UIBlurEffect(style: .dark)
  default: break
  }
}
```

In case the animation was reversed, you remove the blur effect. If it completed successfully, you explicitly adjust the effect to a dark blur.

Give the adjusted animation a try few times; make sure everything goes as expected. It should mostly do that.

Now there's a new issue. If you cancel the press on a certain icon, you cannot press it anymore!

This is because the icon snapshot is still located just over the original icon, and it swallows all touches. To fix that issue, you need to remove the snapshot as soon as the reset animator has completed.

Let's add this code to cancelPreview() back in **LockScreenViewController.swift**, just below previewAnimator.startAnimation():

```
previewAnimator.addCompletion { position in
  switch position {
  case .start:
    self.previewView?.removeFromSuperview()
    self.previewEffectView.removeFromSuperview()
  default: break
  }
}
```

Remember that this call to addCompletion(_:) does not replace the existing completion block, but rather adds a second one.

The goal is to check if the animation has been reversed; and if so, remove the snapshot and the icon frame from the view hierarchy. That's why the only case you're interested in is when position is .start.

Try the app again, and you will see that the icons are interactive again after a canceled gesture. Hooray! You're almost there.

Let's add one more animator to display the icon menu. Switch to **AnimatorFactory.swift** and add to it:

```swift
static func complete(view: UIVisualEffectView) ->
UIViewPropertyAnimator {
  return UIViewPropertyAnimator(duration: 0.3,
    dampingRatio: 0.7) {
    view.contentView.alpha = 1
    view.transform = .identity
    view.frame = CGRect(
      x: view.frame.minX - view.frame.minX/2.5,
      y: view.frame.maxY - 140,
      width: view.frame.width + 120,
      height: 60
    )
  }
}
```

This time you create a simple spring animator. For its animators you do the following:

- Fade in the "Customize Actions" menu item.

- Reset the transform.

- Animate the frame of the view directly to a location just above the icon.

The location of the menu changes depending on which icon the user pressed on.

You set the horizontal position to `view.frame.minX - view.frame.minX/2.5`, which shows the menu to the right if the icon is on the left side of the screen, and shows the menu to the left if the icon is on the right side of the screen. See the difference below:

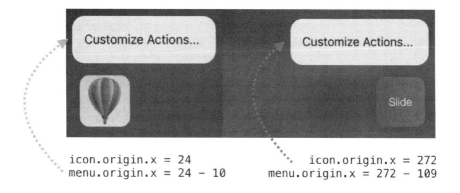

```
icon.origin.x = 24              icon.origin.x = 272
menu.origin.x = 24 - 10         menu.origin.x = 272 - 109
```

The animator is ready to go, so open **LockScreenViewController.swift** and add the last required method in the `WidgetsOwnerProtocol` extension:

```
func finishPreview() {
  // 1
  previewAnimator?.stopAnimation(false)

  // 2
  previewAnimator?.finishAnimation(at: .end)

  // 3
  previewAnimator = nil
}
```

`finishPreview()` is called when the user pushes through the 3D touch gesture, at about the time you feel the haptic feedback.

1. `stopAnimation(_:)` stops the animations currently running on screen and has two different behaviors depending on the boolean parameter you pass in.

2. When you call `stopAnimation(false)`, you put the animator in the `stopped` state. It will wait for you to call `finishAnimation(at:)` at some point later on. If you call `stopAnimations(true)`, this will clear all animations and put the animator in the `inactive` state without calling your completion blocks. Use this to completely cancel the current animations on an animator.

Once you put the animator in the `stopped` state, you have a few options. The one you pursue in `finishPreview()` is to tell the animator to complete at its end state. Thus you call `finishAnimation(at: .end)`; this will update all views with the target values of the scheduled animations and call your completion.

3. You won't need the `previewAnimator` anymore for this gesture, so you can remove it.

You can call `finishAnimation(at:)` with one of the following:

• `start`: To reset the animations to their initial state.

• `current`: To update your views' properties from the current progress of the animation and complete.

After you call `finishAnimation(at:)`, your animator is in the `inactive` state.

Back to the Widgets project. Since you got rid of the preview animator, you can run the complete animator to display the menu. Append the following to the end of `finishPreview()`:

```
AnimatorFactory.complete(view: previewEffectView)
  .startAnimation()
```

That will complete the effect. As soon as you run the app and press on an icon, you will see its menu pop up interactively:

And when the animation is finished, the menu will position itself nicely along the icon:

Congratulations — you deserve a pat on the shoulder. That was a complex effect to develop! But brace yourself — that's just the start! In the next chapter, you are going to work on interactive view controller transition animations!

Meanwhile, work through the challenges provided in this chapter so you can get a bit more experience with adding and re-using animators, and also with using interactive keyframe animations!

Challenges

Challenge 1: Allow the users to dismiss the menu

Once the user sees the complete animation which displays the menu, they can't do anything else with the app.

In this challenge, you are going to reset the UI if the user taps on the blur view or on the menu item. This will allow them to "dismiss" the menu and further interact with the app.

In `finishAnimations()` add the following code to prepare the blur for being interactive:

```
blurView.effect = UIBlurEffect(style: .dark)
blurView.isUserInteractionEnabled = true
blurView.addGestureRecognizer(UITapGestureRecognizer(target:
self, action: #selector(dismissMenu)))
```

Above, you make sure that the blur effect is set to dark and you enable user interactivity on the blur view itself. This will allow the user to tap anywhere around the icon to dismiss the menu. Finally you add a touch recognizer and connect it to a method called `dismissMenu()`.

Next — add `dismissMenu()` on your own:

- Use the `AnimatorFactory.reset(frame:, view:, blurView:)` animator for the dismiss animation.

- Use the `startFrame` property for the `frame` parameter of `AnimatorFactory.reset(frame:, view:, blurView:)`.

- Before starting the animator, add one more completion block which remove `previewEffectView` and `previewView` from the screen. Also disable user interactivity on the blur view so it doesn't swallow any other touches.

Finally, in `viewDidLoad()`, add a tap recognizer on `previewEffectView`, connected to `dismissMenu()` as well. This will allow the users to tap on **Customize Actions...** to close the menu.

Run the app and try opening and dismissing the menu few times. Isn't that jolly old fun?

Challenge 2: Interactive keyframe animations

You've seen how easy it is to add keyframe animations to an animator. If you have an animator with keyframes, you can still use it to create interactive animations. Your users can scrub through the keyframes back and forth.

To give that a try, you will add an extra element to the grow animation — the one you scrub through interactively while the user presses on an icon.

Open **AnimatorFactory.swift** and find the place in `grow(view: UIVisualEffectView, blurView: UIVisualEffectView)` where you add animations to the animator:

```
animator.addAnimations {
  blurView.effect = UIBlurEffect(style: .dark)
  view.transform = CGAffineTransform(scaleX: 1.5, y: 1.5)
}
```

Delete this whole block of code and **replace** it with:

```
animator.addAnimations {
  UIView.animateKeyframes(withDuration: 0.5, delay: 0.0,
animations: {

    UIView.addKeyframe(withRelativeStartTime: 0.0,
relativeDuration: 1.0, animations: {
      blurView.effect = UIBlurEffect(style: .dark)
      view.transform = CGAffineTransform(scaleX: 1.5, y: 1.5)
    }

    UIView.addKeyframe(withRelativeStartTime: 0.5,
relativeDuration: 0.5, animations: {
      view.transform = view.transform.rotated(by: -.pi/8)
    }
  })
}
```

You create an animation with two keyframes:

- The first keyframe goes for the total duration of the animation, and runs the same animation you had previously.

- The second keyframe kicks in the second half of the total duration and rotates the view slightly.

The new element in the animation will help give the user feedback when they are about to complete the gesture. Just before they've pressed hard enough, they'll see the icon frame tilt:

This will also add a bit of playfulness to the complete animations that shows the menu:

With the complete interaction and all animations in place, you are now ready to proceed to the next chapter and dabble on creating view controller transitions with `UIViewPropertyAnimator`.

Chapter 23: UIViewPropertyAnimator View Controller Transitions

While working through Chapters 17 to 19, you learned how to create custom view controller transitions. You saw how flexible and powerful those can be, so naturally you are probably craving to know how to use UIViewPropertyAnimator to create them as well.

Good news — using an animator for your transitions is pretty easy, and there are almost no surprises there.

In this chapter, you are going to review building custom transition animations and create both static and interactive transitions for your Widgets project.

When you've finished working through the chapter, your users will be able to scrub through presenting the settings view controller by pulling down the widget table.

If you worked on the challenges from the last chapter, keep working on the same project; if you skipped over the challenges, open the starter project provided for this chapter.

Static view controller transitions

Currently, the experience is pretty stale when the user taps the "Edit" button. The button presents a new view controller on top of the current one, and as soon as you tap any of the available options in that second screen, it disappears.

Let's spice that up a notch!

Create a new file and name it **PresentTransition.swift**. Replace its default contents with:

```
import UIKit

class PresentTransition: NSObject,
  UIViewControllerAnimatedTransitioning {
  func transitionDuration(using transitionContext:
    UIViewControllerContextTransitioning?) -> TimeInterval {
    return 0.75
  }

  func animateTransition(using transitionContext:
    UIViewControllerContextTransitioning) {

  }
}
```

You are familiar with the `UIViewControllerAnimatedTransitioning` protocol, so you should hopefully be familiar with this piece of code.

> **Note:** In case you skipped the View Controller Transitions section of the book, I'd recommend taking a step back and working through at least Chapter 17, "Custom Presentation Controller & Device Orientation Animations".

In this part of the chapter, you are going to create a transition animation that animates the blur layer and moves the new view controller on top of it.

Add the following method, in the same file you have open, to create an animator for the transition:

```
func transitionAnimator(using transitionContext:
    UIViewControllerContextTransitioning) ->
UIViewImplicitlyAnimating {
    let duration = transitionDuration(using: transitionContext)

    let container = transitionContext.containerView
    let to = transitionContext.view(forKey:
UITransitionContextViewKey.to)!

    container.addSubview(to)
}
```

In the code above, you make all necessary preparations for the view controller transition. You begin by getting the animation duration, you then fetch the target view controller's view, and finally add this view to the transition container.

Next you can set up the animation and run it. Add this code to `transitionAnimator(using:)` to prepare the UI for the transition animation:

```
to.transform = CGAffineTransform(scaleX: 1.33, y: 1.33)
    .concatenating(CGAffineTransform(translationX: 0.0, y: 200))
to.alpha = 0
```

This scales up and moves down the target view controller's view and fades it out. Now it's ready to be animated onto the screen.

Add the animator after `to.alpha = 0` to run the transition:

```
let animator = UIViewPropertyAnimator(duration: duration, curve:
.easeOut)

animator.addAnimations({
    to.transform = CGAffineTransform(translationX: 0.0, y: 100)
}, delayFactor: 0.15)

animator.addAnimations({
    to.alpha = 1.0
}, delayFactor: 0.5)
```

In this code, you create an animator with two animation blocks:

1. The first animation moves the target view controller's view to its final position.

2. The second animation fades the content in from an `alpha` of 0 to 1.

As in the previous chapters you should never forget to wrap up the transition. Add a completion to the animator:

```
animator.addCompletion { _ in
  transitionContext.completeTransition(
    !transitionContext.transitionWasCancelled
  )
}
```

Once your animations complete, you let UIKit know that you're finished transitioning. At the end of your method simply return the animator:

```
return animator
```

Now that you have your animator factory method, you have to also use it. Scroll up to `animateTransition(using:)` and insert this code:

```
transitionAnimator(using: transitionContext).startAnimation()
```

This will fetch a ready-to-go animator, and begin via `startAnimation()`.

That should do it for the time being. Let's wire up the view controller to the transition animator and give the animation a try.

Open **LockScreenViewController** and define the following constant property:

```
let presentTransition = PresentTransition()
```

You will provide this object to UIKit when it asks you for a presentation animation and interaction controller. To do that, add a `UIViewControllerTransitioningDelegate` conformance to `LockScreenViewController`:

```
extension LockScreenViewController:
  UIViewControllerTransitioningDelegate {

  func animationController(
    forPresented presented: UIViewController,
    presenting: UIViewController, source: UIViewController) ->
    UIViewControllerAnimatedTransitioning? {

    return presentTransition

  }

}
```

The `animationController(forPresented:presenting:source:)` method is where you have your chance to tell UIKit that you're planning on spawning a new custom view controller transition. You return the `presentTransition` from that method and UIKit uses it for the animations to follow.

Now for the last step — you need to set `LockScreenViewController` as the presentation delegate. Scroll to `presentSettings(_:)`, and just before calling `present(_:animated:completion:)` set `self` as the transition delegate.

The completed code should look like so:

```
settingsController = storyboard?.instantiateViewController(
    withIdentifier: "SettingsViewController") as!
SettingsViewController
settingsController.transitioningDelegate = self
present(settingsController, animated: true, completion: nil)
```

This should be it! Run the app and tap on the Edit button to try the transition.

The initial result isn't all that exciting (at least not yet!). The settings controller seems to be a bit off:

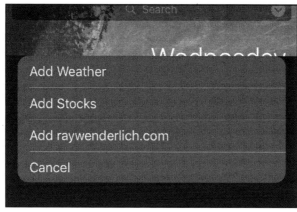

You'll want to take care of few rough edges, but your job here is almost finished.

The first thing to correct is the target view controller doesn't need the solid background color. Open **Main.storyboard** (it's in the Assets project folder) and select the settings view controller view.

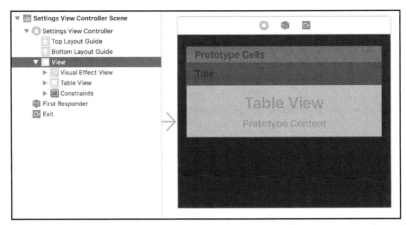

Change the view's Background to **Clear Color** and you should see the storyboard reflect that change like so:

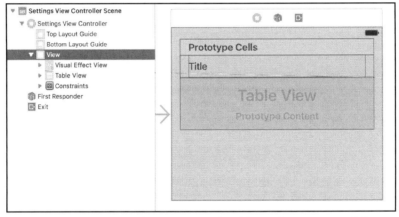

Give that transition another try. This time you should see the contents of the settings view controller appear directly over the lock screen:

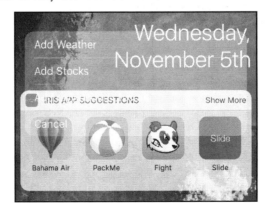

It looks like this transition can do with a few more animations. Wouldn't it be nice, for example, to fade in the blur on top of the widget so that the user can see better the modal view controller on top?

Since you're a pro already, let's do something new — "*animation injection*"!. (No need to look that term up – I just came up with it for this chapter. :])

You will add a new property to the animator that will allow you to inject any custom animation into the transition. This will allow you to use the same transition class to produce slightly different animations.

Switch to **PresentTransition.swift** and add two new properties:

```
var auxAnimations: (()-> Void)?
var auxAnimationsCancel: (()-> Void)?
```

Append this to the bottom of `transitionAnimator(using:)`, just before `return`:

```
if let auxAnimations = auxAnimations {
  animator.addAnimations(auxAnimations)
}
```

In case you've added any arbitrary block of animations to the object, they will be added to the rest of the animator's animations. The cancel block allows you to do any unwinding that might be necessary if the transition is cancelled.

This allows you to, depending on the situation, add custom animations into the transition. For example, let's add a blur animation to the current transition.

Open **LockScreenViewController** and insert the following **at the top** of `presentSettings()`:

```
presentTransition.auxAnimations = blurAnimations(true)
```

This will add the blur animation you created many chapters ago to the view controller transition!

Give the transition another try and see how that one line changed it:

Isn't reusing animations simply amazing?

Now you also need to hide the blur when the user dismisses the presented controller. `SettingsViewController` already has a `didDismiss` property so you simply need to set that property to a block that animates the blur out.

In `presentSettings(_:)` on the second-to-last line before the `settingsController` is presented, insert:

```
settingsController.didDismiss = { [unowned self] in
  self.toggleBlur(false)
}
```

Now tapping on one of the options in the settings screen will dismiss it. The blur will then disappear and the user will be successfully taken back to the first view controller:

This concludes this part of the chapter. Your view controller transition is ready!

Interactive view controller transitions

As the final topic in the `UIViewPropertyAnimator` section of the book, you are going to create an interactive view controller transition. Your user will drive the transition by pulling down the widget table.

First and foremost, let's use the powerful `UIPercentDrivenInteractionTransition` class to enable interactivity for the view controller transition.

Open **PresentTransition.swift** and replace:

```
class PresentTransition: NSObject,
UIViewControllerAnimatedTransitioning
```

with:

```
class PresentTransition:
  UIPercentDrivenInteractiveTransition,
  UIViewControllerAnimatedTransitioning
```

`UIPercentDrivenInteractiveTransition` is a class that defines the "percent" based transition methods such as:

- `update(_:)` to rewind through the transition.
- `cancel()` to cancel the view controller transition.
- `finish()` to play the the transition until it completes.

You may remember these from Chapter 19, "Interactive UINavigationController Transitions", but you didn't look at some of the newly added APIs that accommodate using a `UIViewPropertyAnimator` specifically.

Some of the new functionally built to make animator transitions easier include:

- `timingCurve`: In case your user drives the transition interactively and lets go at a point when you need to play the transition till the end, you can provide a custom timing curve for the animation by setting this property. This can be a cubic, spring, or another custom timing provider.

- `wantsInteractiveStart`: By default this is `true` since you are probably going to use this class mostly for interactive transitions. However, if you set the property to `false`, the transition will start non-interactively and you could pause it and go to interactive mode at a later point.

- `pause()`: Call this method to pause a non-interactive transition and switch to interactive mode.

Add a new method to `PresentTransition`:

```
func interruptibleAnimator(using transitionContext:
  UIViewControllerContextTransitioning) ->
UIViewImplicitlyAnimating {

  return transitionAnimator(using: transitionContext)
}
```

This is a method (new in iOS 10) on the `UIViewControllerAnimatedTransitioning` protocol. It allows you to provide to UIKit an interruptible animator, which it will use for your transition animations.

Your transition animator class has now two different behaviors:

1. If it is used **non-interactively** (when the user presses the Edit button) UIKit will call `animateTransition(using:)` to animate the transition.

2. If it is used **interactively**, UIKit will call `interruptibleAnimator(using:)`, get your animator, and use it to drive the transition that way.

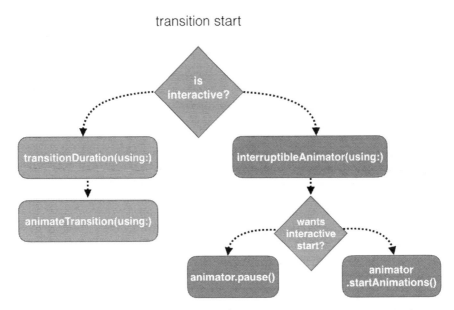

Switch to **LockScreenViewController.swift** and add this new method inside the `UIViewControllerTransitioningDelegate` extension:

```
func interactionControllerForPresentation(using animator:
   UIViewControllerAnimatedTransitioning)
   -> UIViewControllerInteractiveTransitioning? {
   return presentTransition
}
```

This will let UIKit know you're planning some playful interactiveness during the view controller presentation.

Next, still in the file you have open, add two new properties; you will need them to keep track of the user's gesture:

```
var isDragging = false
var isPresentingSettings = false
```

As the user pulls the table down you will set the `isDragging` flag to `true`, and once the user has pulled far enough, you will set `isPresentingSettings` to `true` in turn.

To track how far has the user pulled the table view, you will need to implement some of its scroll view delegate methods. Add a new extension and insert the first of those methods:

```
extension LockScreenViewController: UIScrollViewDelegate {
   func scrollViewWillBeginDragging(_ scrollView: UIScrollView) {
```

```
        isDragging = true
    }
}
```

This might seem a bit redundant since `UITableView` already has a property to track if it's being currently dragged, but this time you are going to do some custom tracking yourself.

Next add the delegate method to track the user's progress:

```
func scrollViewDidScroll(_ scrollView: UIScrollView) {
  guard isDragging else {
    return
  }

  if !isPresentingSettings && scrollView.contentOffset.y < -30 {
    isPresentingSettings = true
    presentTransition.wantsInteractiveStart = true
    presentSettings()
    return
  }
}
```

First, you check if your `isDragging` flag is enabled; you are not interested in tracking the table view's offset otherwise. Then you check if the user has pulled far enough to start the transition.

If both conditions are `true`, you prepare the transition setup. You set `isPresentingSettings` to `true`, you set the transition animator to interactive mode, and finally you call `presentSettings()`.

`presentSettings()` takes care to start the view controller transition in interactive mode because you set the `wantsInteractiveStart` to `true` in advance.

Next, you need to add the code to update it interactively. Append the following to the end of `scrollViewDidScroll(_:)`:

```
if isPresentingSettings {
  let progress = max(0.0, min(1.0, ((-
scrollView.contentOffset.y) - 30) / 90.0))
  presentTransition.update(progress)
}
```

You calculate a progress in the range `0.0` to `1.0` based on how far the user has pulled the table view and call `update(_:)` on the transition animator to position the animation at the current progress.

Give the transition a try right now, and you will see the table view blur progressively as you drag it down.

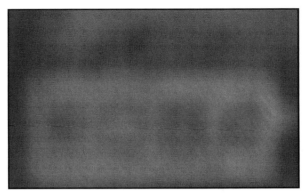

You also need to take care of completing and canceling the transition. Add to the same extension as before:

```
func scrollViewWillEndDragging(_ scrollView: UIScrollView,
withVelocity velocity: CGPoint, targetContentOffset:
UnsafeMutablePointer<CGPoint>) {
  let progress = max(0.0, min(1.0, ((-
scrollView.contentOffset.y) - 30) / 90.0))

  if progress > 0.5 {
    presentTransition.finish()
  } else {
    presentTransition.cancel()
  }

  isPresentingSettings = false
  isDragging = false
}
```

This code should look similar; it's the same approach you employed in Chapter 19, "Interactive UINavigationController Transitions". If the user has pulled through more than half of the distance (that you decided to be "far enough") you consider the transition successful and play the animation to the end. If the user hasn't dragged more than half the distance, you cancel the transition. Either way, you reset the values of the two flags and the interactive part of the transition is over.

The transition, however, is not complete just yet — there are few more things to polish before it's production ready.

Switch to **PresentTransition.swift** and find `transitionAnimator(using:)`. In the completion block, you ignore the parameter and always call `completeTransition(_:)` with the same value.

You can help UIKit by checking at which position the animator completed and provide the relevant value. Replace the existing call to `addCompletion(...)` with:

```
animator.addCompletion { position in
  switch position {
  case .end:
    transitionContext.completeTransition(!
transitionContext.transitionWasCancelled)
  default:
    transitionContext.completeTransition(false)
  }
}
```

Indeed the view controller transition has succeeded only if the animator completes at its `.end` position. Any other case means the transition has been canceled, so you can call `completeTransition(false)` directly.

Try wiggling the table up and down a bit, so the transition starts, but then cancels. Sooner or later you'll see something horrible like this:

This is an issue related to visual effect views. When setting the effect in an animation block, it doesn't seem to get removed properly if the animation is reversed or canceled, so you end up with a mess. Remember the `auxAnimationsCancel` property you added to `PresentTransition`? It's time to use it.

Find the call to `animator.addCompletion` and add this line after the `default:` case:

```
self.auxAnimationsCancel?()
```

If the animator doesn't finish, you'll run anything stored in that block. Switch back to **LockScreenViewController.swift** and find `presentSettings`. Right after you set the `auxAnimations` property, add this line:

```
presentTransition.auxAnimationsCancel = blurAnimations(false)
```

Build and run again and your pixellation wocs should have gone. But there's another problem. Think for a second about your non-interactive transition. Tap on Edit. Something is wrong!

You need to change your code to explicitly set the view controller transition to non-interactive whenever the user taps the button.

Switch back to **LockScreenViewController.swift** and find the widgets table data source method `tableView(_:cellForRowAt:)`. You will see that the code assigns a closure to the Edit button, like so:

```
cell.didPressEdit = {[unowned self] in
  self.presentSettings()
}
```

Just before the `self.presentSettings()` line, insert:

```
self.presentTransition.wantsInteractiveStart = false
```

This ensures that you are presenting the settings view controller non-interactively. Run the app another time and give the transition a try.

Interruptible transition animations

Next you are going to look into switching between non-interactive and interactive modes during the transition.

The integration of `UIViewPropertyAnimator` with view controller transitions aims to solve the issues around situations where the user starts the transition to another controller, but changes their mind mid-way.

In this part of the chapter, you will add code to start presenting the settings controller after a tap on Edit, but pause the transition if the user taps again on the screen during the animation.

Switch to **PresentTranstion.swift**. You will need to alter the animator a bit to handle not only interactive and non-interactive modes separately, but both in the same transition as well.

Add two more properties:

```
var context: UIViewControllerContextTransitioning?
var animator: UIViewPropertyAnimator?
```

You will use these to keep track of the current context of the transition along with the animator taking care of its animations.

Scroll down to transitionAnimator(using:), and towards the bottom just before the return animator line, insert the following:

```
self.animator = animator
self.context = transitionContext
```

Each time you create a new animator for a transition you will also store a reference to it.

It's also important to release those resources when the transition has finished. Add a new completion block just after the two lines you inserted previously:

```
animator.addCompletion { [unowned self] _ in
  self.animator = nil
  self.context = nil
}
```

Now you can add a method to the class to interrupt the transition:

```
func interruptTransition() {
  guard let context = context else {
    return
  }
  context.pauseInteractiveTransition()
  pause()
}
```

You call pauseInteractiveTransitioning() to pause the animator and additionally pause() on the transition animator to put it in interactive mode.

To allow touches during a non-interactive transition, you have to explicitly set the animator as able to handle user activity. Scroll back to transitionAnimator(using:) and insert this line towards the bottom:

```
animator.isUserInteractionEnabled = true
```

You make sure the transition animation is interactive so that the user can continue interacting with the screen after they've paused it.

You will allow the user to scroll either up or down to complete or cancel the transition respectively. To do that, switch back to **LockScreenViewController.swift** and add a new property:

```
var touchesStartPointY: CGFloat?
```

In case the user touches the screen during a transition, you pause it and store the location of that first touch:

```
override func touchesBegan(_ touches: Set<UITouch>,
  with event: UIEvent?) {
  guard presentTransition.wantsInteractiveStart == false,
    let _ = presentTransition.animator else {
    return
  }

  touchesStartPointY = touches.first!.location(in: view).y
  presentTransition.interruptTransition()
}
```

You check if the touch happened during a non-interactive transition and the transition's animator is currently running. In that case, you store the current touch location and then call your custom method `interruptTransition()`. This will pause the transition and leave it in an interactive mode.

Run the app, tap on Edit, and quickly tap again a second time. The transition will freeze onscreen like so:

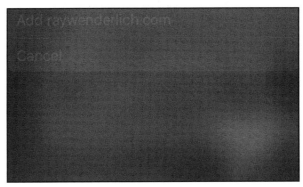

Now you need to track the user touches and see if the user pans up or down. Add the following:

```
override func touchesMoved(_ touches: Set<UITouch>,
  with event: UIEvent?) {
```

```
guard let startY = touchesStartPointY else {
  return
}

let currentPoint = touches.first!.location(in: view).y
if currentPoint < startY - 40 {
  touchesStartPointY = nil
  presentTransition.animator?.addCompletion {_ in
    self.blurView.effect = nil
  }
  presentTransition.cancel()
} else if currentPoint > startY + 40 {
  touchesStartPointY = nil
  presentTransition.finish()
}
}
```

With this rather big chunk of code, your non-interactive-turned-interactive transition is complete!

You observe for two different cases. First, if the user moves their touch downwards more than 40 points, you cancel the transition and reset the blur effect. If the user moved their touch upwards more than 40 points, you complete the transition successfully.

Give the app a try one last time. Tap on Edit, tap again to pause the transition, and either cancel or complete it depending on the direction you pan.

And that's all for this section of the book!

You've learned plenty about `UIViewPropertyAnimator` and how to make the best of it. You've worked through a rather lengthy four chapters but you achieved a lot, and the project looks amazing:

Section VI: 3D Animations

Up to this point in the book you've only worked with animations in two dimensions, and for good reason – this is the most natural way to animate elements on a flat device screen. After all, buttons, text fields, switches, and images in the flat post-iOS 7 world don't have a third dimension; these elements exist in a plane defined by X and Y axes:

Core Animation helps you float free from this two dimensional world; although it isn't a true 3D framework, Core Animation has a lot of smarts to help you position two-dimensional objects in 3D space.

In other words, your layers and animations still take place in two dimensions, but you can rotate and position each element's 2D plane in a 3D space like so:

Shown above are two 2D images that are rotated in 3D space. The perspective distortion gives you an idea of how they are positioned from the renderer's point of view.

This section of the book will show you how to position and rotate layers in 3D space. You'll work with a special property of CATransform3D: namely, the transformation class applied to layers. CATransform3D is similar to CGAffineTransform, but in addition to letting you scale, skew and translate in the x and y directions, it also brings in the third dimension: z. The z-axis runs straight out of the device screen towards your eyes.

CATransform3D lets you determine where the rendering camera is located respective to the device's screen; this affects the amount of perspective distortion Core Animation applies to your views.

Consider the following few examples to better understand how perspective works. If you stand very, very close to an object, such as right in front of a skyscraper, the object will take up most of your view and you'll see a lot of perspective as the lines of the skyscraper recede into the distance.

In a similar way, setting the camera very close to the screen distorts your layer's perspective accordingly:

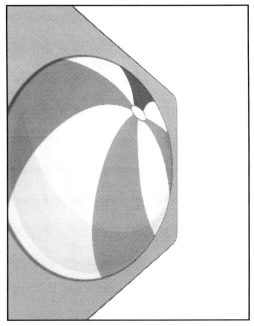

If you move the camera back from the object, there is less perspective distortion applied, just as you don't see as much perspective distortion when you view a skyscraper from a few blocks away.

Finally, if you set a great distance between the camera and the screen there won't be any noticeable perspective – just as you won't notice any perspective distortion on a skyscraper you view from across the city:

The image is still distorted, but notice how the top and bottom lines of the image frame are almost parallel. You're still looking at it at an angle, but the perspective distortion is very minor.

In the next two chapters you'll learn how to set up your layers in 3D space, how to choose the distance from the camera to your layer, and how to create animations in your 3D scene. With a bit of knowledge about perspective under your belt, the rest of this chapter should be a walk in a three-dimensional park! :]

Chapter 24, "Simple 3D Animations" — Try out your newfound knowledge about camera distance and perspective. Set up your layer's perspective, work on the layer's transform to rotate, translate and scale your layer in three dimensions.

Chapter 25, "Intermediate 3D Animations" — Building on the previous chapter, now that you know the secret of m34 and camera distance you can create all kinds of 3D animations with more than one view.

Chapter 24: Simple 3D Animations

In this chapter you'll get to try out your newfound knowledge about camera distance and perspective.

Once you set up your layer's perspective, you can work on the layer's transform as you usually would; but now you can rotate, translate and scale your layer in three dimensions.

The project for this chapter features a folding pull-out menu as popularized in many apps, such as Taasky:

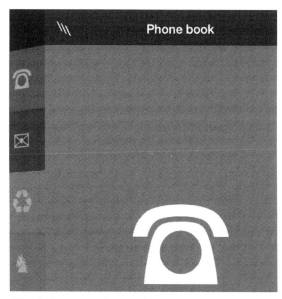

Office Buddy is an office helper app for employees to access categorized information about day-to-day company life.

The starter project already has all the code to make the menu functional, but it only works in 2D. Your task is to bring the menu into the third dimension and give it life!

Creating 3D transformations

Open the starter project for this chapter and build and run it to see what the initial version of the Office Buddy app looks like:

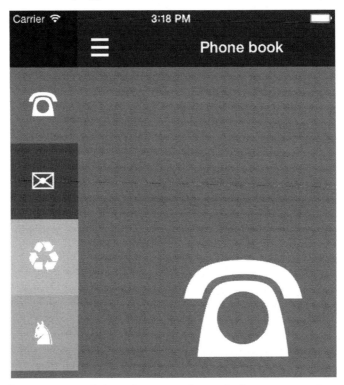

Tap the menu button to reveal the side menu; alternatively, you can swipe right to reveal the side menu.

As you can see, this app is as flat as they come. But armed with your new insight on 3D perspective, you're going to add some depth to the menu.

Open **ContainerViewController.swift**; this controller displays both the menu view controller and the content view controller on the screen. It also handles pan gestures so the user can open and close the menu.

Your first task is to build a class method that creates the corresponding 3D transform for a given percentage of "openness" of the side menu.

Add the following method declaration to **ContainerViewController.swift**:

```
func menuTransform(percent: CGFloat) -> CATransform3D {

}
```

The above method accepts a single parameter of the current progress of the menu, which was calculated by the code in `handleGesture(_:)`, and returns an instance of `CATransform3D`. You're going to assign the result of this method directly to the menu layer's transform property.

Add the following code to your new method:

```
var identity = CATransform3DIdentity
identity.m34 = -1.0/1000
```

This code might look a bit surprising; so far you've only used *functions* to create or modify transforms. This time, however, you're modifying one of the class' *properties*.

Note: Why is this property called m34? View and layer transforms are expressed as two-dimensional math matrices. In the case of a layer transform matrix, the element in the **3rd** row at the **4th** column sets your z-axis perspective. You can set this element directly to apply the desired perspective transform.

So you create a new `CATransform3D` struct and you set its m34 property to −1.0/1000...

Keep explaining, dude.

Okay, I'll back up a little. To enable 3D transforms on a layer you need to set `m34` to −1.0 / [camera distance]. Since you read through the introduction for this section, you have some understanding of how the camera distance affects the scene perspective.

But why are you using **1000** for the camera distance? The distance is expressed in points between the camera and the front of the scene. As to what value to use, the truth is that you need to try different values and see what looks good for your particular animation.

Working with camera distance

For UI elements in an average app you can consult the following reference table for some guidelines on an appropriate camera distance:

distance

- **0.1...500**: Very close, lots of perspective distortion.

- **750...2,000**: Nice perspective, content is clearly visible.

- **2,000** and up: Almost no perspective distortion.

For the Office Buddy app, a distance of **1000** points will give the menu a nice subtle perspective. You can see it in action once you finish working on the current method.

Add the following code to the bottom of `menuTransform(percent:)`:

```
let remainingPercent = 1.0 - percent
let angle = remainingPercent * .pi * -0.5
```

In the above code you calculate the current angle of the menu based on its "openness" value.

Now add the following code to the bottom of `menuTransform(percent:)`:

```
let rotationTransform = CATransform3DRotate(
  identity, angle, 0.0, 1.0, 0.0)

let translationTransform = CATransform3DMakeTranslation(
    menuWidth * percent, 0, 0)
return CATransform3DConcat(
  rotationTransform, translationTransform)
```

Here you use `rotationTransform` to rotate the layer away from you around its y-axis. The menu is moving in from the left, so you also create a translation transform to move it along the x-axis, eventually to `menuWidth` at **100%**. Finally, you concatenate the two transforms and return the result.

Now you can use `menuTransform(percent:)` to update the menu transform as the user pans right or left.

Remove the following line from setMenu(toPercent:) that modifies the menu's origin:

```
menuViewController.view.frame.origin.x =
    menuWidth * CGFloat(percent) - menuWidth
```

You don't need the above line anymore because you will move the menu via its transform. Add the following code to setMenu(toPercent:):

```
menuViewController.view.layer.transform =
    menuTransform(percent: percent)
```

Build and run your project; pan right to see how the menu rotates around its y-axis:

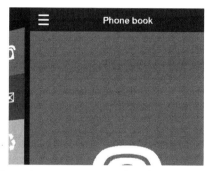

The menu rotates in 3D, but it's rotating around its horizontal center, which separates the menu from the content view controller.

Moving the layer's anchor point

By default, the anchor point of a layer has an x coordinate of 0.5, meaning it is in the center. You need to set the x of the anchor point to 1.0 to make the menu rotate around its right edge like a hinge, as shown below:

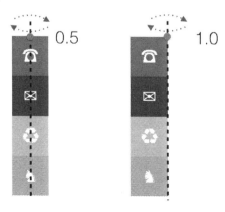

All transforms are calculated around the layer's anchor point. You also use the anchor point as your reference point when setting the position of the layer. This means it's best to change the layer's `anchorPoint` before you set its position on the screen.

Find the following line in `viewDidLoad()` where you set the menu frame:

```
menuViewController.view.frame = CGRect(
    x: -menuWidth, y: 0,
    width: menuWidth, height: view.frame.height)
```

Now insert the following code just **above** that line (it's important to insert the line before you set the view frame because otherwise setting the anchor point will offset the view — if you're curious to see the different give both ways a try):

```
menuViewController.view.layer.anchorPoint.x = 1.0
```

This rotates the menu around its right edge.

Build and run your project again, then pan horizontally through the view and observe how the effect has changed:

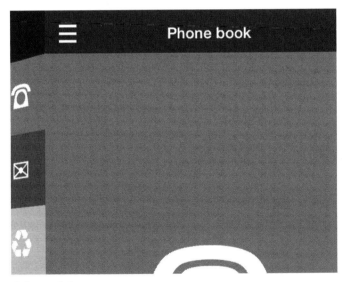

That looks much better! :]

You're almost done — there's just a few more bits to take care of.

Creating perspective through shading

Shading lends a lot of realism to 3D animations; to that end, you will rotate the menu out of the "shadow" of the left side of the content view controller.

You're not using any advanced shading techniques here; instead, you can simulate this by changing the alpha of the menu as it rotates.

Add the following code to `setMenu(toPercent:)`:

```
menuViewController.view.alpha = CGFloat(max(0.2, percent))
```

In the code above, you assign the percent value directly to the layer's alpha, but you limit it to `0.2` to ensure the menu remains visible when it's edge-on to the user and doesn't disappear completely.

Since the background of this app is black, lowering the alpha of the menu view makes the black color show through the menu and simulates a shadow effect.

Build and run your project and observe the effect:

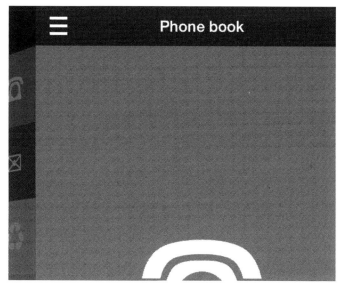

It's a small detail, but it really makes your 3D animation "pop"! :]

You might have noticed that when you tap the menu button the first time, the animation does not play in 3D. The effect only kicks in on the second and subsequent animations.

That's because you're not setting the 3D animation parameters and the layer transforms until *after* the first time you toggle the menu. This is easy to fix: As soon as the menu view controller loads, set the menu progress to 0.0 to set the proper menu layer transform.

Add the following to the bottom of `viewDidLoad()`:

```
setMenu(toPercent: 0.0)
```

This will get the starting frames and layer transforms in place from the start. Build and run your project again; tap the menu button and you'll see that the animation works properly the first time through.

Rasterizing for efficiency

There's one last task to make your animation "perfect". If you starc at the menu long enough while you pan back and forth you'll notice the borders of the menu items look pixelated, as shown below:

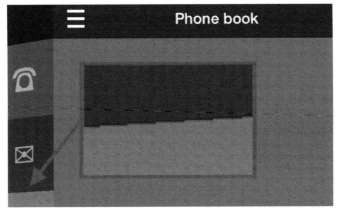

Core Animation continually redraws all contents of the menu view controller and recalculates the perspective distortion for all elements as it moves, which isn't terribly efficient — hence the jagged edges.

It's better to let Core Animation know that you won't change the menu contents during the animation so that it can render the menu once and simply rotate the rendered and cached image.

That sounds complicated at first, but you'll see it's quite easy to implement. Scroll to `handleGesture()` and find the `.began` case block; this code executes when the user starts the pan action. This is where you'll instruct Core Animation to cache the menu.

Add the following code to the end of the `.began` case block:

```
// Improve the look of the opening menu
menuViewController.view.layer.shouldRasterize = true
menuViewController.view.layer.rasterizationScale =
  UIScreen.main.scale
```

`shouldRasterize` instructs Core Animation to cache the layer contents as an image. You then set `rasterizationScale` to match the current screen scale and you're golden!

Build and run your project again to see how your graphics have improved:

Core Animation really shines in this instance. Working with 2D images is one of the things this framework really does well! :]

To avoid any unnecessary caching while using the app, you should turn off rasterization as soon as the animation is done.

Find the empty animation completion closure inside the `.failed` case and add the following code:

```
self.menuViewController.view.layer.shouldRasterize = false
```

Now you're only activating rasterization during the animation. How efficient of you!

In only a few pages, you learned about camera distance, perspective, and how to set up your 3D scene and apply animations to it.

There's one more chapter in this section, which contains some more 3D fun — but before you go, take a look at this chapter's challenge first.

Challenges

Challenge 1: Create your own 3D animation

For this challenge you are going to create a 3D rotation animation for the menu button. As the user pans the button will rotate alongside the menu view controller.

Specifically, you will create a rotation around both the x- and y-axes to make the menu button flip on its diagonal.

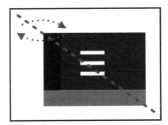

Add the following code to setToPercent() in **ContainerViewController.swift**:

```
let centerVC = centerViewController.viewControllers.first as?
CenterViewController
```

This fetches the current content view controller so you can work with it.

The menu button is accessible via the menuButton property of CenterViewController. For this challenge, adjust the 3D transform of the button's imageView.

If you directly rotate the button rather than use the 3D transform, it will clash with the navigation bar views underneath and might get partially obscured by the navigation bar.

In contrast, the button's own 2D space is already positioned on top of all navigation bar views before you rotate it — so if you rotate menuButton.imageView, it rotates within the button's own plane, which is on top of the navigation bar at all times.

Another gotcha is that the first time the code runs menuButton will be nil, so you should treat it like an optional, even though it is implicitly unwrapped.

For the rotation, create a transform just like you did earlier in this chapter, but this time rotate the view around the x- and y-axes. If necessary, have a look at the documentation for CATransform3DRotate().

This time you don't need to calculate the remaining percentage; to get the rotation angle, simply multiply the progress by .pi.

When you are finished with your solution the button image should flip around while you pan through the screen like so:

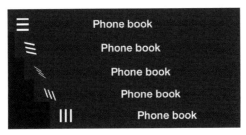

That's it! Head on in to the next chapter for more awesome animations in 3D!

Chapter 25: Intermediate 3D animations

In the previous chapter, you learned that applying perspective to a single view isn't a complicated task; in fact, once you know the secret of m34 and camera distance you can create all kinds of 3D animations.

This chapter builds on what you've already learned and shows you how to create convincing 3D animations with more than one view.

The starter project for this chapter is a simple hurricane image gallery. By the end of this chapter, you'll have a 3D effect to get an overall view of the images in the gallery:

You'll be able to tap on a photo to bring it full screen, and tapping the top right button fans all the images open again — with a cool animation to take you between the two states, of course!

Ready to get started? Hang on to your hat and prepare to get blown away by this "stormy" project ! :]

Exploring the starter project

Open the starter project from the Resources folder for this chapter; build and run it to see what you have to start with:

All you have is a blank screen with two bar buttons on top: the left one shows the NASA image credits and the right one invokes the method that shows or hides the gallery as appropriate.

First, you'll need to display all images on the screen and set them up so they're ready for your "fan" animation.

Open **ViewController.swift** and inspect the class code. You'll see an array called `images`; this array contains some slightly customized image views. The `ImageViewCard` class inherits from `UIImageView` and adds a string property `title` to hold the hurricane title, and a property called `didSelect` so you can easily set a tap handler on the image.

Your first task is to add all images to the view controller's view. Add the following code to the end of `viewDidAppear(_:)`:

```
for image in images {
  image.layer.anchorPoint.y = 0.0
  image.frame = view.bounds

  view.addSubview(image)
}
```

In the code above, you loop over all images, set each image's anchor point to `0.0` on the y-axis and resize each image so it takes up the full screen. When that's done, you add each image to view.

Setting the anchor point lets the images rotate around their upper edge rather than the default of the center, as illustrated below:

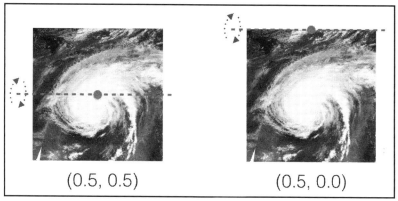

(0.5, 0.5)   (0.5, 0.0)

This will make it a lot easier to fan out the images in 3D space.

Build and run your project to see what you've achieved so far:

Hmm — you only see the last image you added to view. That's because all images have the same frame, so you only see the last image you added: Hurricane Irene.

To make it more obvious which hurricane image is being displayed, add the following line at the end of `viewDidAppear(_:)`:

```
navigationItem.title = images.last?.title
```

This code takes the name of the last hurricane image in the collection and sets it as the navigation title of the view controller, like so.

Build and run again to familiarize yourself with Irene:

Notice that you didn't set any perspective transforms on the images; you're going to set a perspective directly on the view controller's view instead.

In the previous chapter you adjusted the transform property on a single view and then rotated it in 3D space. But since your current project has more individual views that you'd care to manipulate in 3D, you can set the perspective of their parent view instead to save yourself a bunch of work.

Add the following code to `viewDidAppear(_:)`:

```
var perspective = CATransform3DIdentity
perspective.m34 = -1.0/250.0
view.layer.sublayerTransform = perspective
```

Here you use the layer property `sublayerTransform` to set the perspective of all sublayers of the view controller's layer. The sublayer `transform` is then combined with each individual layer's own `transform`.

This lets you focus on managing the rotation or translation of your subviews without having to worry about perspective. You'll see how this works in more detail in the next section.

Transforming the gallery

`toggleGallery(_:)` is hooked up to the Browse bar button on the right and is where you'll apply your 3D transform to the four images.

Add the following variable to `toggleGallery(_:)`:

```
var imageYOffset: CGFloat = 50.0
```

Since you don't just rotate all images in place but simply move them around to produce the "fan" animation, you use `imageYOffset` to set the offset of each image.

Next you need to iterate through all the images and run their individual animations.

Add the following code to `toggleGallery(_:)`:

```
for subview in view.subviews {
  guard let image = subview as? ImageViewCard else {
    continue
  }

  // more code here
}
```

Here you loop through all subviews of the view controller's view and act only on the subviews that are instances of `ImageViewCard`.

Add the following code inside the if block you added above, to replace the `more code here` comment:

```
var imageTransform = CATransform3DIdentity

//1
imageTransform = CATransform3DTranslate(
  imageTransform, 0.0, imageYOffset, 0.0)

//2
imageTransform = CATransform3DScale(
  imageTransform, 0.95, 0.6, 1.0)
```

```
//3
imageTransform = CATransform3DRotate(
  imageTransform, CGFloat(M_PI_4/2), -1.0, 0.0, 0.0)
```

You start by assigning the identity transform to `imageTransform` and then add a series of adjustments to it. This is what each individual adjustment does to the image:

1. Move the image on the y-axis with CATransform3DTranslate; this offsets the image from its default 0.0 y-coordinate as shown below:

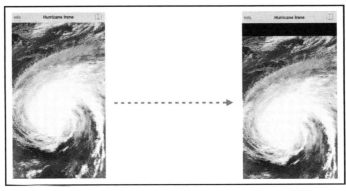

Later, you'll calculate the `imageYOffset` of each image separately; for now all images move by the same amount so you'll still see only the top one for the moment.

2. Scale the image by adjusting the scale component of the transform using `CATransform3DScale`. You shrink the image just a little on the x-axis, but you scale it down to **60%** on the y-axis to enrich the rotation 3D effect:

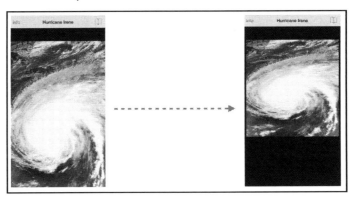

3. Finally you use `CATransform3DRotate` to rotate the image by `22.5` degrees to give it some perspective distortion as shown below:

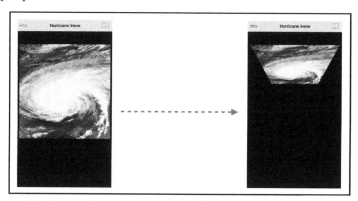

Remember, you already set the anchor point so the image rotates around its top edge.

Now you see the value of setting the `m34` value above via `view.layer.sublayerTransform`; your rotation transform simply re-uses the `m34` value from the sublayer transform, without the need to apply it here. That's handy!

Now all that's left is to apply the transform to each image. Add the following line to the end of the `if` block:

```
image.layer.transform = imageTransform
```

Build and run your project; tap the Browse button to see the result of your transforms:

Again, you only see the top image as all other images behind it have the same transform applied. Now is a perfect opportunity to customize the transform for each image.

Add the following line to the end of the `if` block:

```
imageYOffset += view.frame.height / CGFloat(images.count)
```

This adjusts the y-offset of each image depending on where it is in the stack. You divide the screen height over the number of images so they distribute themselves evenly over the screen.

Build and run your project to see your views fan out:

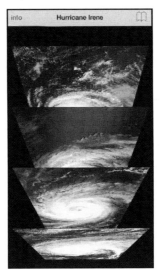

Sweet — the gallery looks just as you intended! But as this is a book about animations, it would be a shame if you didn't animate the transition to the fanned-out view, wouldn't it? :]

Animating the gallery

Find the following line in `toggleGallery(_:)` where you set `transform` on each image:

```
image.layer.transform = imageTransform
```

Insert the following code **above that line** to animate transform:

```
let animation = CABasicAnimation(keyPath: "transform")
animation.fromValue = NSValue(caTransform3D:
  image.layer.transform)
animation.toValue = NSValue(caTransform3D: imageTransform)
```

```
animation.duration = 0.33
image.layer.add(animation, forKey: nil)
```

This code is definitely familiar: You create a layer animation on the transform property and animate it from its current value to the imageTransform you designed earlier.

Build and run your project once more; tap the Browse button and enjoy your completed animation:

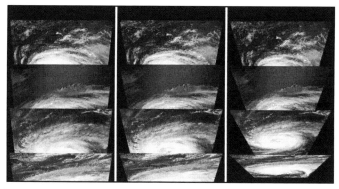

You're finished with the gallery for now; you'll revisit it in the Challenges section when you add the ability to close the fan when the user taps the Browse button.

Bringing an image to the front

In this final section, you'll add a bit of interactivity to the image gallery: tapping an image will make it jump in front of the other images so that the user can get a better look at it.

ImageViewCard already features a closure expression property named didSelect; this fires when the user taps on the image and receives the tapped image view as an input parameter.

To add this feature, you'll add a method to ViewController and assign it to didSelect on all the image views.

First add the following code to viewDidAppear(), inside the for loop body:

```
image.didSelect = selectImage
```

Xcode will complain that selectImage doesn't exist, but you'll fix this in the next step.

Add the following method to `ViewController`:

```
func selectImage(selectedImage: ImageViewCard) {

  for subview in view.subviews {
    guard let image = subview as? ImageViewCard else {
      continue
    }
    if image === selectedImage {
      //selected image
    } else {
      //any other image
    }
  }
}
```

This is the skeleton of `selectImage(selectedImage:)`; when the user taps one of the images, you loop over all subviews and get the `ImageViewCard` instances just like you did earlier. Then you check each `ImageViewCard` to see if it's the selected image.

Now you need two more animations: one to animate the selected image, and another to animate all the other images in the gallery.

You'll tackle this in reverse and fade out the unselected images first.

Replace the `//any other image` comment in `selectImage(selectedImage:)` with the following code:

```
UIView.animate(withDuration: 0.33, delay: 0.0,
  options: .curveEaseIn,
  animations: {
    image.alpha = 0.0
  },
  completion: {_ in
    image.alpha = 1.0
    image.layer.transform = CATransform3DIdentity
  }
)
```

This is a simple animation to fade out each image. In the completion block, you reset its transform to the identity transform and alpha to fully opaque. By the time the above animation is done, the selected image will be in front of all others — so transparent or not, you won't see any of the unselected images. Resetting `alpha` here saves you from having to remember to reset it when you want to see the image again.

Build and run your project; open the gallery and tap on an image to see all the other unselected images fade from view.

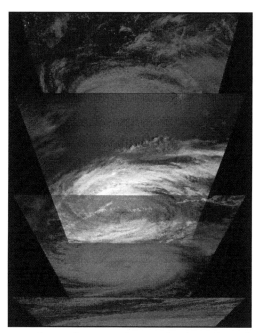

When that animation completes, the view changes back to show the top image at full-screen — because you haven't done anything with the selected image! You'll fix that now.

You'll animate the selected image's `transform` back to the identity transform and pull the image to the front when the animation completes.

Replace the `//selected image` comment in `selectImage(selectedImage:)` with the following code:

```
UIView.animate(withDuration: 0.33, delay: 0.0,
  options: .curveEaseIn,
  animations: {
    image.layer.transform = CATransform3DIdentity
  },
  completion: {_ in
    self.view.bringSubview(toFront: image)
  }
)
```

Here, you're un-doing the 3D transform for the animation, and then ensuring the image is at the top of the view stack at the end so it's visible.

Finally, add the following code to the end of `selectImage(selectedImage:)`:

```
self.navigationItem.title = selectedImage.title
```

This will update the navigation bar with the currently selected image title.

Build and run your project; tap the various images to see how they zoom to full screen. How does it look?

I *thought* you'd enjoy this classy little animation! :] That's a wrap; there's one small bit of functionality to clean up in the Challenge section below, but other than that, you have a really stunning animation at your fingertips. I suspect you can think of many ways to use it in your own projects!

Challenges

Challenge 1: Toggle the gallery with the Browse button

Right now the user must choose an image from the gallery once they open it. In this challenge, you'll make the Browse button work like a toggle to close the gallery view as well.

Add a new property to `ViewController` named `isGalleryOpen` and set its initial value to `false`. You need to update the value of this property in couple of places in the code:

• Set it to true at the end of `toggleGallery(_:)`

• Set it to false at the end of `selectImage(selectedImage:)`

At the top of `toggleGallery()`, add a check to see if the gallery is already open. If so, loop over all images and animate their `transform` back to its original value. Don't forget to reset `isGalleryOpen` and return so the rest of the method code doesn't execute as well.

That's it — if you like, play around with the animations in this project and see what other flashy elements you can add on your own!

Section VII: Further Types of Animations

In the first four sections of this book, you learned about the core APIs and classes behind iOS animations.

There are two more specialized topics that don't fit in with any the previous sections, so you get a bit of a breather from keyframes and 3D animations!

Chapter 26, "Particle Emitters" will show you how to create particle emitters and create the following snowfall effect:

Core Animation includes a particle , which you'll use to generate a virtual blizzard full of unique snowflakes that have their own lifespan, color tint and direction.

Chapter 27, "Frame Animations with UIImageView" will walk you through sequencing multiple images together into a flipbook-style animation like so:

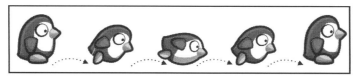

By combining frame animation with traditional view animations, you can create a cartoon-like effect with good old `UIImageView` and make the first steps to creating a game in UIKit.

These two chapters are the dessert after a multi-course meal of view and layer animations! :]

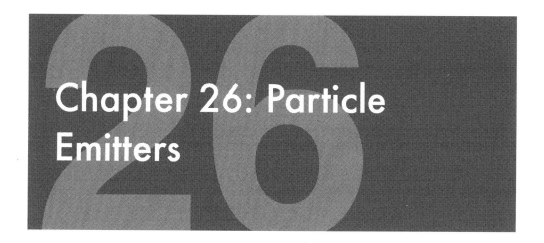

Chapter 26: Particle Emitters

Simulated fiery explosions, driving rain and choking smoke make us *ooh* and *aah* at the action on the big screen. In this chapter, you'll become a one-person Special Effects Team as you bring your own effects to the "small screen" and learn how to create your own special effects using particle emitters.

Waterfall, fire, smoke and rain effects all involve a large number of visual items — particles — that share common physical characteristics but may still have their own unique size, orientation, spin and trajectory.

Particles work really well to create realistic effects, as each particle can be random and unpredictable, just as objects are in nature. For example, each raindrop in a thunderstorm may have a unique size, shape, and velocity.

Here are just a few examples of the visual effects you can achieve with particle emitters:

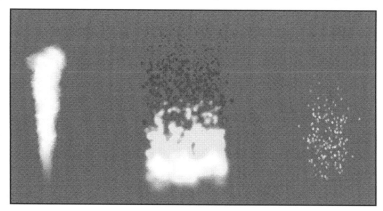

You'll revisit one of the earlier projects in this book – the Bahama Air flight info – and recreate the snow effect from Chapter 4, "View Animations in Practice" using particle emitters.

You'll learn how particle systems work as you experiment with different emitter properties and observe the effect they have on the resulting animation.

By the time you're done you'll be putting on your hat and gloves after seeing your particle emitter snow effect as shown below:

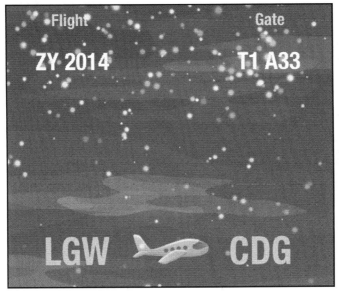

This chapter will be a lot of fun; read on to get started!

Creating your emitter layer

Although by this point in the book you've covered a lot of animation topics, there's a layer class for creating animations that you haven't seen yet: CAEmitterLayer. You can use this class to create particle effects natively in Core Animation.

> **Note**: There are a number of third-party classes for creating particle effects, but they're usually targeted towards integration with game frameworks. For particle animations in your UIKit apps, CAEmitterLayer is a great choice since it's built in and simple to use.

Open the starter project and run the app to see what you've been given to start with:

There's your London-Paris flight information screen with a gloomy weather background. The flight information on this version of the screen doesn't change; this way, you can focus on the snow effect alone.

Open **ViewController.swift** and add the following code to the bottom of `viewDidLoad()`:

```
let rect = CGRect(x: 0.0, y: 100.0,
   width: view.bounds.width, height: 50.0)
let emitter = CAEmitterLayer()
emitter.frame = rect
view.layer.addSublayer(emitter)
```

This code creates a new `CAEmitterLayer`, sets the layers' frame to take up the full width of the screen and positions the layer near the top of the screen.

Next you need to set the type of emitter to use with your particle effect.

Add the following code to `viewDidLoad()`:

```
emitter.emitterShape = kCAEmitterLayerRectangle
```

The shape of your emitter generally affects the area where new particles are being created, but it also can affect their z-position in situations where you're creating 3D-like particle systems.

Here's a look at the three simplest emitter shapes:

Point shape

An emitter shape of `kCAEmitterLayerPoint` causes all particles to be created at the same point: the emitter's position. This is a good choice for effects that involve sparks or fireworks.

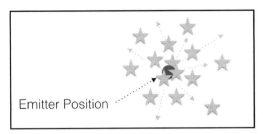

As an example, you could create a spark effect by creating all particles at the same point and making them fly in different directions before they disappear.

Line shape

An emitter shape of `kCAEmitterLayerLine` creates all particles along the top of the emitter frame.

This is an emitter shape useful for waterfall effects; the water particles appear at the top edge of the waterfall and cascade down like so:

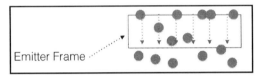

Rectangle shape

Finally, an emitter shape of `kCAEmitterLayerRectangle` creates particles randomly through a given rectangular area:

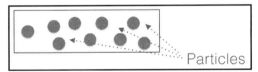

This emitter shape is great for many different effects, including bubbles in a carbonated drink and popping popcorn.

Since snow appears randomly from the whole sky, the rectangle emitter shape is a good choice for your project.

> **Note:** There are a few more emitter shapes — cuboid, circle and sphere — but these are out of the scope of this chapter. Check out the *CAEmitterLayer Class Reference* in Apple's documentation for more information.

Adding an emitter frame

Add the following code to the end of `viewDidLoad()`:

```
emitter.emitterPosition = CGPoint(x: rect.width/2,
    y: rect.height/2)
emitter.emitterSize = rect.size
```

Combining the shape, position and size properties defines the emitter frame. Here you set the position of the emitter to the center of the layer and set the emitter size equal to the size of the layer.

This means the emitter takes up the entire layer frame like so:

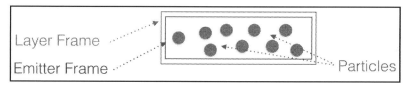

Creating an emitter cell

Now that you have configured the location and size of the emitter, you can move on to adding an **emitter cell**.

An emitter cell is the data model representing one source of particles. It's a separate class from `CAEmitterLayer` because a single emitter layer can contain one or more cells.

For example, in a popcorn animation you can have three different cells that represent the different states of a popcorn kernel: fully popped, half popped and those stubborn unpopped kernels:

In this chapter you will use only one emitter cell; you'll have an opportunity to work with multiple cells in the Challenges section of this tutorial.

Add the following code to the bottom of `viewDidLoad()`:

```
let emitterCell = CAEmitterCell()
emitterCell.contents = UIImage(named: "flake.png")?.cgImage
```

In the code above, you create a new cell and set **flake.png** as its contents. The contents property holds the template from which new particles will be created.

Below is a scaled up flake.png screenshot on a dark background:

Your emitter will create multiple varying copies of this image to mimic real snowflakes.

Add the following code to the bottom of `viewDidLoad()`:

```
emitterCell.birthRate = 20
emitterCell.lifetime = 3.5
emitter.emitterCells = [emitterCell]
```

The above code instructs your cell to create **20** snowflakes every second and keep them on the screen for **3.5** seconds. This means there will be **70** snowflakes on the screen at any given time, except for the first few seconds of the animation before the oldest particles start to disappear.

Finally, you set the `emitterCells` property with an array of all your emitter cells. Remember, you can have multiple emitter cells but you're starting with one so the array has as a single value. The emitter will begin to create particles as soon as you set the list of emitter cells.

Build and run your app; check out the pseudo-snowflake effect you have so far:

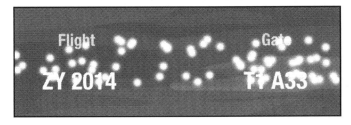

Multiple copies of flake.png show up and disappear after 3.5 seconds. However, the snow is oddly static – it's not falling anywhere. Do you have the development chops to turn this into a believable snow scene?

Great! Time to investigate some more properties of CAEmitterCell.

Controlling your particles

At this point in the chapter the snow particles appear, float in space for a few seconds, then disappear. That's incredibly boring — even for a particle with a lifespan of 3.5 seconds! Your next task is to give these aimless particles some direction in their lives.

Changing particle direction

Add the following code to the bottom of viewDidLoad():

```
emitterCell.yAcceleration = 70.0
```

This will add a little acceleration in the y-direction so the particles will drift downwards like real snow.

Build and run your project to see the effect:

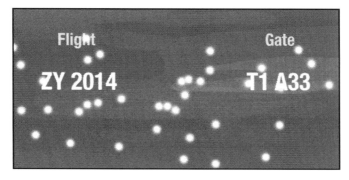

That looks a little more like snow — but snow seldom falls straight down.

To fix this, add the following bit of horizontal acceleration to your particles:

```
emitterCell.xAcceleration = 10.0
```

Build and run your project again; the snowflakes should be moving in a downward diagonal direction:

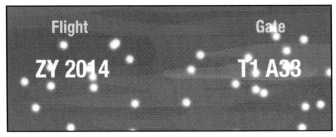

To create a gentle falling effect, you'll shoot the particles straight up and let the yAcceleration pull them down.

Add the following code:

```
emitterCell.velocity = 20.0
emitterCell.emissionLongitude = .pi * -0.5
```

The emission longitude is the initial angle of the particles, and the velocity parameter sets the initial speed of the particle like so:

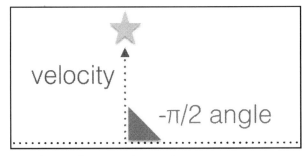

Build and run your project again to see the result:

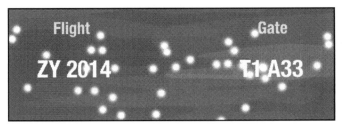

Your animation looks better and better with each change. But these particles look like snowflake-sized kill-bots moving in mechanical unison. This is because each particle has the exact same initial angle, velocity, and acceleration. You need to add some randomness to the particle creation process.

Adding randomness to your particles

Add the following code to `viewDidLoad()`:

```
emitterCell.velocityRange = 200.0
```

This tells the emitter what the randomized range of values should be. Since random ranges for particle animations are used frequently throughout this chapter, it's worth taking a bit of time to explain how they work.

All of your particles have the same initial velocity of 20; adding a velocity range assigns a random velocity to each particle as illustrated below:

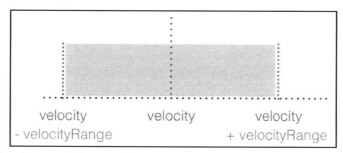

Each particle's velocity will be a random value between (`20–200`) = `–180` and (`20+200`) = `220`. The particles with negative initial velocity will not fly up at all; they'll start floating down as soon as they appear on the screen. The particles with positive velocity will fly up first, then float down.

Build and run your project to see what your changes have wrought:

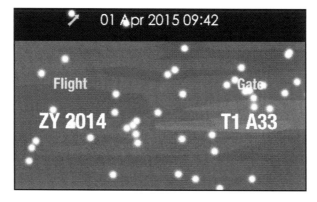

Okay, things are definitely random: some snowflakes jump as high as the top edge of the screen, while others appear, hang around for a moment, and fall down.

The initial particle direction is the next thing to randomize.

Add the following code to `viewDidLoad()`:

```
emitterCell.emissionRange = .pi * 0.5
```

Originally, you configured all particles to shoot straight up (at a −π/2 angle) as they appear. The above line of code instructs the emitter to pick a random angle for each particle within the range of (−π/2 − π/2) = 180 degrees and (−π/2 + π/2) = 0 degrees as illustrated below:

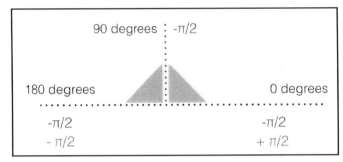

The particles will end up moving up from the x-axis in different angles rather than straight up.

Run the project again to see how the animation has changed:

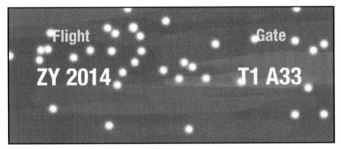

Now THAT's random! :] Your virtual snowstorm has really come to life.

Changing particle color

One of the handy features of `CAEmitterLayer` is the ability to set a tint color for your particles. For example, you could tint your snowflakes light blue instead of stark white, as the color blue is often associated with rain, water, snow or ice.

Add the following code to the bottom of `viewDidLoad()`:

```
emitterCell.color = UIColor(red: 0.9, green: 1.0, blue: 1.0,
alpha: 1.0).cgColor
```

Build and run your project to see the tint effect on your particles:

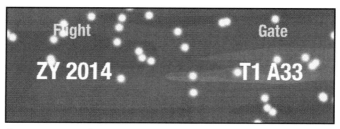

The change looks interesting, but all the snowflakes are a uniform shade of blue. Wouldn't it be great if you could randomize the color of each snowflake?

You can! All you need to do is define three separate ranges for your particle color: one each for the red, green, and blue color components.

Add the following code to the end of `viewDidLoad()`:

```
emitterCell.redRange   = 0.3
emitterCell.greenRange = 0.3
emitterCell.blueRange  = 0.3
```

This code defines the following range for each color value:

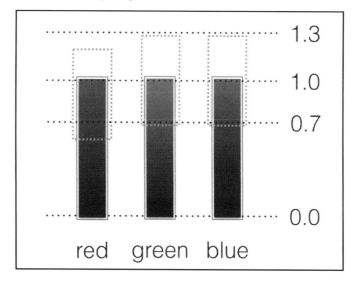

Green and blue component values will now be a random value between 0.7 and 1.3; however, values higher than 1.0 are capped at 1.0 so the effective range is 0.7 to 1.0. The red component will be capped between 0.6 and 1.0 since its "normal" value is 0.9. These are relatively narrow ranges so the resulting random color will still be quite light.

Build and run your project to see the result of your snowflake dye-job:

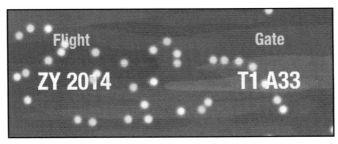

Um, well, this *is* random. Is it just me, or does it look like it's raining candy sprinkles? :]

You can experiment with the various ranges on each individual color component to bias your color towards a particular tint if you like. For now, just replace the code you added above with the following:

```
emitterCell.redRange   = 0.1
emitterCell.greenRange = 0.1
emitterCell.blueRange  = 0.1
```

Build and run to see a much more subtle color variation:

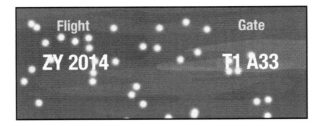

Randomizing particle appearance

Even after all the customization you've added, the snowflakes still look relatively uniform. In this section of the chapter you'll make each of your particles a beautiful and unique snowflake — and that starts with assigning a random size to each snowflake.

Add the following code to `viewDidLoad()`:

```
emitterCell.scale = 0.8
emitterCell.scaleRange = 0.8
```

Here you set the base particle size as 80% of the original size, then you assign a wide range for the random size:

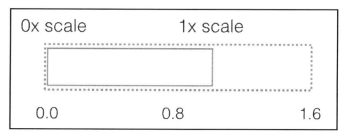

This produces big fluffy snowflakes `1.6` times the original size, all the way down to microscopic flakes with zero size that disappear as soon as you create them.

Build and run your project to see your new snowflake sizes in action:

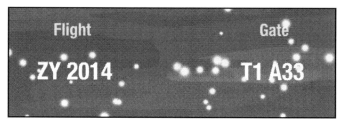

Not only can you set the initial size of your snowflakes, but you can also modify the size of the snowflake as it falls. Perhaps it's melting in the warm foggy air as it nears the ground? :]

Add the following line to `viewDidLoad()`:

```
emitterCell.scaleSpeed = −0.15
```

The `scaleSpeed` property above instructs your particles to scale down by 15% of their original size per second.

Big particles will shrink substantially before they disappear from sight, while small particles will completely disappear before the end of their lives. Don't feel bad, it's just the snowflake circle of life.

Build and run your project to see how your snowflakes melt as they fall:

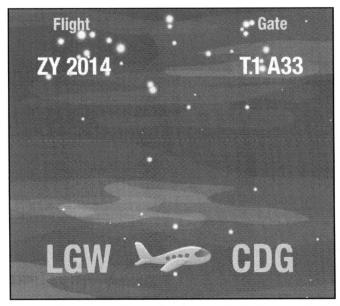

The snowflakes get smaller and smaller as they approach the bottom half of the screen. That's a neat effect — but now the bottom half of the screen looks a bit empty. I've got a fever, and the only prescription is...more snowflakes! :]

Find the line where you set emitterCell.birthRate and replace the value with 150 like so:

```
emitterCell.birthRate = 150
```

Build and run to see your blizzard take shape:

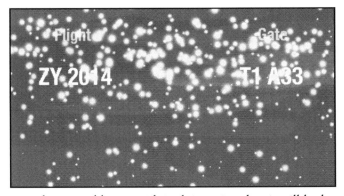

Your animation gets better and better with each iteration, but it still looks a little flat. You can add a lot of depth to the scene by randomizing the alpha value of each snowflake.

Add the following to the bottom of `viewDidLoad()`:

```
emitterCell.alphaRange = 0.75
emitterCell.alphaSpeed = -0.15
```

You set a wide alpha range, from `0.25` to a capped value of `1.0`. `alphaSpeed` works much like `scaleSpeed` to change the alpha of the particle over time.

Build and run your project again to see the depth effect that a simple alpha animation lends to your snowfall:

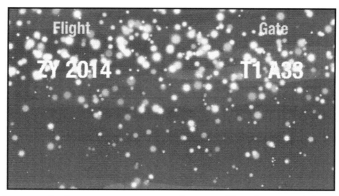

You've covered most of what `CAEmitterCell` has to offer; the rest of this chapter is about adding polish to your animation.

Adding some final polish

Find the line in `viewDidLoad()` that sets emissionLongitude and change it to the following:

```
emitterCell.emissionLongitude = -.pi
```

Remember, the emission longitude is the starter angle for the particles. This change will make the snowflakes swirl a bit as if pushed around by the wind.

Next, find the line in `viewDidLoad()` that declares `rect` and **modify it** as follows:

```
let rect = CGRect(x: 0.0, y: -70.0, width: view.bounds.width,
height: 50.0)
```

This moves the emitter off-screen so the user doesn't see where the particles come from.

Finally, add the following bit of code to `viewDidLoad()` to randomize the length of time that a snowflake remains on the screen:

```
emitterCell.lifetimeRange = 1.0
```

This sets each snowflake's lifetime to a random value between `2.5` and `4.5` seconds.

Build and run the app to see these final bits of polish in effect.

Although this chapter was pretty heavy on the snow effect, each concept is completely applicable to other particle systems. Every particle implementation I've seen so far has worked in a similar fashion. You always have a set of features to configure per particle, and the emitter randomizes the system as it creates large amounts of copies of the original particle.

If you worked through this chapter, then you're in good shape to start exploring *any* particle system, whether it's in SpriteKit, Unity, or any other custom particle emitter class.

Once you understand how particle systems work, it's a ton of fun to design and implement particle effects! To that end, work through the following challenge where you can customize your snowfall effect.

Challenges

Challenge 1: Add more cells to the emitter layer

This challenge is more free-form than most; your task is to add one or more cells to the emitter you just developed.

The starter project includes a number of snowflakes to choose from for your challenge cells: flake1.png, flake2.png, flake3.png and flake4.png.

Before you add more cells to the emitter, consider the effect of overcrowding on the screen. The one existing cell emits `150` snowflakes per second, which results in a dense snowfall. If you add two more cells to your emitter, you'll want to throttle back each emitter to about `50` particles per second to maintain approximately the same density of snowflakes in your system.

Play around with the properties of each cell: make some flakes swirl around, while others fall quickly to the ground. The snowflake shape flake2.png isn't symmetrical so try to set its cell's spin and spinRange properties to make those particles spin around as if blown by the wind.

There's no right or wrong solution to this challenge; simply stop playing with the effect when you're satisfied. I've included one of my favorite solutions with this chapter, which you can have a look at once you're done changing your particle system:

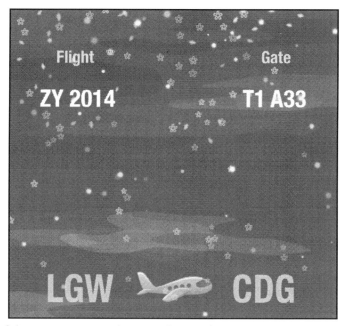

In the spirit of the snowy season, the next chapter showcases some creatures who would fully appreciate your snowfall effect: penguins!

Chapter 27: Frame Animations with UIImageView

It's finally time to learn how to create a very special type of animation. **Frame animation** is the type of animation you enjoyed as a kid and probably still adore today; it's the way Disney's *Duck Tales*, Hanna-Barbera's *Tom and Jerry* and *The Flintstones* cartoons were created.

This is also the kind of animation you use to animate characters in your games. It's not enough to simply translate your static game characters from one location to another. you need to move a character's feet or spin the aircraft's propeller to give a realistic sense of motion.

To create the effect of character movement, you break the animation into **frames**, which are still images that represent stages of the action. When you display the frames quickly, one after the other, it will look like your character is moving:

The project in this chapter is set at the South Pole and the player gets to control Pengui, the penguin. You will start with a static scene and work through the chapter to make Pengui walk and slide around his world.

Project basics

Open the starter project for this chapter and select **Main.storyboard** to see the initial game scene:

The penguin and buttons are all connected to the code in **ViewController.swift**, but nothing happens at the moment if you tap them. Open **ViewController.swift** and take a look at the guts of the code.

You'll see two outlets: one for the penguin image view (`penguin`) and one for the slide button (`slideButton`). You also have two properties, `walkFrames` and `slideFrames`, which contain the `UIImage` frames of the walking and sliding animations respectively.

The HUD buttons on the left side of the screen are connected to `actionLeft(_:)` and `actionRight(_:)`; you'll add some animation code to these two methods to make the penguin walk.

The HUD button on the right hand side of the screen is connected to `actionSlide(_:)`, where you'll add some code to make the penguin jump and slide on the ice.

Open **Images.xcassets** and browse through the frame images to see the individual frames of walking and sliding animations like so:

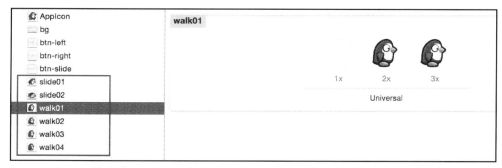

You need to walk before you can run — and in this game, your penguin needs to walk before he can slide! :] Your first task is to make the penguin walk when the player taps the HUD buttons.

Setting up your frame animation

Add the following code to the `loadWalkAnimation()` stub in **ViewController.swift**:

```
penguin.animationImages = walkFrames
penguin.animationDuration = animationDuration / 3
penguin.animationRepeatCount = 3
```

This code sets a number of properties on `UIImageView` that you might have not seen before. Here's what each of them does in turn:

1. `animationImages`: This stores all the frame images of your frame animation. `walkFrames` is declared earlier in the code as an array containing `UIImage` objects, so here you just need to assign it to `penguin.animationImages` to set up the animation frames.

2. `animationDuration`: This tells UIKit how long one iteration of the animation should last; since you will have the animation repeat three times (see below), you set this to one-third of the length of the total `animationDuration`.

3. `animationRepeatCount`: This controls the repeat count of the animation; in this case, the animation will repeat three times.

Finally, you need to call `loadWalkAnimation()` from `viewDidLoad()` in the view controller so that the image view will be ready whenever the player taps the left arrow button.

Add the following code to the bottom of `viewDidLoad()`:

```
loadWalkAnimation()
```

Build and run the project; tap the left arrow button to set your penguin in motion:

Oh — nothing happens when you tap the left arrow button. Did you do something wrong? No; you only *configured* the image view for a frame animation, but you never started the animation. If you don't start the frame animation, the image view continues to show the contents of its image property.

Time to get this penguin waddling.

Add the following code to `actionLeft(_:)`:

```
isLookingRight = false
```

To track which way the penguin faces, you'll set `isLookingRight` to `false` or `true` inside `actionLeft(_:)` and `actionRight(_:)` respectively.

Since you need to update the penguin's transform and the button transform every time you change the penguin's direction, you'll need to add some code to the `didSet` observer of `isLookingRight`.

Find the following property near the top of the class definition:

```
var isLookingRight = true
```

...and replace it with the code below:

```
var isLookingRight: Bool = true {
  didSet {
    let xScale: CGFloat = isLookingRight ? 1 : -1
    penguin.transform = CGAffineTransform(scaleX: xScale, y: 1)
    slideButton.transform = penguin.transform
  }
}
```

This code sets the x-axis scale of the penguin and the slide button to either 1 or −1 depending on the value of `isLookingRight`. Setting that transform will then flip the view so the penguin can face the correct direction:

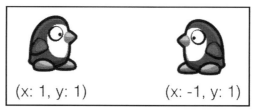

Now you need to call the animation code. Add the following to the bottom of `actionLeft()`:

```
penguin.startAnimating()
```

When you call `startAnimating()` the image view plays the animation as you configured it: Each frame in the `animationImages` array displays in order for a total of three times over 1 second.

Once the animation has finished, the image view will once again display its initial contents – the `image` property.

Build and run your project; tap the left arrow button to see your penguin in action:

Your chilly friend is walking — but he's going nowhere fast! :] You'll need to move the penguin across the screen as the walking animation plays.

Translating your view

Add the following code to `actionLeft(_:)`:

```
UIView.animate(withDuration: animationDuration, delay: 0,
  options: .curveEaseOut,
  animations: {
    self.penguin.center.x -= self.walkSize.width
  },
  completion: nil
)
```

This is familiar code that needs little explanation by this point in the book; you simply animate your view across the screen. You use the width of the walking image to determine how far the penguin will move during the length the animation plays.

Run the project again; how do things look now?

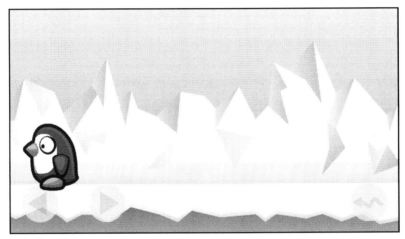

That's more like it! Walking in the other direction is pretty similar code-wise.

Add the following code to `actionRight(_:)`:

```
isLookingRight = true
penguin.startAnimating()

UIView.animate(withDuration: animationDuration, delay: 0,
  options: .curveEaseOut,
  animations: {
```

```
      self.penguin.center.x += self.walkSize.width
  },
  completion: nil
)
```

It's almost the same code as before: you change the character orientation, play the frame animation and move it towards the right edge of the screen.

Build and run your project and play around a bit with the game. Can you think of other frame animations the character could perform?

Playing different frame animations

Now that Pengui can walk around, it's time for him to jump and slide. You'll face some new frame animation issues in this section and learn how to solve them in an elegant manner.

To make the image view play a different frame animation, you need to change the contents of the `animationImages` property. Conveniently, the `slideFrames` property of `ViewController` already contains the images for the sliding animation.

Add the following code to `loadSlideAnimation()` to load the new frame sequence:

```
penguin.animationImages = slideFrames
penguin.animationDuration = animationDuration
penguin.animationRepeatCount = 1
```

In the code above, you assign the `slideFrames` array to `animationImages`, then set the animation duration to the predefined 1 second time span. Finally, you set the repeat count to 1.

It looks like you've taken care of everything you need above, so you can move on the code to load and play the animation.

Add the following code to `actionSlide(_:)`:

```
loadSlideAnimation()
penguin.startAnimating()
```

Build and run your project; tap the slide button on the right hand of the screen and you'll see Pengui jump on his tummy and bounce back to his feet.

Hmm, there's something weird going on in that animation. Pengui gets real chubby as the animation runs; in fact, while he's lying on the ground he looks totally round! What gives?

Well, check the most obvious thing first: are the slide images correct? Take a peek at **slide01** and **slide02** and you'll see that the penguin is the right shape and size. So something in your project must be sabotaging Pengui's figure. Either that or he's been eating a few too many fish lately. :]

The sliding animation looks off because the frame images aren't the same between the two animations:

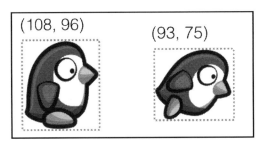

The walk frame images are 108 x 96, while the slide images are 93 x 75. If they were all the same size, you'd end up with a lot of empty space in each image. Imagine a character with five, six, or more frame animations; you'd end up with huge image dimensions to fit in all the possible animation frames.

> **Note:** An easy solution to this problem is to set the content mode of the image view from its default value of Aspect Fill to Center or Top Left. But since you're an animation ninja, you'll implement a slightly different and more flexible solution.

In this part of the chapter, you'll manually resize and reposition the image view to create a beautiful animation that flows nicely.

First, you'll need to set the desired image view frame before you play any animations; this ensures the frames are the correct size when they're visible on the screen.

Add the following code to `actionSlide(_:)`, just before the point where you start the animations:

```
penguin.frame = CGRect(
    x: penguin.frame.origin.x,
    y: penguinY + (walkSize.height - slideSize.height),
    width: slideSize.width,
    height: slideSize.height)
```

This code moves the penguin image view down a little bit to compensate for the shorter frames of the slide animation and resizes the image view to match `slideSize`.

`slideSize` contains the size of **slide01.png**; `viewDidLoad()` already contains the code to fetch the image.

Now add the following code to the bottom of `actionSlide(_:)`:

```
UIView.animate(withDuration: animationDuration - 0.02, delay:
0.0,
  options: .curveEaseOut,
  animations: {
    self.penguin.center.x += self.isLookingRight ?
      self.slideSize.width : -self.slideSize.width
  },
  completion: {_ in
    // animation is complete
  }
)
```

In the code above, you create a view animation to move the penguin image view and simulate the jump action. You also add or subtract one penguin length (would that be a "penguimeter"?) depending on which way the penguin is facing.

You'll notice there's a small adjustment to the animation duration and you're making it a bit shorter. You'll see why this is necessary in just a moment.

Build and run your project; your animation should look nice and sleek at this point.

But poor Pengui is stuck on the ice; once you do a slide, all animations become slide animations, even if you tap the left and right arrow buttons.

Whoops — you didn't reset the image view frame and reload the walking frames. That's pretty easy to fix.

Replace the `// animation is complete` comment in the piece of code you added above with the following:

```
self.penguin.frame = CGRect(
  x: self.penguin.frame.origin.x,
  y: self.penguinY,
  width: self.walkSize.width,
  height: self.walkSize.height)
self.loadWalkAnimation()
```

This resets the image view frame to its initial size and loads up the walking frame sequence.

The small time interval you subtracted from the animation duration comes into play here; without it, the frame animation and the movement animation end at the same time, which sometimes results in a little glitch where the penguin returns to standing before the frame has been adjusted. Adding the little offset ensures the new frame is ready before the previous animation ends.

Build and run the project one last time; you should see that Pengui now returns to his upright position once he's done sliding.

Where to go from here?

Frame animations with `UIImageView` are simple, but they are a great addition to your already impressive animation skill-set.

You might think UIKit isn't suited for games but you'd be surprised to learn this isn't the case! Core Animation is a more powerful engine than many other platforms have and as you've seen throughout this book it can run particles, multiple animations, fades, etc. just fine :)

Conclusion

We hope you're excited about the breadth of animations available to you in iOS! Animations bring life and playfulness to touch-based interfaces; this makes people feel more connected to your interface and creates memorable app experiences for your users.

You're now equipped to use and understand the animation tools available to you, from layers to 3D effects and beyond. It's up to you now to couple your creativity with the things you've learned in this book and create some impressive effects of your own!

If you have any questions or comments about the projects in this book or in your own animations, please stop by our forums at http://www.raywenderlich.com/forums.

Thank you again for purchasing this book. Your continued support is what makes the books, tutorials, videos and other things we do at raywenderlich.com possible. We truly appreciate it!

May all your animations be fun and fluid, with furiously high frame rates!

— Marin, Erik, Richard, Chris, and Vicki

The *iOS Animations by Tutorials* team

Made in the USA
Lexington, KY
08 August 2017